PHIL GORDON'S
LITTLE GOLD
BOOK

Previous Titles by Phil Gordon

Poker: The Real Deal
(*a k a Phil Gordon's Little Black Book*)

Phil Gordon's Little Green Book:
Lessons and Teachings in No Limit Texas Hold'em

Phil Gordon's Little Blue Book:
More Lessons and Hand Analysis in No Limit Texas Hold'em

PHIL GORDON'S

LITTLE GOLD

BOOK

Advanced Lessons for Mastering Poker 2.0

Phil Gordon

WITH ANDERS TAYLOR

Gallery Books

New York   London   Toronto   Sydney   New Delhi

This publication contains the opinions and ideas of its author. It is intended to pro-
vide helpful and informative material on the subjects addressed in the publication.
The strategies outlined in this book may not be suitable for every individual, and are
not guaranteed or warranted to produce any particular results. The book is sold with
the understanding that the authors and publisher are not engaged in rendering any
kind of personal professional services in the book.

The author and publisher specifically disclaim all responsibility for any liability, loss
or risk, personal or otherwise, which is incurred as a consequence, directly or indi-
rectly, of the use and application of any of the contents of this book.

G

Gallery Books
A Division of Simon & Schuster, Inc.
1230 Avenue of the Americas
New York, NY 10020

Copyright © 2011 by Phil Gordon

First Gallery Books hardcover edition October 2011

GALLERY BOOKS and colophon are registered trademarks of
Simon & Schuster, Inc.

For information about special discounts for bulk purchases,
please contact Simon & Schuster Special Sales at 1-866-506-1949
or business@simonandschuster.com.

The Simon & Schuster Speakers Bureau can bring authors
to your live event. For more information or to book
an event contact the Simon & Schuster Speakers Bureau at
1-866-248-3049 or visit our website at www.simonspeakers.com.

Designed by Peng Olaguera/ISPN

Manufactured in the United States of America

10 9 8 7 6 5 4 3 2 1

Library of Congress Cataloging-in-Publication Data

Gordon, Phil, 1970–
    Phil Gordon's little gold book : advanced lessons for mastering
poker 2.0 / by Phil Gordon.
    p.   cm.
    1. Poker. I. Title.
    GV1251.G659 2011
    795.412—dc23   2011031197
ISBN 978-1-4516-4159-2
ISBN 978-1-4516-4160-8 (ebook)

To Xander and Zachary,

With everything you do in your lives,
go all-in.

Daddy loves you.

CONTENTS

PHIL GORDON'S
LITTLE GOLD
BOOK

INTRODUCTION

I've said it before and I'll say it again: poker is a very difficult game. It has been six years since my *Little Green Book* was published, and in that time the game has morphed considerably. The prevalence and importance of Internet poker have fueled most of the changes. Pot Limit Omaha (PLO) has become the game of choice at nosebleed stakes. The players are more aggressive, the games more volatile, and the decisions tougher. With all that in mind, I thought it was time to reexamine the game from the ground up with an update to the *Little Green Book*. To write this book, I had to do some soul-searching and take a critical look at my own game. In many ways, "new poker" has passed me by in a flash. At forty plus years old, I'm ancient in the poker world. The kids are now dominating. From 2008 to 2010, thirty-six players made the final table of the World Series of Poker Championship Event—twenty-four were under the age of thirty, and twelve of those twenty-four players were twenty-five years old or younger. These "kids" are good.

To give my readers the best possible insight, I knew that I needed to completely relearn the game. And I needed some help. Fortunately, that was relatively easy to find. I owe a debt of gratitude to my friends and mentors Anders Taylor, Phil Galfond, Annette Obrestad, Daniel Cates, and Austin Schaff. They are the ones who gave me the insights and impetus to write this book. With their help, my goal is to shorten your learning curve. If you haven't read and studied the *Black, Green*, and *Blue* books, I suggest you do so before taking on this more challenging material, as the fundamentals laid out there will still serve you well in the new poker ecosystem.

We will begin with the foundations of Poker 2.0. We'll examine some of the mathematics and concepts behind the new poker theory: range, combinatorics, and expected value. For the mathematically minded, much of this material will be easy. For others, it will be a real struggle, but perseverance will make the effort worthwhile.

Next, I'll introduce you to the modern poker player's toolkit. Heads Up Displays are the biggest innovation. Using them properly can take your game to an entirely different level almost immediately. I'll also show you how to effectively use range simulation tools to your advantage. These new computer models are essential in today's poker world.

We will reexamine No Limit Hold'em, tackling both cash games and tournaments with rigorous detail. The strategies of yesteryear have been replaced by new thought processes, new lines of play, and new insights. Think of this section as the *Little Green Book*, version 2.0. (Note: When advice varies between the *Green* and *Gold* books, go for the *Gold*.)

In the next section, we turn to Pot Limit Omaha, the new game of choice for most high-stakes cash games. PLO is fast and furious, with some huge bankroll swings and a strategy all its own. I'm still working on my PLO game and I'm no world-beater. But I'm confident that the fundamentals in this section combined with good game selection will turn a profit in all but the toughest PLO games.

In the "Meta-Game" section, we'll talk about the game-within-the-game and some important non-strategy concepts that need to be mastered. We'll also take a look at the remarkable Chris Ferguson and his quest to turn zero dollars into one million by utilizing excellent bankroll-management rules.

Last, we'll hear from three poker "whiz kids" and learn what makes them tick and their strategies for success, as we get coached by the best in the game. Much of the material presented in the first sections of this book stems from the advice and counsel of my mentors. We'll talk with Phil Galfond, Annette Obrestad, and Daniel Cates. Phil is one of the best PLO players in the world. Annette is a multi-table tournament genius. And at the ripe old age of twenty-two years, Daniel is widely considered the best Heads Up No Limit Hold'em specialist in the world. Their contributions and willingness to share their insights were invaluable to me, and I know you're going to find this material very helpful as well.

The golden age of poker is upon us. For those willing to put in the time and work, big bankrolls await.

Let's go for the gold.

JARGON

If you listen to the Internet kids talk poker and you're not familiar with their terminology, you can quickly get overwhelmed and lost. They have a language all their own. Some of it is downright cute.

6-Max: A poker game with six seats

Agro: Aggressive

Barrel, Barrel off: Another phrase for bet, usually with some connotation of a bluff

Blocker: A card in your hand that reduces the chance your opponent holds a hand that has you beat

Bluff-catcher: A hand that only beats a bluff

Button: Player seated in the dealer position, the best position at the table

C-Bet: A continuation-bet

Cutoff: Player just to the right of the button

Deep: Playing with more than 150 big blinds in your stack

Defend: Call or re-raise a pre-flop opening raise from the small or big blind

Donk Bet, Donk, Donked: An out-of-position bet into an opponent when you do not have the lead in the betting. (Example: You raise from late position and get three-bet by the button. You call. The flop comes, 8-6-2 rainbow. You bet. This is a donk bet.)

Effective Stack Size: The size of the smallest stack belonging to a player still playing in the hand

Expected Value: A probabilistically weighted average of all possible results

Fish: A bad, losing player

Flat-Call, Flat, Flatted: Just call a raise or bet

Float: To flat-call an opponent's flop continuation-bet with a relatively weak hand

Four-Bet: The re-re-raise. (Example: In a $5–$10 NLH game, you raise to $30 from late position. The button three-bets to $100. When the action gets back to you, you four-bet to $300.)

Full Ring: A poker game with nine seats

Hi-Jack: Player two to the right of the button, just to the right of the cutoff

ICM: The Independent Chip Model for tournament poker, a method for calculating tournament equity based on the payout structure and the number of chips remaining for each player

LAG: A loose, aggressive player. Typically, LAGs play too many hands and play them very aggressively

LAGtard: A super LAGgy player—plays tons of hands and plays them hyper-aggressively

Lead, In the Lead: The player who took the last aggressive action in the hand. (Example: If I raise pre-flop and my opponent called from the blind, I have the betting lead. If I raise pre-flop and my opponent three-bets and I call, my opponent has the lead.)

Merge: To have a range of hands that will include more medium-strength hands in the "value range." (*See* Polarize.)

MP1: Player four to the right of the button, just to the right of MP2, just to the left of UTG+1

MP2: Player three to the right of the button, just to the right of the Hi-Jack

Monotone: A flop that contains three cards of the same suit (i.e., A♣ J♣ 4♣ or 8♥ 9♥ 2♥)

Nit, nitty: Very tight, not playing many hands. A player with no gamble—if he puts chips in the pot, he is almost certain to be ahead.

NLH: No Limit Hold'em

Nosebleeds: Very high stakes, usually $100–$200 or higher online

Nuts: The best hand possible or, more commonly, one of the best hands possible

Offsuit: Two cards with different suits (i.e., A♣ and J♦—denoted with a lower-case *o*, as in AJo. AJ denotes both suited and unsuited varieties.)

Over-call: To call a pre-flop raise when at least one other player has already called the pre-flop raise in front of you

Play-back: To call or raise a bet

Play-back Range: The range of hands that a player will play-back with, either calling or raising

PLO: Pot Limit Omaha

Polarize: To divide a range of hands into two sub-sets, bluff hands and value hands, leaving out most medium-strength hands

Pop It: Raise

Rainbow: A flop that contains three cards of different suits (i.e., A♣J♦4♠ or 8♥9♦2♣)

Range: Set of all possible hands for a player given all previous actions in the hand

Shallow, Short: Playing a stack size of less than 30 big blinds

Shove: Move all-in

Spewtard: A poker player who is giving money away with reckless, hyper-aggressive play

Stacked, Felted: Get it all-in and go broke

Steal: Usually refers to a pre-flop raise in an effort to win the blinds and antes

Suited: Two cards of the same suit (i.e., Ace of Clubs and Jack of Clubs—denoted with a lower-case *s*, as in AJs)

TAG: A tight, aggressive player; typically a good, solid player

Thin: A really close decision, usually in reference to a bet made by a weak, made hand. (Example: "He made a really thin value bet with third pair.")

Three-Bet: Re-raise pre-flop. (Example: In a $5–$10 NLH game, a player raises to $30 from late position. You re-raise—three-bet—from the button and make it $100.)

Triple Barrel: To bet the flop, turn, and river

Two-Tone: A flop that contains two cards of the same suit (i.e., A♣J♣4♥ or 8♥9♥2♠)

UTG: Under the gun, first player to act; UTG is always directly to the left of the big blind

UTG+1: First player to act after the UTG

Value-Own: Betting a hand that will get called by a better hand more than 50% of the time

x: Sometimes refers to the size of the previous bet, or the size of the blind. (Example: If the big blind is $20, a raise to 3x would be $60. If a player faces a bet of $50 and makes it 2.5x, he'd be raising to $125.)

X: Any small card "kicker." For example, AX could be A2, A3 . . . A9

Try this on for size—if you can make sense of it, you won't have any problems at the bar after Day One of the WSOP Main Event:

So I'm UTG, deep stacked, and playing like a nit. I pump the pot 3x. LAGtard button three-bets me. My four-bet range was very tight, so I flatted with AQ suited. The flop was Q-9-4 rainbow. I donked half pot. He raised, I flatted. Turn was a suited 8. I checked, he barreled. His range was pretty polarized, so I called again. River came 7. I checked again, he overbet the pot and shoved, and I thought I had to bluff-catch. He showed me the nuts. Guess I played this hand like a monkey.

FOUNDATIONS OF POKER 2.0

Poker has changed dramatically and quickly in the last few years. The game is much tougher than it used to be. Version 2.0 of the game is characterized by very high aggression, off-the-charts variance, and relentless pressure. This is not the same game I played back in the day, not at all.

In the old days, if you had good pre-flop fundamentals, you were a cinch to win. That is why most of the material written about the game (including my previous books) has focused on the pre-flop game. Now, most people play well pre-flop, but the edge comes from post-flop play. Post-flop is where the pros are separated from the posers.

Table composition has also changed dramatically. As late

as 2007, I could easily find a nine-handed game with three, four, even five weak spots. These "fish" were easily fried, and you didn't even have to be that good a fisherman to fill your quota. There was plenty of money to go around. These days, we've depleted the ocean, and fish are simply not as plentiful. Now, at a nine-handed table, there might only be one fish, and all the fishermen are fighting to get him on the line first.

Much of this change has been fueled by a rigorous scientific study of the game through simulation and mathematics. It is no longer good enough to know my Rule of 4 and 2. To really understand Poker 2.0, you need to get more comfortable with the math underlying this new playing style. If you are less mathematically gifted, don't be intimidated—I have made this material as approachable and simple as possible.

RANGE

"Range" is the set of all possible hands an opponent can have based on your knowledge of their playing style and all actions that have taken place during the play of a hand. A typical pre-flop range might sound something like this: "He's on, at worst, any pocket pair, AJ offsuit,* or, better, KQ suited, or QJ suited."

---

* Denoted throughout the rest of the book as AJo, KQs, with the *o* representing offsuit hands, the *s* representing suited hands.

Poker players routinely use "range" when thinking about or discussing a hand:

PLAYER: He's got a really wide range here.
TRANSLATION: He can be playing almost any two cards.

PLAYER: I'm at the top of my range.
TRANSLATION: Of the hands that my opponent suspects I could be playing, this hand is one of the best I could have.

PLAYER: He's playing about 10% of his hands pre-flop from early position.
TRANSLATION: His range is pocket sevens or better, AT offsuit or better, A8 suited or better, KQ suited, QJ suited, and JT suited.

It is very important to think about an opponent's range throughout the play of a hand. It is also vitally important that you consider what range of hands your opponent is putting *you* on.

Range analysis, often through computer simulation (and later, experience), has intensified and become one of the most important tools in NLH2.0—without it, you'll have little or no chance to succeed. I'll show you how to do these range analyses later in the book.

STANDARD RANGE NOTATION

When writing about range, it is helpful to have a standard-ized notation. The Internet whiz kids quickly figured out a range notation that is very useful. Here is a quick rundown, via example:

Any pocket pair: 22+

Pocket nines or better, AJ or better (meaning AK, AQ, AJ), KJ suited or better (KQ, KJ): 99+, KJs+, AJ+

Top 20% of all possible hands: 20%+

Some 30% of all possible hands, but not AA or KK: 30%+ - KK+

A "very tight" under-the-gun range in a full No Limit Hold'em ring game: TT+, AQs+, AK

A "loose button-position" range: 22+, A2+, K2+, Q2+, J8+, J5s+, T9s, 85s+, 74s+, 63s+

Note: In all cases, a range of A2+ denotes all un-suited combinations and automatically includes all suited combinations as well. So, A2+ is the same as A2s+, A2o+. This is the notation I'll be using throughout the rest of the book.

STANDARD POSITION
NOTATION

Position is extremely important. We need some common terminology and abbreviations to be able to talk about position intelligently. Refer to this chart for the names of certain seats with respect to the button. Also, I'll be discussing 6-max games* quite a bit. When thinking about 6-max, I simply visualize a 9-player table where the UTG, UTG+1, and MP1 players have folded. In a 6-max game, the UTG position is the MP2 position at a full ring.

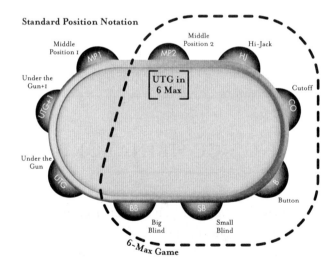

Standard Position Notation

Middle Position 1 — MP1
Middle Position 2 — MP2
Hi-Jack — HJ
Under the Gun+1 — UTG+1
Cutoff — CO
UTG in 6 Max
Under the Gun — UTG
Button
Big Blind — BB
Small Blind — SB

6-Max Game

---

* A game with a maximum of 6 players seated.

FUNDAMENTAL MATHEMATICS

NLH2.0 is based largely on mathematics. Without the "reads" and "tells" commonly associated with live play, the Internet poker geniuses had no choice but to adapt and find other ways to win, and they focused most of their efforts on the mathematics of the game.

To understand and ultimately be successful in the new poker world, you're going to have to expand your math repertoire beyond the basics of the Rule of 4 and 2 and Pot Odds. Your new weapons will include three concepts: combinatorics, expected value (EV), and combined probability. If you haven't mastered simple pot odds calculations or you have a hard time figuring out your chances of winning after the flop or turn, go back and study my *Green Book* for a detailed explanation.

RANGE COMBINATORICS

Combinatorics means listing all possible two-card combinations and then figuring out the likelihood of any given combination or range of combinations being dealt. Let's start with the basics: There are 1,326 possible two-card starting hands in Texas Hold'em. How do we know that?

Well, there are 52 cards in the deck. After you select a single card from the 52, there are 51 cards possible for your second hole card. So, the total number of combinations is: 52 x 51 = 2,652.

However, there is no difference if we're dealt the Ace of Clubs first followed by the Seven of Diamonds or if we're dealt the Seven of Diamonds first followed by the Ace of Clubs—it is the same hand. Clearly, each possible two-card combination has been counted twice.

So, the total number of two-card combinations in Texas Hold'em is: 2,652 ÷ 2 = 1,326.

Now, with that under our belts, let's take a look at all the ways we can be dealt the best possible hand, AA: A♣A♦, A♣A♥, A♣A♠, A♦A♥, A♦A♠, A♥A♠.

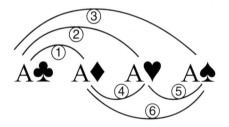

Of the 1,326 possible two-card starting hands, there are clearly six ways to be dealt AA, so the chances are: 6 ÷ 1,326 = 0.0045 = 0.45%.

Now, let's move on to a slightly worse hand, Ace-King, either suited or unsuited.

17

	A♣	A♦	A♥	A♠	
K♣	A♣ K♣	A♦ K♦	A♥ K♥	A♠ K♠	← suited
K♦	A♣ K♦	A♦ K♣	A♥ K♣	A♠ K♣	← unsuited
K♥	A♣ K♥	A♦ K♥	A♥ K♦	A♠ K♦	← unsuited
K♠	A♣ K♠	A♦ K♠	A♥ K♠	A♠ K♥	← unsuited

There are sixteen ways to be dealt AK; four are suited, and twelve are unsuited. Indeed, there are sixteen ways to be dealt every unpaired hand. There are sixteen combinations of 7-2, sixteen combinations of QT, and sixteen combinations of 9-5. The probability of being dealt any specific unpaired hand like AK is:

$$16 \div 1,326 = 0.012 = 1.2\%$$

With 1,326 combinations possible, every 13 combinations account for 1% of the possible hands, every 66 combinations represent 5% of the possible hands, every 132 combinations is equivalent to 10% of the hands, and so on.

These two basic combinatorics are the essential building blocks for advanced Poker 2.0 calculations. Now, let's try a few examples . . .

Example 1:

What are the chances of being dealt a pocket pair?

13 different pairs (or ranks) × 6 combinations for each rank = 78

$$78 \div 1,326 = 0.0588 = 5.88\%$$

Example 2:

What are the chances of being dealt a hand in the following range: 77+, ATs+, KQs, AQo+?

77–AA = 8 ranks × 6 combinations = 48

ATs+ = 4 kickers × 4 combinations = 16 (ATs, AJs, AQs, AKs)

KQs = 4 combinations (K♣Q♣, K♦Q♦, K♥Q♥, K♠Q♠)

AQo+ = 2 kickers (K, Q) × 12 combinations = 24 combinations

---

48 + 16 + 4 + 24 = 92 combinations

92 ÷ 1,326 = 0.0694 = 6.94%

Example 3:

What are the chances of being dealt a "suited" hand?

Ranks	A	K	Q	J	T	9	8	7	6	5	4	3	
Kickers	12	11	10	9	8	7	6	5	4	3	2	1	
× Suits	4	4	4	4	4	4	4	4	4	4	4	4	
= Total	48	44	40	36	32	28	24	20	16	12	8	4	= 312

312 total combinations ÷ 1,326 = 23.5%

Example 4:

If we think our opponent is playing 12% of their hands from under the gun, how many combinations does that represent?

1,326 × 12% = 159.12 ≈ 159 combinations

Example 5:

If an opponent is playing all pocket pairs and is playing 12% of his hands from under the gun, how often will he be unpaired?

12% range = 159 combinations (see Example 4)

From Example 1, we know that there are 78 pair combinations.

159 − 78 = 81 unpaired hands

81 unpaired combinations ÷ 159 total combinations = 0.509 = 50.9%

Our opponent will be unpaired a little more than half the time.

RANGE COMBINATORICS AFTER CARD REMOVAL

At first blush, 1,326 looks like the magic number for poker combinatorics. It certainly is when evaluating your hand or range of hands. But, as you well know, more often than not what we're more concerned about is the possible hands our opponents can hold. That means we need to make some minor adjustments to our calculations.

After you look at your hole cards, you have some vital information: your opponent can't be dealt either of the two cards you hold in your hand. There are 50 cards left in the deck. That means that the number of remaining two-card combinations decreases from 1,326 to 1,225.

$50 \times 49 \div 2 = 1,225$

Obviously, the possibilities for your opponent's hand are affected after the removal of your known hole cards from the deck. Intuitively, you know that if you have an Ace in your hand, it is much less likely that any one of your opponents will be dealt one as well. Let's take a look at a few examples:

Example 1:

You are dealt A♥Q♠. What are the chances that your opponent was dealt AA?

3 combinations of AA $\div$ 1,225 = 0.0024 = 0.24%

(Notice that by being dealt an Ace, thereby removing it from the deck, the number of combinations of AA decreases by 50%—there are six combinations of AA if you don't have an Ace in your hand, three if you do: A♣A♦, A♣A♠, A♦A♠.)

Example 2:

You have A♠K♠. What are the chances that a single opponent has AA or KK?

As we learned above, once the A♠ and K♠ have been dealt to you, your opponent's chance of having either pocket pair is cut in half.

AA, KK = 3 combinations each = 6 combinations total

$6 \div 1,225 = 0.0048 = 0.48\%$ or about 1 out of 204

Example 3:

You're in the small blind with A♣2♣. What are the chances that your opponent in the big blind has a better hand (pocket 22+, A3–AK)?

Well, you're in the lead against all non-pair, non-Ace hands, which are easy to count.

22, AA = 3 combinations each = 6 combinations

33–KK = 6 combinations each × 11 ranks = 66 combinations

A3–AK = 12 combinations of each × 11 ranks = 132 combinations (3 remaining Aces combined with 4 of each kicker)

6 + 66 + 132 = 204 combinations ÷ 1,225 = 16.65%

Example 4:

Your opponent has a hand in the following range: 88+, ATs+, AQo+, KQs, QJs, JTs

You are dealt QQ. What are the chances that you have the best hand right now?

First, we'll count the combinations in our opponent's range that have us beat:

AA, KK = 6 combinations each = 12 combinations beat us

Now, let's count the other combinations in the range:

88–JJ = 6 combinations of each × 4 ranks = 24 combinations

QQ = 1 combination

ATs, AJs, AKs = 12 combinations

AQs = 2 combinations (2 queens gone)

AQo = 6 combinations (2 queens gone)

AKo = 12 combinations

KQs = 2 combinations (2 queens gone)

QJs = 2 combinations (2 queens gone)

JTs = 4 combinations

24 + 1 + 12 + 2 + 6 + 12 + 2 + 2 + 4 =
   65 combinations we are ahead against

We beat 53 of the 65 combinations:
   53 ÷ 65 = 0.815 = 81.5%
With QQ vs. this range, we expect to be "ahead"
   81.5% of the time.

EXPECTED VALUE

Expected Value (EV) is a term from probability theory with a splash of economics. Essentially, EV is a probabilistically weighted average of all possible outcomes. You can think of EV as the "long-term outcome" of a play.

First, an example where you have nothing to lose (unfortunately, these situations don't come up often in poker):

Example 1:

There is $100 in the pot, and you compute that you have a 60% chance of winning. What is your EV?

Answer:

60% of the time, you'll win $100. 40% of the time, you'll win $0.

$$\begin{array}{r} \$100 \times 60\% = \$60 \\ +\ \$0 \times 40\% = \$\ \ 0 \\ \hline EV = \$60 \end{array}$$

Over the long run, you can expect to win $60.

Example 2:

I have three piggy banks. Piggy bank A has $50 in it. Piggy bank B has $100 in it. Piggy bank C has $1,000 in it. You randomly select a bank and get to keep whatever you find. What is your EV?

Answer:

33% of the time, you'll choose Piggy A and get $50
33% of the time, you'll choose Piggy B and get $100
33% of the time, you'll choose Piggy C and get $1,000

$$\begin{array}{r} 33.3\% \times \ \ \ \ 50 = \$\ \ 16.67 \\ 33.3\% \times \ \ 100 = \$\ \ 33.33 \\ +\ 33.3\% \times 1{,}000 = \$333.33 \\ \hline EV = \$383.33 \end{array}$$

If you played this game thousands of times, you'd expect to win, an average of $383.33 each time.

Example 3:

You bet $250 on the LA Lakers to win the NBA championship with your best friend. You think you have a 52% chance of winning that bet. What is your EV?

Answer:

52% of the time, you'll win $250.

48% of the time, you'll lose $250.

$$52\% \times \quad \$250 = \quad \$130 \leftarrow \text{You win}$$
$$\underline{+48\% \times -\$250 = -\$120 \leftarrow \text{You lose}}$$
$$EV = \quad \$ \ 10$$

On average, this bet is worth $10. In other words, you are risking $250 for the expectation of winning $10 over the long run.

Example 4:

You are heads up at the river and your opponent bets $700 into a $1,000 pot. You can beat a bluff, but only a bluff. What percent of the time must your opponent be bluffing to make this a profitable call?

Answer:

If he has the best hand, you will lose $700. If he was bluffing and you have the best hand, you will win $1,700, the $1,000 in the pot before his bet plus the $700 bluff.

The key now is to determine the Break Even
   Percentage (BEP):
Let B = the percent chance that he is bluffing
So, 100% − B = the percent chance that he has the
   best hand and we lose
We are searching for the equilibrium point where:
0 = EV(winning) + EV(losing)
EV(winning) = 1,700 × B
EV(losing) = −700 × (100% − B)

Now, time for some algebra:
0 = (1,700 × B) −700 + (700 × B)
0 = (2,400B) − 700
700 = 2,400 × B
700 ÷ 2,400 = B
0.292 = B
29.2% = B

What this shows us is that if our opponent is bluffing
29.2% of the time and we call each and every time, we will
break even over the long run.

   Quick double-check:

29.2% × $1,700 =	$496	←	EV of catching a bluff
+70.8% ×− $700 =	−$496	←	EV of losing
EV =	0		

Since this situation comes up so much, it is useful to
generalize the BEP formula like this:

   BEP = Amount of Bet ÷ Total Pot, including my call

So, let's try a few more of these river situations and apply the BEP formula:

Example 4a:

Pot is $500, opponent bets $500. What percent chance do you need to justify a call?

River Bet = $500

Total Pot if I call = $1,500

BEP = $500 ÷ $1,500 = 33%

Example 4b:

Pot is $10,000. River Bet is $1,000. What percent chance do you need to justify a call?

River Bet = $1,000

Total Pot if I call = $12,000

BEP = $1,000 ÷ $12,000 = 1 ÷ 12 = 0.125 = 12.5%

We'll see BEP in action in later sections. If these formulas make your head spin, here is a chart of river bet sizes and the associated BEP:

River Bet Size	BEP
1/2 pot	25%
3/4 pot	30%
POT	33%
1.5x Pot	37.5%
2x Pot	40%

Example 5:

Putting EV together with Combinatorics

A player moves all-in pre-flop for $100. Like Phil Hellmuth, you look deep into their soul and know that they have AA or AK. You have QQ. Should you call?

There are 6 combinations of AA. If they have AA, you're going to suck-out and win about 18.5% of the time and lose about 81.5% of the time.*

There are 16 combinations of AK. If they have AK, you're going to win about 56% of the time.

So, there are 22 total combinations to consider:

AA, Suck-out $(6 / 22) \times 18.5\% \times +\$100 =$		$5.04
AA, Lose $(6 / 22) \times 81.5\% \times -\$100$	$=$	$-\$22.28
AK, Win $(16/22) \times 56.0\% \times +\$100$	$=$	$40.73
AK, Lose $(16/22) \times 44\% \times -\$100$	$=$	$-\$32.00
	$EV =$	$-\$8.51

Remember, this is weighted probability. For this situation if you decide to call in this spot, you are essentially "giving" your opponent $8.51. You should not call.

Players in Poker 2.0 are always thinking about EV. If they believe a play has a positive EV, they make the play. They know that at "Internet speed," they'll get to make that same play thousands of times, and over the long run, they'll be big winners.

---

* These situations are widely known and are easily calculated through some of the simulation tools I'll introduce you to in the Poker Toolkit.

One key concept about EV worth noting: the results of any one particular hand aren't all that important. If you have AK and get it all-in against QQ and win the hand, that is excellent in the short term—you doubled up! But, if you keep doing the same thing over and over and over, you'll end up broke—your opponent is getting the best of every hand a little bit at a time. Bottom line: getting lucky doesn't mean that you played well.

COMBINED PROBABILITIES

I'm in the cutoff seat (just to the right of the button) and I'm thinking about moving all-in for my last 12 big blinds with A♠T♣. I'd like to figure out how often I'm going to get called by a dominating hand (AJ, AQ, AK, TT, JJ, QQ, KK, AA) by one of three players remaining. Here, I need to use combinatorics (see pages 16–23) and approach the problem as if there were a single player left to act:

3 Aces are left in the deck.

AJ, AQ, AK = 12 combinations of each =

36 total combinations

AA, TT = 3 combinations each = 6 combinations

KK, QQ, JJ = 6 combinations each =

18 combinations

A total of 60 combinations have me dominated.

As I've shown, after my A♠T♣ have been removed from the deck, there are 1,225 possible combinations (50 × 49 ÷ 2) for my opponent.

60 dominant combos ÷ 1,225 total combos =

0.0489 = 4.89% chance I'm dominated.

100% − 4.89% = 95.11% chance I'm *not* dominated by a single player.

So, there is a 95% chance I'm not dominated by the button, a 95% chance I'm not dominated by the small blind, and a 95% chance I'm not dominated by the big blind. We combine these probabilities by multiplying them all together:

95% × 95% × 95% = 85.7% chance I'm not dominated by *any* of the remaining three players.

Example 1:

You own two stocks. You estimate a 10% chance the price of Stock A will increase. You estimate a 30% chance the price of Stock B will increase. What is the probability of both stocks increasing?

10% chance Stock A increases × 30% chance Stock B increases = 0.10 × 0.30 = 0.03 = 3%

Example 2:

You purchase a "parlay" card at the sports book. You have to pick three games correctly in order to win. You are an excellent handicapper and believe that you have a

55% chance of picking Game A correctly, a 52% chance of picking Game B correctly, and a 59% chance of picking Game C correctly. What is the probability that you'll win the parlay?

55% × 52% × 59% = 0.168 = 16.8%

Combined probabilities are very useful in multi-way pots and in all spots where there are multiple players left to act. In general, be more careful and conservative when there are multiple players left to act.

UTILITY

Utility is the measure of how important an outcome is to an individual player. For some, there is a substantial difference between coming in fifth place and cashing for $3,000 and coming in fourth place for $4,500. Some might place great importance on winning the extra $1,500, while others will find very little value or utility in the extra money.

Here's a typical utility problem, as seen every day on the show *Deal or No Deal.* Suppose you're in deep on the show with two choices remaining on the board. One box contains $10 and the other box has $250,000 in it. The banker offers to settle with you for $100,000. Deal or No Deal?

The expected value for just choosing a box is about

$125,000. If you take the deal, you are essentially giving away $25,000 in expectation. Clearly, if you could get in this spot thousands of times, you'd just keep picking boxes and would never settle for $100,000. But, this is your only shot. The problem you face is simple: is the guaranteed usefulness of $100,000 worth giving up $25,000 in expectation? Many people, myself included, would probably just take the $100,000 and give Howie Mandel a hug.

Now, suppose the remaining two boxes contained $90,000 and $130,000 and the banker offered $100,000. The expected value is $110,000, but I suspect that not many people would take the deal—there simply isn't much of a difference between the utility of the $90,000 minimum and the $100,000 offer. The usefulness of the guaranteed extra $10,000 won't be enough to convince many people to give up the chance at an extra $30,000 for a total of $130,000.

Understanding utility and how it affects decision making at the poker table is critical. There are many utility points, and many are exploitable. Here are some of the more common spots:

♦ Near the end of a tournament day. The utility of "making Day 2" in a big tournament is important to some players, a milestone worthy of bragging rights. You can often get them to lay down big hands or expect them to play very tight near the end of the day.

♦ Near the bubble in a tournament. On the bubble, many players, especially satellite winners, believe that cashing, even for the minimum, is the most important thing they can do. The utility for getting in the money can make them do some crazy, mostly nitty things.

♦ Moving up a place in a tournament. In many tournaments, the difference in prize money between rankings can become quite substantial. Suppose 4th place pays $50,000 and 3rd place pays $100,000. For many, many players, that extra $50,000 is extremely important, and they will play a strategy counter to pure expectation in order to secure the utility of that extra $50,000. Usually, they will play tighter than they should from a pure EV perspective.

♦ Protecting winnings in cash games. If I'm playing in a $1–$2 cash game and I know that a guy is up $800, I know he will be cautious about dipping below his initial buy-in of $200. The utility of being a "winner" in the game is more important to him than making a winning decision in the current hand.

Players who base their decisions on utility instead of expected value aren't necessarily making a mistake. Yes, they are making an expected-value error. But that doesn't mean they are making a mistake with respect to their *life goals*. If a guy owes $20,000 in credit card debt and is folding every hand on the bubble to make enough money to get out of debt, who are we to say that he's making a mistake by folding Aces? Perhaps the utility of being out of debt is more important to him than maximizing his expectation. Expected value is objective, while utility is subjective and personal.

EXPLOITABLE, UNEXPLOITABLE, EXPLOITATIVE

No, this isn't some kind of Latin conjugation exercise. These terms come from the branch of mathematics called "game theory" and, as you might expect, they are very important in poker, particularly in "the game" of Poker 2.0.

In game theory, a "strategy" is a plan of attack, a method of play, or your game plan. A strategy is said to be "exploitable" if an opponent can implement a counter-strategy that is certain to triumph in the long run. A strategy is said to be "unexploitable" if there is no strategy that an opponent can come up with to beat it over time.

To simplify it, let's see this concept in the context of Roshambo, or Rock-Paper-Scissors. In Roshambo, say you're playing against a "Bureaucrat" who only knows one move: paper. Obviously, this is an exploitable strategy—all you have to do to win is always go scissors.

A slightly more sophisticated player randomly decides to go either paper or scissors. Again, this strategy is easily exploitable. You simply always go scissors—you will either tie or win and you'll never lose.

In Roshambo, an unexploitable strategy is to go completely random with your throws. Over time, a random strategy will break even—there is no exploitative strategy that a player can implement to counter and get the best of a random strategy.

In poker, there are two basic approaches: you're trying to play either an unexploitable strategy or an exploitative strategy (which, in turn, will probably make you exploitable).

An exploitative strategy seeks out holes and weaknesses in an opponent's strategy and then counters with the highest possible EV play. Below are some clear-cut exploitable strategies and their associated exploitative counterstrategies that will crush.

Exploitable Strategy	Exploitative Counterstrategy
Wait for Aces	Play every hand and steal like a bandit
Raise with strong hands, limp with weak hands	Fold when they raise, raise when they limp
Never bluff	Fold when they bet or raise
Go all-in every hand	Wait for the nuts
Bluff too much	Call with more bluff-catchers

BALANCE

I love to watch great tennis players battle on the court. Take a classic pairing that almost always produces an awesome, strategic battle: Roger Federer vs. Rafael Nadal. Nadal has what is probably the best forehand in tennis, while Federer has an absolutely deadly backhand. For each of them, there is a better chance that they will win the point on any given shot if they hit a shot to their opponent's weakest side: Nadal tries to hit shots to Federer's forehand and Federer wants to hit shots to Nadal's backhand. Accurate as these guys are, it is no surprise that matches between them feature an alarmingly large number of Federer forehands and Nadal backhands.

They each know their opponent's strategy—this is where "balance" enters the game and makes things very interesting. See, in order to catch their opponent off guard, occasionally, they have to hit a ball to his stronger side. By mixing their strategies, they prevent their opponent from accurately anticipating where the next shot will be placed. Although the chances of them winning a particular point decreases substantially on that particular stroke (because they are hitting to the strong side), the *overall* chance of winning the point increases dramatically because they keep their opponent guessing.

In poker, balancing the range of hands you play and the way you play them is important—you simply must keep your opponent guessing. Most of the time, you play a hand in the most profitable way possible, but occasionally, you should mix it up and deviate from the "normal" line of play to make your *overall game* more profitable. In most cases, there is a "best play" available for a particular situation. Using experience, reads, game flow, and some randomness to deviate from the normal, best play will make you much, much tougher to read and a much stronger player.

——BALANCE IN GAME THEORY——

In order to explain the merits and principles of balance, I want to walk you through a simple game. Let's say there is $100 in the pot. Half the time (50%) your opponent has the nuts (and you'll lose), and the other half of the time (50%) he has air (and you'll win). Your opponent has the option of betting $100 or checking.

One unbalanced strategy your opponent might use would be to always bet the nuts and always check with air. You can counter that strategy by always folding if they bet. That should be clear—calling a bet if they always have the nuts is suicidal. By adopting this strategy, you will play the game absolutely perfectly against this opponent.

Now, let's say the villain complicates life a little and implements another unbalanced strategy—betting every single hand. What is your best counterstrategy? Well, if you call every single hand, 50% of the time (they were bluffing) you'll win $200 ($100 in the pot and the $100 bet) and 50% of the time you'll lose the $100 bet (they had the nuts), for an expected value of $50 per hand. Clearly, if they bet every single hand, calling every bet is correct and will show the highest profit.

A balanced strategy for our opponent requires that he bet every good hand and *some* bad hands—his best strategy is to keep us guessing. Let's see what happens if he bets all his good hands and half of his bad hands, and we call every bet.

What should be clear is that he's bluffing one-third of the time when he bets the river. He's betting all of his good hands (50%) and half of his bad hands (25%). Overall, he's betting 75% of the time, and 25% of those bets are bluffs. $25\% \div 75\% = 33.3\%$. So, if he's bluffing 33% of the time, he has the nuts 66.6% of the time.

Expected Value:
$$66\% \times -100 = -66.66$$
$$\underline{33\% \times +200 = +66.66}$$
$$= \quad 0$$

By bluffing one-third of the time, he essentially gives us no way to "win" on the river. We can call every single time and the best we can do is break even. This balanced strategy is said to be unexploitable.

——BALANCE IN PRACTICE——

Balance is overused, in general, except against the very best players. Bad players tend to make bad mistakes, and they don't adjust their strategy, so with them you don't need to balance your game. Think about it this way: should you ever bluff on the river against a guy who is going to call every bet? Of course not! Bluffing against players who won't and can't fold is moronic. They are going to call! You don't need to balance your river play against this type of opponent—in fact, doing so will cost you dearly. Against this type of opponent, you simply bet everything that will beat 50% of their range and check everything else. That should be obvious, and yet, it is a mistake that I see world-class players making all the time. You simply can't bluff someone who is incapable of folding.

Use a balanced strategy against the best players, and just play an exploitative game against the rest. As I said in my *Green Book*, 90% of the money you win at the table will come from the few bad players. Bottom line: strive to play an unexploitable, balanced strategy against the great players, and a straightforward exploitative strategy against the weak players.

POKER 2.0 TOOLKIT

Winning at Poker 2.0 necessitates being a great player, but it also requires using all of the tools available to you. For example, Heads Up Displays (HUDs) are computer programs that analyze opponents' play in real time, and range simulation programs give you deep insight into how certain hands play against ranges of hands. If you're not using these tools correctly, it will be very difficult to win regardless of how well you play.

HEADS UP DISPLAYS (HUDS)

The most useful tool developed for online poker is the HUD. HUDs look through each hand that you've played and extract vital information about each of your opponents. The HUD then displays that information in real time, directly on top of the window while you're in action. In one quick glance, you can tell how often players are opening the pot, how often they three-bet, and other important stats.

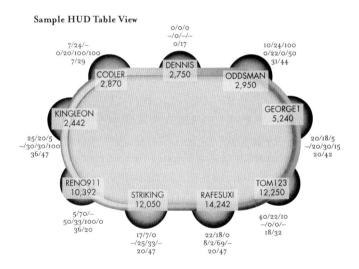

Sample HUD Table View

HUDs are completely legal to use with most online poker sites, including Full Tilt Poker, and do not violate

41

any terms of service. If you're not using a HUD today, you are at a serious disadvantage. All the cool, good players are doing it.

HUDs analyze every hand history file saved on your computer. If you replay a former opponent, their stats will automatically pop up next to their icon. HUDs are fully customizable. You'll get to know these stats in the following pages. Here is how I have mine set up:

```
┌─────────────────────┐
│     USER NAME       │
│    CHIP COUNT       │
└─────────────────────┘
```

VPIP / PFR / 3 BET
AF / UOPFR / FOLD3BET / FLOPCB
TURN CB / C-R

These stats give you a quick overview of the type of player you're up against, and enable you to form a solid strategy for breaking down their game and finding exploitable weaknesses. It's like having a little devil on your shoulder, whispering: "Pssst! He raises 32% of his hands from this position and only four-bets with AA and KK . . . looks like a good time for a three-bet! You can win this pot! Hit the raise button, buddy!"

There are literally hundreds of stats that HUDs track, but here are the most useful, along with a brief analysis of their applicability and ranges. When you find an opponent with a stat outside the common range, you can be sure that opponent is exploitable. In the examples below we're assuming a 6-handed NL cash game.

VPIP, Money Voluntarily Put in Pot

VPIP tracks how often a player voluntarily commits chips to the pot pre-flop. If a player limps, raises, calls a pre-flop raise, three-bets, or puts in any money other than the blinds, that will be reflected in this stat. The smaller the VPIP, the tighter the player is pre-flop. Think of it this way: a player with a VPIP of 11 is voluntarily putting chips into the pot about 11% of the time, or about 1 out of 9 hands.

- 0–5: Complete and total nit, playing way, way too tight. Probably only playing TT+, AK, and occasionally a "bad" hand like AQs
- 5–15: Playing too tight, not much of a factor—he won't be in enough hands for you to worry about, and when he is, he will have a very good hand
- 15–20: A tight, solid player, probably a little hesitant to get involved with speculative hands

20–27: A normal, solid player with good hand selection skills; not afraid to mix it up a bit

27–35: A normal player who is very active and seeks conflict and will be involved in quite a few hands

35+: Playing too loose, probably very exploitable; fishy

Most of the best players online have a VPIP between 18 and 25. There are winning players with a VPIP above 30, but they are hard to find as it is a very difficult style to play well.

PFR, Pre-flop Raise %

PFR tracks a player's percentage of raising before the flop, either as the opening raiser or three-bettor.

0–18: Either plays way too tight or limps quite often

18–25: Normal, solid; plays an appropriate number of hands

25–30: Aggressive player not afraid to get involved in hands and willing to put on some pressure with light three-bets and many steal attempts

30+: Playing way too loose

The difference between VPIP and PFR indicates how often a player calls a pre-flop raise. A 22/18 player will be playing 22% of his hands pre-flop and will be raising with 18% of his hands—that means he must be calling a pre-flop raise (or limping) with 4% of his hands.

- 22/21: Almost never calls pre-flop; this player has a "raise-or-fold" strategy
- 22/5: Limps or calls way too much, and is only raising with 5% of hands

Most good players have a gap of 4–5% between their VPIP and PFR.

AF, Aggression Factor

AF tracks the ratio of bets and raises to calls throughout the course of an entire hand. AF gives you a sense of a player's aggressiveness, not only pre-flop, but post-flop as well.

AF = (%Bet + %Raise) ÷ (% Call)

For example:

Player A raises pre-flop, Player B calls.

Player A bets post-flop, Player B raises, Player A calls.

Player A checks the turn, Player B bets, Player A calls.

Player A checks the river, Player B bets, Player A raises, Player B calls.

	Pre-Flop	Flop	Turn	River
Player A	Raise	Bet/Call	Raise	Raise
Player B	Call	Raise	Bet/Call	Bet/Call

AF (Player A): 1 Bet, 3 Raises, 1 Call = $(1 + 3)/1 = 4$
AF (Player B): 2 Bets, 1 Raise, 3 Calls = $(2 + 1)/3 = 1$

In this example, the AF calculation shows what we already know: Player A was much more aggressive in this hand.

AF is correlated to VPIP and PFR, but reveals more about a player's post-flop character as well. For instance, take a look at the two profiles:

	VPIP	PFR	AF
Player A	22	18	0.5
Player B	22	18	3.0

They both play the same number of hands pre-flop, but Player A is a nitty, passive post-flop player. Player B will be putting on lots of post-flop pressure with continuation-bets, double-barreled bluffs, and thin river value bets. Player A will likely be showdown-oriented and less likely to continuation-bet on boards they miss. Most winning players have an AF between 2.0 and 2.5. That is, good players are betting and raising about twice as often as they are calling.

UOPFR, Unopened Pre-Flop Raise Percentage

This stat tracks how often you raise pre-flop if you are the first player to commit chips to the pot voluntarily—a more accurate way of determining a player's actual opening range, since PFR includes times that a player three-bets and four-bets. Some HUDs have the capability of displaying this stat for each position at the table. With that level of detail displayed, you can see at a glance that a player open-raises 5% from under the gun, 8% from UTG+1, 14% from MP1, and 32% from the button.

3Bet, Three-Bet Percentage

This stat tracks how often a player is three-betting pre-flop. Among good players, expect a three-bet percentage between 5% and 9%. Any more than 9% and your opponent is three-betting way too frequently and light. Below 5% and they are probably playing a little too weak-tight.

This is a very important stat. Recently, I was playing in a six-handed cash game with an aggressive Norwegian pro, Thomas Wahlroos. I opened from the cutoff with AJs and he three-bet me from the button with what I believed to be about a 15% range. I wasn't at all concerned. AJs is a favorite over that range. I four-bet and took the pot. If I were playing that same hand against Dan Harrington and Dan was three-betting a 6% range, the AJs would hit the muck—and fast.

Fold3Bet, Fold to 3Bet

This is the percentage of times the pre-flop raiser folds to a three-bet. Players react very differently after they open the pot and get three-bet:

- 0–60%: Calling three-bets quite often (especially out of position)—you will crush them.
- 60–70%: Normal, good players. They are folding the bottom of their range and continuing with the rest.
- 70%+: These players are afraid to get involved and fold too much—without a big hand they will fold to a three-bet. Against these nits, you can three-bet mercilessly and be sure that you'll pick up the pot often enough to justify the risk.

FlopCB, Flop Continuation

This stat tracks how often a player with the betting lead makes a post-flop continuation-bet.

- 0–55%: Not being aggressive enough post-flop or playing to trap too often. With low FlopCB stats, they are likely just betting when they hit the flop. I'd be very unlikely to go for a check-raise against these types of players.
- 55–75%: Normal continuation-bet percentages for most good players.

75%+: Highly exploitable. These guys are betting way too much post-flop. You can check-raise them quite profitably. You can also float more often in position.

It is important to use the FlopCB stat in conjunction with the PFR stat. A tight player with a low PFR will, on average, have a much stronger hand post-flop—they are playing only good hands pre-flop. I expect players with a low PFR to have a very high FlopCB.

TurnCB, Turn Continuation-Bet (Double Barrel)

This stat tracks how often a player will bet the turn after raising pre-flop and then making a continuation-bet on the flop. Essentially, how much follow-through do they have? Are they the type of player that likes to take a stab on the flop and then give up, or are they going to double-barrel quite often?

You'll see most good players with a TurnCB that is somewhat inversely correlated to their FlopCB.

FlopCB	TurnCB
55%	75%
60%	70%
65%	65%
70%	60%
75%	55%

If a player is making a reasonable but high number of flop continuation-bets (75%), I'd expect them to need to slow down a little on the turn. If a player is somewhat reluctant to make a continuation-bet on the flop, they will have a hand more often and I'd expect them to barrel the turn more often.

When I run across a player with a high FlopCB and a high TurnCB, I can profitably call the flop, expect to get a turn bet, and then raise with my good hands. Semi-bluffing the turn is a very profitable play against these types of players as well.

Against players with low FlopCB and low TurnCB, I think twice before calling on the flop and the turn—they have the goods more often than not. With a FlopCB of 60% and a TurnCB of 60%, they are only betting *both the flop and the turn* about 36% of the time—most likely, those are very strong hands.

C/R, Flop Check-Raise

This stat tracks how often a player will check-raise after the flop. Good players seem to have a C/R stat of around 10%. If you see a player with a C/R of 5% or less, that means they very rarely check-raise the flop. If they check to me, I can bet with almost every hand—I'm not going to get check-raised, and if I am, they almost certainly aren't bluffing. My opponent will either be check-folding or check-calling. Against these types of players, I consider making my continuation-bets smaller than normal. When they do check and call the flop, they are very likely to check the turn as well.

If I see a player with a C/R stat of around 15%, I know they are check-raising the flop too much. They simply must be check-raise-bluffing quite often. I avoid slow-playing big hands against these types of players. When I do get check-raised, I have to either call or re-raise lighter than normal.

Most regulars who have a C/R stat of 8% or higher are check-raising most of their flush draws. On a two-tone board, if I don't get check-raised by a player with a C/R of 10%, I am pretty confident they don't have a flush draw.

FFB, Fold to Flop Bet

This stat tracks the percent of time that a player folds when facing a bet on the flop.

- 0–50%: Too loose. Open up your value betting range against players who call too many flop bets. Betting second or even third pair on the flop is profitable against these guys.
- 50–65%: Just about right, a typical good player.
- 65%+: Too tight. I make more continuation-bets than usual against these types and bluff far more often. Bluffing with most of my range will be profitable. These players rarely "float" and are "fit or fold" types who are easy to play against and are almost always raising or folding. Most players with this high an FFB stat are weak, tight, and highly exploitable.

When first using a HUD, some players will focus on individual stats and lose sight of the entire picture of the player. They'll also lose their bankrolls. It is vitally important to understand that stats are interrelated, and that focusing solely on one stat will give you an incorrect assessment of what is going on at the table.

Say I told you that you were playing against a player who had a FLOPCB % (Flop Continuation-Bet Percent) of 100%. You'd probably think, *Sweet, I'm going to own this guy!* If you plopped down in the middle of a hand and this was the only thing you knew about this guy, you'd definitely raise JT on a QT2 board, right? Now, what if I told you that this guy was only playing 2% of his hands pre-flop, would you still raise? I didn't think so. He's only playing TT+. Raising is silly (so was playing JT!) He has a 100% FLOPCB range because he always has a strong hand post-flop!

There are many instances when you can look at a particular stat and become convinced to make a play that is incorrect because you didn't take the player's entire profile into account. Context is king.

Players will not always be playing the style that the stats display, either. Perhaps they are on tilt. Or drunk. Or perhaps they are a big winner today. Or maybe they are adjusting their play to exploit someone else at the table. So although the stats are based on every hand I've played against that player, they don't necessarily reflect what is *presently* happening at the table.

If you rely too much on your HUD, you'll likely ignore your intuition. Don't stop being a poker player just because you have some stat staring you in the face—you are making the decisions, the stats are just another variable to consider, not a mandate.

You need thousands of sample hands to accurately judge a player's style of play. Without a lot of data, the randomness of the game can and will skew the stats and lead you to make some crazy, negative-EV plays. Rely on your poker skills and instincts to tell you when to ignore the HUD.

If you play online and keep seeing the same players over and over, you can be sure that they are using a HUD, too. They know your stats, they are looking for your exploitable weaknesses, and they are adjusting their game plan. They are also fully aware of each fishy spot at the table—and are aware that you are also in the know.

——HUD OPTIONS——

There are a few quality HUD packages on the market, with more on the way. I don't have a strong preference, but the true HUD power users tell me that Hold'em Manager is the best, as of this writing.

My website has an up-to-date link to the best HUD options available. And if you purchase one through my website, all of the proceeds from those sales go to the Bad Beat on Cancer initiative: www.philnolimits.com.

——HUDS FOR LIVE PLAYERS——

Even if you never play online and devote yourself fully to the live game, you can start playing live as if you were using a HUD. For instance, when I sit down with Gus Hansen in a full ring game, I think, *Ah, Gus, he's a 30/20/10* type player.* When Dan Harrington is seated at my table, I think, *Okay, Dan the Man, you're playing a 19/17/5 style.* When I'm in a $5–$10 game at the Bellagio at 3 a.m. on a Tuesday night and a drunk tourist sits down, before he plays a single hand I'm thinking, *Drunk, loose-passive, I hope he's a 60/20/20.*

Against unknown opponents, I'll start developing a profile as quickly as possible. After a few hours, I will have a pretty good idea what they're doing—essentially, my live HUD will have all the data it needs.

By breaking down opponents' games, you will be able to find exploitable weaknesses and capitalize. While the HUD is much more accurate, that doesn't mean that the principles and techniques we explore later in the book can't be used in a live setting.

---

* 30/20/10 = voluntarily committing chips to the pot pre-flop with 30% of his hands, raising pre-flop with 20% of his hands, and three-betting with 10% of his hands.

RANGE AND SIMULATION

Most players know that if I have pockets 5's and you have two over-cards, like AK, we both have about a 50/50 chance to win. This is a classic "coin flip" situation that comes up millions of times every day online and in live tournaments. As players progress, it's necessary to run more advanced calculations and simulations. For instance, what are the chances that JJ will win if I put it all-in against a range consisting of AA, KK, AK, QQ, and AQ? The only way to do this with any accuracy and speed is to use a simulator:

Results:

Hold'em Simulation

513,691,200 trials (Exhaustive)

Hand	Equity	Wins	Ties
JJ	*42.60%*	217,768,764	2,127,612
AA, KK, AK, QQ, AQ	*57.40%*	293,794,824	2,127,612

In a tenth of a second, this simulator played out all 513,691,200 combinations of starting hands and flops and calculated the expected value of JJ and QQ+, AQ+. As you can see from the results, the JJ is a slight underdog, winning 42.6% of the time.

I often use range simulation tools to determine expected value. Using these tools can give you insight into situations where your intuition and experience will lead you astray. Here is an introduction to some of the best tools available with tips on how to use them effectively. (Again, up-to-date links to all of these websites and tools can be found at my website: www.philnolimits.com.)

——PROPOKERTOOLS.COM——

This free website is extremely useful for performing hand vs. hand equity analyses. It also offers some truly innovative and useful features: Say we are in early middle position and we open the pot with J♣J♦. A tight player behind us calls. From our experience, we believe that he would make this call with a range of 88–QQ, AK, AQ, AJs, ATs, KQs. Everyone else folds. Before the flop comes down, how do you like this hand? The only way to know for sure is to run the simulation:

Simulator 2.0 Help/Docs

game:	Hold'em
syntax:	generic
board:	
dead	
hand:	Jc Jd
hand:	88-QQ, ATs, AJs, AQ+, KQs
More hands	Simulate Clear All
	Graph HvR Graph HvH Count Rank
	Unroll

Hit the "Simulate" button and check out the results:

Hold'em Simulation

90,752,112 trials (Exhaustive)

Hand	Equity	Wins	Ties
Jc Jd	**62.36%**	55,542,633	2,092,959
88-QQ, ATs, AJs, AQ+, KQs	**37.64%**	33,116,520	2,092,959

Against this flat-calling range, we're looking pretty good! No worries so far.

Now, down comes the flop: K♦4♠4♦. I'm worried about the King and that flush draw out there. Let's see how this flop affected our equity. I plug the flop into the "board" field:

Simulator 2.0 Help/Docs

game:	Hold'em
syntax:	generic
board:	Kd 4s 4d
dead	
hand:	Jc Jd
hand:	88-QQ, ATs, AJs, AQ+, KQs
More hands	Simulate Clear All
	Graph HvR Graph HvH Count Rank
	Unroll

After hitting "Simulate," we learn that our equity actually improved against this range of hands:

Hold'em Simulation

51,480 trials (Exhaustive)

board: Kd 4s 4d

Hand	Equity	Wins	Ties
Jc Jd	70.33%	35,574	1,260
88-QQ, ATs, AJs, AQ+, KQs	29.67%	14,646	1,260

I bet and get called. I think he'd raise with AK. I seriously doubt that my opponent has AT, AJ, or AQ, but I think it is likely that he'd call with the rest of the pairs in his range, as well as the diamond flush draws. Now that we've narrowed the range a bit with our post-flop bet, let's see how we're doing:

Hold'em Simulation

29,700 trials (Exhaustive)

board: Kd 4s 4d

Hand	Equity	Wins	Ties
Jc Jd	63.60%	18,326	1,128
88-QQ, KQs, AdTd, AdJd, AdQd	36.40%	10,246	1,128

Not great, but not terrible either, assuming that all of our estimates are correct. We're still in the lead!

We hold our breath and here comes the turn: the A♠. You know the drill . . . back to the simulator:

Hold'em Simulation

1,320 trials (Exhaustive)

board: Kd 4s 4d As

Hand	Equity	Wins	Ties
Jc Jd	**60.61%**	778	44
88-QQ, KQs, AdTd, AdJd, AdQd	**39.39%**	498	44

Hmm, what looked like a "scare card" isn't so scary. That turn card didn't really change much. There are only three hands in my opponent's range that hit that Ace: A♦T♦, A♦J♦, A♦Q♦, which means I'm still a favorite.

Looking through the combinations, I see that I'm either really, really far ahead when my opponent has 88–TT, or I'm really far behind when he has QQ, KQ, AT, AJ, or AQ. Betting might get QQ and KQ to fold.

Putting it all together, I believe my best plan of attack is to bet small, maybe half the pot, and try to get QQ and KQ to make a tight fold, but give up if I get called again.

As you can see, these tools can give you some valuable insight into the game that would be hard to come by otherwise.

One of the things I like to experiment with is running different types of flops against my opponent's expected hand range to see how board texture affects my equity. Take this same pre-flop matchup, JJ vs. 88–QQ, ATs+, AQ+, KQs, and a slightly different flop: A♠4♦4♥.

Hold'em Simulation
46,530 trials (Exhaustive)

board: As 4d 4h

Hand	Equity	Wins	Ties
Jc Jd	**46.48%**	21,024	1,204
88-QQ, ATs, AJs, AQ+, KQs	**53.52%**	24,302	1,204

What this shows me is that an Ace-high dry board is much worse for my hand than a King-high dry board. I have just 46.48% equity against this range, whereas with the K-4-4-flop, I had 70% equity!

Try this one on for size: A late position opener raises with the top 20% of his hands. I decide to flat-call on the button with J♣T♣. Let's see how different flops affect my equity:

board: Ad Js 4c

Hand	Equity	Wins	Ties
Jc Tc	**48.17%**	88,005	5,220
20%	**51.83%**	94,875	5,220

board: Kd Js 4c

Hand	Equity	Wins	Ties
Jc Tc	**56.67%**	108,927	4,321
20%	**43.33%**	82,772	4,321

board: Qd Js 4c

Hand	Equity	Wins	Ties
Jc Tc	**60.26%**	118,756	3,519
20%	**39.74%**	77,705	3,519

By doing this sort of work, it is easy to see that Queen-high and King-high boards are less threatening than an Ace-high board. I can call or raise post-flop much more frequently on those boards.

Here is a somewhat surprising result I found recently. You're playing in a three-way pot and you get to choose a hand:

Which hand would you choose?

I was shocked to find out that the answer is that the "worst" hand of the three, K♥Q♥, actually has the highest equity:

Hand	Equity	Wins	Ties
Ac Tc	33.40%	456,470	4,090
Kh Qh	35.77%	488,952	4,090
8c 8d	30.83%	421,242	4,090

It seems that one pair will rarely win at showdown. With K♥Q♥, you have two shots at making an over-pair to the 88 and still have outs when the AT flops a pair of tens. If you can get a sucker on the line with this bet, please send me a small cut.

Amarillo Slim's Hussle

Here's a hussle that WSOP champ Amarillo "Slim" Preston used to run (and no, I never lost money to him on it). Slim would produce three Hold'em hands: 4♣4♦, J♠T♠, A♣K♥.

He'd give you first choice, and then he'd choose a hand. He'd then deal out a flop, turn, and river, with the best poker hand winning $100.

If you chose the 44, he'd take the J♠T♠ and have the edge.

Hand	Equity	Wins	Ties
Js Ts	**52.85%**	897,075	15,602
4c 4d	**47.15%**	799,627	15,602

If you took the A♣K♥, he'd take the 44 and make a few bucks.

Hand	Equity	Wins	Ties
4c 4d	**54.03%**	920,845	8,630
Ac Kh	**45.97%**	782,829	8,630

And if you took the J♠T♠, he'd get the best of it by taking the A♣K♥.

Hand	Equity	Wins	Ties
Js Ts	**41.18%**	701,504	7,241
Ac Kh	**58.82%**	1,003,559	7,241

That's the kind of gambler Slim was—he was always looking for a champion and turning him into a sucker.

Other Simulation Tools

There are plenty of other features at ProPokerTools that are interesting and useful. I encourage you to check them out—CardRunnersEV and PokerStove, in particular. Both are simulation engines that give you different looks at equity and hand playability.

NO LIMIT
HOLD'EM 2.0

Although No Limit Hold'em (NLH) has evolved substantially in the last five years, it is still incredibly fun and potentially profitable. But the games are much tougher than they were just a few years back. The Internet geniuses have really done an incredible amount of work on NLH theory; as a result, the players are more aggressive and playing a much less exploitable game. They are unpredictable and tough to read. At a $5–$10 table, online or live, you're going to face relentless pressure and be forced to make tough decisions.

My *Little Green Book* was a good start to NLH. But the advances that have been made in the last few years require rethinking and retooling to win at the mid-stakes games or higher.

PRE-FLOP RANGES TABLE

As we'll be using discussions of pre-flop ranges quite often throughout the book, here are two different looks at the top Hold'em hands:

Standard Pre-flop Ranges

5% 99+, AJs+, AQ+
10% 77+, A9s+, AJ+, KTs+, KQ, QJs
15% 66+, A4s+, AT+, K9s+, KJ+, QTs+
20% 55+, A2s+, A9+, K7s+, KT+, Q9s+, QJ, J9s+, T9s
25% 44+, A2s+, A8+, K5s+, KT+, Q8s+, QT+, J8+, JT, T8+, 98s
30% 33+, A2s+, A4+, K3s+, K9+, Q8s+, QT+, J8s+, JT, T8s+, 98s
40% 22+, A2+, K2s+, K8+, Q4s+, Q9+, J7s+, J9+, T7s+, T9, 97s+, 87s, 76s
45% 22+, A2+, K2s+, K5+, Q2s+, Q9+, J5s+, J9+, T6s+, T9, 96s+, 86s+, 75s+, 65s
50% 22+, A2+, K2s+, K5+, Q2s+, Q8+, J4s+, J8+, T6s+, T8+, 96s+, 98, 85s+, 75s+, 65s, 54s
55% 22+, A2+, K2s+, K4+, Q2s+, Q7+, J2s+, J8+, T4s+, T8+, 95s+, 98, 85s+, 87, 75s+, 64s, 54s
60% 22+, A2+, K2+, Q2s+, Q6+, J2s+, J7+, T3s+, T8+, 94s+, 97+, 85s+, 87, 74s+, 64s, 53s+
70% 22+, A2+, K2+, Q2s+, Q3+, J2s+, J6+, T2s+, T7+, 92s+, 96+, 84s+, 86+, 73s+, 76, 63s+, 52s+, 43s
80% 22+, A2+, K2+, Q2+, T2s+, T6+, 92s+, 95+, 82s+, 85+, 72s+, 75+, 62s, 65, 52s+, 54, 42s+, 32s
90% 22+, A2+, K2+, Q2+, T2+, 92s+, 94+, 82s+, 84+, 72s+, 74+, 62s+, 64+, 52s+, 53+, 42s+, 32s, 43

	A	K	Q	J	T	9	8	7	6	5	4	3	2
A	5	5	5	5	10	10	15	15	15	15	15	23	20
K	5	5	10	10	10	15	20	20	25	25	30	30	35
Q	5	10	5	10	15	20	25	35	35	35	40	45	45
J	10	15	20	5	15	20	25	35	45	45	50	55	55
T	15	20	25	25	5	20	25	35	45	55	55	60	65
9	20	30	35	40	40	5	25	35	45	50	60	65	70
8	25	40	50	50	50	50	10	35	45	50	65	75	75
7	30	45	55	60	65	60	55	10	40	45	60	70	80
6	35	45	60	70	75	70	65	65	15	45	55	65	80
5	30	45	65	75	85	80	80	75	75	20	50	60	70
4	30	55	70	80	85	90	90	90	85	80	25	65	75
3	35	55	70	85	90	95	100	95	95	85	90	30	80
2	40	60	75	85	90	95	100	100	100	95	100	100	40

Unsuited hands (left) / Suited hands (right)

It is important to understand that a 20% range doesn't necessarily mean that a player is playing only the top 20% of hands. In many cases, the 20% will be composed of the top 15% of hands by rank, and 5% of smaller suited-connector and suited-one-gapper hands that have excellent playability post-flop. Still, these charts and hand ranks should be quite useful—study them until you are able to take any hand and tell within 5% what range it falls into. For example, if I see a player opening J6s from late position, I know that player is opening at least 45% of the hands.

Here are some interesting observations that might help you memorize this hand-ranking chart:

♦ All pocket pairs are in the top 40% of hands
♦ Suited cards with a 4 aren't in the bottom 40% of hands (mnemonic: 4–40)
♦ Suited cards with a 5 aren't in the bottom 50% of hands (mnemonic: 5–50)
♦ 33 is top 30% (mnemonic: 33–30)
♦ Suited Aces are always top 20%

RANGE VS. RANGE

Ten years ago, players were content to "put you on a hand" and didn't think that much about range. "I put you on AK," you'd hear them say as they stacked off with pocket 9s.

If you showed up with KK or QQ, they *really* believed they were unlucky and just made a bad read.

Five years ago, as the Internet whiz kids started analyzing the game, they figured out that trying to put a player on a single hand didn't make sense. It was much more valuable to calculate against the entire set of hands that a player could have based on their profile and actions. "I put him on a range of 77+, AQo+, ATs+, KQs, QJs, JTs. My 99 against that range only wins 44% of the time, so I mucked it."

Now, in Poker 2.0, players are talking about "range vs. range." How the range of hands their opponent expects them to play does against their opponent's range. "He raised with the top 20% from the Hi-Jack; I called from the big blind. The flop was Q-J-8. I check-raised. There are so many more hands that make two pair in my range than there are in his range, and I was pretty sure I could get a fold from a hand as good as KQ."

To do well in this new poker landscape, you simply must make the transition from a hand vs. hand mentality and begin thinking in terms of range vs. range.

PRE-FLOP PLAY

In the early days of the poker boom, improving your pre-flop fundamentals was the quickest way to fix your game.

Today, almost everyone plays a good pre-flop game. Sure, there are still the fishy weak spots, but for the most part, you don't see people limping under the gun with 75s any more.

In NL 2.0, pre-flop play has changed significantly. I see more three-betting, more aggression, and lots more pre-flop shoving in tournaments. Here's the thing: sound, fundamental pre-flop play is still the foundation of every great player's game. If you don't have a good pre-flop game, it is very unlikely that you can be a winning player no matter how good your post-flop skills are.

——PRE-FLOP FUNDAMENTALS——

If you're going to be a winning player, you simply must have these basics mastered:

- ♦ You need to be selectively aggressive—wait for good spots and then raise.
- ♦ You must avoid playing dominated hands, especially out of position. Practice sound hand selection. Simple.

Limping Is for Losers

This is *the most important fundamental* in poker—for every game, for every tournament, every stake:

If you are the first player to voluntarily commit chips to the pot, open for a raise.

Limping is inevitably a losing play. If you see a person at the table limping, you can be fairly sure he is a bad player. Bottom line: If your hand is worth playing, it is worth raising.

When I raise before the flop, I get five main benefits:

♦ I can steal the blinds. Everyone might fold and I might just stack some chips without a fight. If I limp, I don't give myself a chance to steal.

♦ I take control of the betting. When I raise, I announce to the rest of the table, "I think I have the best hand. If you want this pot, you're going to have to do something extraordinary or get lucky." If I limp, I announce to the table, "I don't like my hand all that much, here is some free money if you want it."

♦ I disguise the strength of my hand. I raise with all the hands, whether it is AA or 86s. I don't give away any information about the strength of my hand, and I force my opponents to guess. If I limp with my bad hands and raise with my good hands, my opponents know exactly what type of hand I have and they almost never make a mistake.

♦ I define the strength of my opponent's hand. If I raise and the big blind calls, I know he probably doesn't have a hand strong enough to three-bet. I know that he doesn't have a hand weak enough to fold. He has a pretty narrow range of medium strength, somewhat speculative hands. If I limp and get a check from the big blind, I have no idea what two cards he has.

♦ I limit the competition. When I limp, I will be playing a ton of multi-way pots, and most of the time I'll be out of position. The more players in, the more likely I will face a tough decision and lose. Ideally, I want to raise and play in position against a single player.

Now, if a fish limps into the pot ahead of you, do whatever you want. I suggest raising, and doing so quite liberally, but you can call behind a limp without getting scorned. In my book, it only counts as limping if you are open-limping, that is, you are limping as the first player to enter the pot voluntarily.

There are certainly a few famous, great players who regularly limp in cash games and tournaments. I've seen Daniel Negreanu, Gavin Smith, and quite a few others make it work. However, just because it works for a very small number of players doesn't mean it will work for you. Those two (and others who limp and can still win) are some of the best post-flop players in the world. They give up all the advantages of raising pre-flop and can get back lost expectation with spectacular post-flop play. It is extremely difficult to play that style and win. Raising pre-flop is a much better approach for all but the very best of the best.

Avoid Domination

If a player opens the pot for a raise, avoid playing hands that aren't currently ahead of at least a decent percentage of your opponent's opening range. Your calling and three-betting range should be much tighter than their opening range. For example, if your opponent opens 88+, ATs+, AQo+, KQs, QJs, JTs and you call with KTo, you are making a pretty big mistake. You only dominate three of those combinations, the JTs. You are behind to AA, KK, AK, QQ, JJ, TT, and KQ—48 combinations. You are going to have an extremely hard time making money on this hand. In reality, playing KT against this range is suicidal. Using a range simulator, you can see that KT only has 33% equity against that range. If you're going to play KT against this range, you might as well play 52o as well—they have fairly similar equity.

The big problem when you play these dominated hands comes when you actually flop something. Say you play KT against this range and the flop comes K-9-8—a great flop, right? Well, if you face any significant action, you are going to be crushed. You might be drawing dead, and at best you'll be drawing to 5 outs.

Hand Selection

Much has been written about proper pre-flop hand selection, but in brief: Tight, *very tight*, is right from early position. As players fold and there are fewer players left to act behind me, I loosen up my starting-hand requirements. If the action folds to me in late position, I get aggressive. (If you need a starting-hand guide, you can get one here: www.philnolimits.com.)

A word about starting-hand guides: they are just that— a start. In some games, you should be playing much, much looser from all positions; in some games, you should be playing tighter. In Poker 2.0, good starting-hand-selection skills are assumed. Remember, everyone plays pretty well pre-flop these days.

——NEW STEAL POSITIONS——

Blind stealing, once the bread and butter of top tournament players, is getting more and more difficult. These days, re-steal three-bets are very profitable, and today's top players employ that counterstrategy quite effectively. It is very difficult to find a "good spot" these days.

As players got tougher and late position three-bets became more commonplace, the standard steal positions migrated counterclockwise around the table toward the blinds. Rather than stealing from the button, cutoff, and Hi-Jack quite liberally, steals from positions as early as under the gun are the most effective, and steals from late position are unprofitable, as a three-bet forces a fold and takes the pot away. Opponents give me more credit for a real hand when I open from early position, and they are less likely to three-bet.

I was talking with Australian superstar Mark Vos

recently. Mark has had tremendous tournament success by looking for weak spots: "Phil, I'm just targeting the weakest players at the table. When it is their big blind, I'm raising pre-flop with almost every single hand, regardless of my position. If there are two or three really bad players at the table, I'm in there with a pre-flop raise with every hand when they are in the big blind as well. My pre-flop hand selection has less to do with my hand than it does with the quality of the player in the big blind."

This makes total sense to me. Still, it is hard to do in practice—looking down at 7-4 offsuit in early position and firing a pre-flop raise is tough. But if that player in the big blind is bad enough, it is probably a winning long-term strategy—that is, at least, until the other players catch on to your shenanigans. When they figure I'm picking on the fish, I expect to get three-bet quite liberally. Everyone fights tooth and nail to get the fishy chips.

The new most effective steal position is probably the big blind. How can you steal from the big blind? By cultivating a tight image and then three-betting a late position player who opens way too many pots.

Stealing blinds is much more important in tournament play, particularly after the antes have kicked in. In cash games, stealing blinds just isn't that necessary but raising pre-flop is still valuable and serves to isolate the fish and narrow the field.

In late position, when there are competent players with short stacks behind me holding less than 20 big blinds, I am extremely cautious. When I open for a pre-flop raise in middle or late position, I'm expecting a short-stacked player to move all-in. So I lock it down and only open with hands that are willing to call the inevitable shove. Trying to steal the blinds in these spots when I am unwilling to call a 20 big-blind shove is just asking to make a donation to the short stacks, making them even more difficult to combat on subsequent orbits. I save my chips, keep them short-stacked, and wait for the right hand to call an all-in three-bet.

50–100

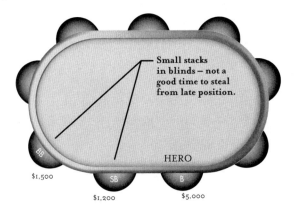

75

——CALLING A PRE-FLOP RAISE——

Even in hyper-aggressive poker games, the Gap Principle still reigns supreme: you need a better hand to call a pre-flop raise than you need to open the pot for a raise. If my opponent is open-raising with a 15% opening range, I should be calling that pre-flop raise with a range much, much tighter than 15%.

Good players simply don't call pre-flop raises very often. Typical winning players call a late position opening raise between 5% and 7% of the time. Great players three-bet or fold unless very specific conditions are met. I call a pre-flop raise with small pocket pairs, but only if the implied odds* are 20 times the opening raise. This is a big leak for many players—they call with too many weak pocket pairs when the effective stack sizes are less than 50 big blinds, especially from the small or big blind (out of position).

Here are some other good spots to flat-call an opening raiser:

♦ I flat-call with speculative hands against players who open with a wide range (30%+) and play a very exploitable post-flop game.
♦ I flat-call with quite a few more hands than normal

---

* The amount of money I can expect to win if I flop a set and my opponent has a premium hand like KK or AA on an 8-5-2 board.

against calling stations. When I hit a hand, I'm going to get paid off.

♦ I flat-call with more hands in medium-stacked situations where I simply can't three-bet effectively. With stack sizes less than about 35 big blinds, a three-bet is effectively an all-in. In these spots, I start flat-calling more.

♦ I flat-call on the button against a wide cutoff or Hi-Jack opening range. I can make this play with a "narrower gap"—position helps immensely and will compensate.

♦ I flat-call with very strong hands when there are many short stacks behind me. I'm trying to set up a reverse squeeze (see page 116)—that is, calling a pre-flop raise with a strong hand and hoping that a player will try a squeeze play.

I was recently in a $10–$20 ring game and I had Phil "Unabomber" Laak on my right. Phil was really splashing around in late position and opening a very wide range. I was eager to flat-call his middle position opener with KTs. To Phil's right was one of the nittiest guys around, Tony Cousineau. When Tony opened the pot from middle position, I had no problem folding AJo from the button.

When flatting an opening raise, I am careful to look for potential squeezers behind me. Flatting and then folding to a 20-big-blind squeeze is just silly. When there are many short stacks behind me, I save my money and eliminate speculative flat-calls. I also avoid flat-calling nits who make continuation-bets on almost every flop. I'll almost never be in a good spot to make a post-flop move against a nit with a tight range.

Against loose, aggressive players (LAGs), I flat-call liberally when I'm in position. I can maneuver post-flop because my opponent will rarely have a hand that can stand up to significant post-flop pressure. I flat-call a late position LAG with hands like A5s, ATo, 55, QJs, 96s, and because most of my range is so weak, I balance those calls with very, very strong hands, like AA, KK. Having these strong hands in my range will make me much harder to play against post-flop and may also invite a reverse squeeze.

From the small and big blinds, I will call a late position pre-flop raise with lots of speculative hands: 97s, KTs, 22–66 (assuming deep stacks). To balance those "bad" hands, I also like to flat-call with AQ and QQ. Having those hands in my flat-calling range will make my opponent think twice before pulling any ridiculously fancy plays post-flop. These hands help me slow them down a bit when I'm out of position. Of course, my opponent may not be aware that I can have QQ and AQ in my flat-calling range, but after I shove it down their throat a few times, they'll think twice about raising my blind and then barrel away.

——THREE-BETTING——

Pre-flop three-bets are becoming increasingly common as the game evolves. If you're unfamiliar with a three-bet, let me lay out a quick example. You're seated in a nine-handed tournament table, 100–200 blinds, and you're in middle position. You have AQo and you raise three times the big blind to 600, just like you're supposed to. The player on the button re-raises and makes it 1,800 to go. That re-raise is known as a three-bet, and it is nasty.

Three-betting is essential for success, and a proper defense strategy is also mandatory.

Four Factors

There are four main factors to consider when three-betting:

♦ My opponent's playback range—how often will they four-bet?
♦ My opponent's opening range—how often are they entering the pot?
♦ How often will my opponent call and take a flop with me? How well do they play post-flop?
♦ How will players behind me react? How often will they pick up a monster and get involved?

There are many different types of players, each with a specific pre-flop style. These differences in play will lead to huge three-betting strategy deviations (or at least they should). Let's examine some common player types.

Three-Betting vs. Nits

My opponent is the king of nits. He prides himself on his patience. Pre-flop, this player will limp in with all his small pocket pairs in hopes of hitting a set, and he'll raise big with the big pairs, KK+.

If this opponent opens the pot for a raise, I never three-bet unless I'm dealt AA. I never bluff a three-bet. His opening raise range is KK+. This player never folds to three-bets, has a 100% playback range, and a 0% calling range.

Three-Betting vs. Gamblers

My opponent is the king of gamblers. He loves seeing flops. He opens pre-flop with a very wide range of hands, will call three-bets with almost every hand, and only four-bets with premium hands.

I three-bet these gamblers with a wide range of hands for value, isolating my prey from the rest of the good players. This player doesn't fold to three-bets, has a 2.6% playback range, QQ+, AK, and calls the other 97.4% of the time. I am going to crush him.

Three-Betting vs. Loose-Passive Limpers

These players define their range by limping into the pot with medium-weak hands and raising with strong hands. These players typically only raise with QQ+, AK and limp pre-flop with the rest. Loose-passive limpers rarely fold to three-bets, even out of position.

Against these players, I only three-bet pocket Aces. But, I will raise their opening limps quite liberally in an attempt to isolate them. Post-flop, I will make very thin value bets against these players.

Three-Betting vs. Loose-Passive Raisers

These loose-passive types open around a 15% range for a raise—TT+, JT+, QT+, KT+, AT+—but still only four-bet with QQ+, AK. My three-betting range against this type of player consists strictly of value hands: JJ+, AJs+, KJs+, QJs, AJo+, KQo. There are a few reasons this three-betting range wins money:

♦ Loose-passive players have a wide gap between their opening range and playback (four-bet) range, so I'll frequently get to see the flop in position with a hand that dominates their range. These players usually do not slow-play AA, KK, or AK versus three-bets.
♦ Loose-passive players rarely fold to three-bets. By three-betting hands that make good top-pair hands, I get value from a wide calling range. So when I three-bet AJ, I expect to get calls from their KJ, QJ, and JT.

They play a straightforward post-flop game, and when they do decide to bluff, it is usually quite obvious. These are the type of players that check down J high to the river and let me win with K high. The key to winning against loose-passive players is to go for thin-value post-flop.

Three-Betting vs. LAGtards

LAGtards are the wannabe smart loose-aggressive players. They're posers. They've seen hyper-aggressive poker on television and try to emulate Phil Ivey and Tom Dwan by making sick bluffs. It is common to see a LAGtard raising with a 40–50% range from the cutoff and button.

There is no point in three-betting these players light. I three-bet them for value with about the same range as I do the more aggressive loose-passive players: JJ+, AJs+, KJs+, QJs, AJo+, KQo. Many of the LAGtards play a decent post-flop game. Against these players, there are some tricky situations post-flop, but a wide value three-betting range is still correct.

If the LAGtards are very good, aggressive, post-flop players, I narrow my three-betting range a little bit and avoid the difficult decisions. Even three-betting a very tight range of JJ+, AK against these geniuses who try to outplay me post-flop can be very profitable.

Recently, I was playing at the Wynn in a $5,000 buy-in tournament. In the first level, a LAGtard opened from the Hi-Jack. I three-bet from the button with QQ and expected him to call. He didn't disappoint. The flop was

Q-9-2. He checked, I bet, he called. I put him on AQ, KQ, JJ, TT, KT, JT. Turn was a 2. He checked, I bet pot, he called. My assessment of his range didn't change much. River was a K. He checked, I overbet the pot, praying that he had a straight, KQ, or KT. He moved in and of course I snap-called. He had JT and got what he deserved, and I got an early double up.

Three-Betting vs. Weak-Tight Players

A weak-tight player might open 25% of hands from the cutoff. Weak-tight players don't really know how to respond to three-bets: their default response is to fold all but the best hands.

They fold KJs and QJs to a three-bet because they fear domination, but they gladly call with pocket pairs (22–TT) in an attempt to set-mine.* A weak-tight player typically calls a three-bet with a range of 22–TT, KQs, AQs+, AK (94 combinations), and they four-bet with JJ+ (24 combinations).

I pound relentlessly on weak-tight players—three-betting against them is very profitable. The only thing I really worry about is getting four-bet by a player who has noticed that I've been overly active against the weak-tight guy.

---

* Set-mine: To play small pocket pairs pre-flop in an attempt to flop a set.

Against weak-tight players, I polarize my range to include bluffs and high-value hands.

Value hands are KK+ against their early position openers, and QQ+ against middle and late position opening raises. My bluff hands include trash like 56o, 96s, 86s, and such. Weak-tight players fold so much pre-flop that three-betting with hands like this (and worse!) becomes nearly automatic.

I definitely do not want to three-bet with hands like KQs, QJs. With these hands I will simply call and take a flop if I'm in position. I'm hoping that I can flop a pair with KQ, like K-9-5, and get paid off against the KJ or KT hands my opponent would have folded to a pre-flop three-bet. Often, there is more value in calling with these hands that dominate the opening range than there is in three-betting and winning a small pot pre-flop.

Three-Betting vs. Tight-Aggressive Players

A TAG, tight-aggressive player, opens 25% of their hands in the cutoff seat, but they have a dramatically different (and better) response to three-bets. These players are extremely prevalent at the mid- and high-stakes games, and therefore deserving of detailed attention.

In contrast to the weak-tight player, the tight-aggressive player has a much smaller gap in their opening range compared to their play-back range. In other words, they have a well-balanced four-bet range and could be four-betting as much as 25% of their opening range. Four-bet ranges could look like any of these profiles:

- Pure Value: QQ+, AK, usually when opening from early position
- Polarized: JJ+, AK, A2s–A5s, A5o when they open from late position and get three-bet from the button
- Merged: 88+, AK from late position against an aggressive three-bettor capable of five-bet shoving with hands like A5s and 44

When out of position, TAGs call three-bets less often than most players. For example, when a TAG opens from the cutoff seat and calls your button three-bet out of position, they are probably doing so with about a 10% range—usually something like 88–TT, KQs, AJs, AQs.

TAG, in Late Position, Facing Early Position Opening

When I'm on the button and a TAG opens UTG, I three-bet them with a highly polarized range of KK+, 54s, 64s+, 74s+, 85s+. Most TAGs play very straightforwardly when they open from UTG and get three-bet. They know that I know that their range is tight and they don't believe that I would be suicidal enough to three-bet them with a hand like 85s. I expect them to fold all but the very top of their range, JJ+, AK. After I employ this tactic a few times, I realize a thinking TAG will adjust, so I try to stay one step ahead of them and adjust my three-betting tendencies just before they adjust theirs.

TAG, on the Button, Facing Cutoff or Hi-Jack Opening

When I'm on the button and a TAG opens from the Hi-Jack or cutoff seat, I've found that a mixed three-betting strategy is the most effective. About 75% of the time, I play a very straightforward, no-nonsense three-bet range of JJ+, AK, AQ, AJs. The other 25% of the time, I switch gears dramatically and three-bet like a crazy monkey with a very polarized range of 22–66, QQ+, AK, 43s, 53s+, 64s+, 74s+, 85s+. Here's a good way of doing this: When considering my action, I look down at my watch. If the second hand reads 0–45, I play the tight and straightforward. If the second hand reads 46–60, I turn into a simian.

In combination, these ranges have me three-betting at right around 5% of the time. When I mix it up like this and I show down a few 64s-type hands, I expect to get four-bet quite liberally. What my opponents don't know is that I'll "have the goods," QQ+, about 50% of the time I'm three-betting! My random, mixed three-betting strategy is very difficult to counter.

TAG, from the Blinds Against any Opening

Out of position (from the SB or BB) against a TAG, I employ a very standard three-betting strategy: I re-raise to a little more than pot,* and *never* as a bluff.

Against a TAG who opens 35% of his hands on the button, a reasonable three-bet range is 22–77, JJ+, AJs+, KQs, AQ. Notice that all of these hands are value hands; there aren't any 65s or 86s in that range. I don't call with many hands out of position, but a range of 88–TT, ATs, KJs, QJs, JTs seems fine. I don't like to three-bet with those hands because I often won't know what to do if I get four-bet.

TAGs can vary widely in how they react to three-bets when they're in position. I vary the three-betting range after I get an idea about their tendencies. If they are flatting with many hands when I three-bet, I'll make some slight adjustments to my standard three-betting range:

♦ Remove 22–77. Those hands will be very difficult to play post-flop.
♦ Add some suited-connectors, like 54s, 65s, 76s, 87s, 98s. These hands aren't going to be easily dominated by the TAG's calling range, and they have excellent playability post-flop. If I catch a piece of the flop (top pair, flush draw, or straight draw), I can barrel away and put

---

* If my opponent opens for 3x the blind, I'll raise to 11 or 12 blinds.

tons of pressure on my opponent. With a hand like this, I'll hit the flop hard enough to fire a few shells about 40% of the time.

If my TAG opponent is a frequent four-bettor, there simply must be some bluffs in his range. Here are the appropriate adjustments against this agro-four-bettor:

♦ Fold 22–44 pre-flop.
♦ Add some A-X (A2–A5) hands to my three-betting mix. The Ace serves as a blocker and reduces the number of strong four-betting combinations that will be in his range, such as AA, AK, AQ, or AJs.
♦ If I've seen him four-bet and then call a five-bet shove with small pocket pairs, I merge my five-bet shoving range and get it in with 88+.
♦ Against tricky TAGs that will flat-call with monster hands like KK+ quite frequently and four-bet with the lesser hands, I will start five-bet-shoving hands like A2–A5 and AQ. Since they won't have monsters in their four-bet range, these five-bet shoves are very effective, assuming appropriate stack sizes and fold equity.

Three-Betting Against Smart LAGs

If I were to pick a type of player to avoid three-betting light, this would be the one. Unfortunately, these players are quick to isolate the fish, take their money, and kill the game. I want the fish's money first, so I need to put these LAGs in their place and stop letting them run the table.

LAGs are much more likely than the average player to play-back and four-bet when they suspect that I am three-betting light against them. Smart LAG players are very quick to adjust and change gears. So, if I see any exploitable tendency, I must pounce immediately. Timing is imperative—if I wait too long, they will change gears and the opportunity will evaporate. Against smart LAGs, I don't have time to confirm my read with more information and *then* make a move.

Against smart LAGs that are four-betting frequently, the five-bet becomes a tool that must be used. Against an aggressive player, I create a volatile dynamic pre-flop by three-betting and five-bet shoving more frequently. Getting all-in pre-flop with AQ, 88, and even 22 can be the right (but scary!) play. For example, if my smart LAG opponent is opening the button with a 67% range, I will be three-betting around 25% of the time. If he responds by four-betting with a 15% frequency, five-bet shoving with all pocket pairs becomes quite profitable. But getting into pre-flop shoving wars is not advisable unless there is quite a bit of history with an opponent. Remember, small samples can be very deceptive and lead to catastrophic, stack-ending mistakes.

As a default, I three-bet a wide-range smart LAG

opener with 99+, AJo+, ATs+, KQo+, KJs+, QJs. I will call most small four-bets with most of this range as well, but five-bet shove QQ+, AK. After calling a four-bet a few times, I tighten up my four-bet-calling range a bit—my opponent will know that I'm not folding and will likely reduce his four-betting frequency or do so only with stronger hands. My willingness to "gamble" with him will also probably lead him to tighten up his opening-raise requirements as well. These changes effectively turn my smart LAG into just another TAG. Finally, I'll be the "table captain" and control the action.

Against smart LAGs, I'm playing a continuous game of cat and mouse. I try to stay one step ahead and force them into playing a more predictable, exploitable style. These smart LAGs are chameleons and will adjust their pre-flop style quickly. I'll adjust as well and find more exploitable weaknesses . . . and the dance continues until one of us says "uncle" and gives up.

Three-Betting with a Short Stack

If my stack is less than 25 big blinds and I'm going to three-bet, I simply ship it in. I can't commit anywhere near a third of my stack to the pot and then fold. So I might as well get it in and apply maximum pressure and give myself maximum fold equity. In some situations, a very small three-bet might be preferable with a monster hand. In tournaments partic-ularly, I really need to get full value from QQ+ when short stacked. In these instances, I don't mind a min-three-bet, an attempt to build the pot and trap my opponent rather than just moving my stack all-in.

In an online tournament recently, I took a bad beat and was down to 18 big blinds. A very loose, very aggressive player opened from late position and I was dealt AA on the button. I believed that if I just moved in my opponent would fold way too often and I'd lose value. But I didn't want to call either, and give the small and big blind really good odds to come along. So, I min-three-bet and made it 6 big blinds to go. With J9s, my opponent couldn't resist the great odds he was getting to see the flop. He flopped a pair, all the money went in on the flop, and I doubled up.

Summary

Since three-betting is an integral part of Poker 2.0, here is a summary of the key points:

♦ I polarize my three-betting range against solid players. I three-bet for value with very good hands and bluff-three-bet very weak hands that won't be dominated if my opponent decides to call.

♦ If my opponent decides to four-bet, my decision is automatic. If it's close, and I won't know what to do against a four-bet, I don't three-bet.

♦ Against most opening-range profiles, merging hands like QJ, KQ, and KJ into my three-betting ranges, even in position, is a big, costly mistake. The exception to this is when a player opens an extremely wide range, calls three-bets with a very large portion of their opening range, and rarely four-bets.

♦ I am more selective with my three-bets as the number of players yet to act increases.

♦ If my opponent is going to fold a high percentage of their opening range to a three-bet, I am very aggressive and start three-betting with a very wide range.

——THREE-BET DEFENSE——

When I open for a raise and get three-bet, there are three possible responses: fold and give up, take a flop, or four-bet (re-re-raise). Position is the most important factor to consider when weighing these options. When out of position, I will occasionally take a flop, but I'm much more apt to fold or four-bet. If I'm in position, I'm much more likely to call and less likely to fold or four-bet. Three-bet pots will quickly escalate post-flop and increase the potential for getting stacked, which is why position is so important.

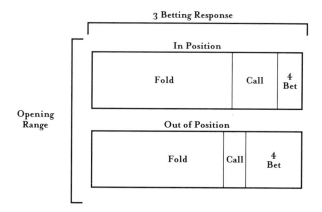

As always, it is critical to consider my opponent's pre-flop three-betting range. Also, understand that range will vary dramatically based on the position of my opening raise. If I raise from early position, my opponent needs a much better hand to three-bet me than he needs if I open from the Hi-Jack or cutoff seat.

When I open from early position in a full ring game, I only expect to get three-bet by hands like QQ+, AK. If I open from the cutoff with a TAG-like 25% range, I expect to get three-bet by a wide 10–12% of hands from the button and maybe a 5–7% range from the small or big blind.

When I'm trying to figure out how often I'll be up against a "monster," QQ+, I think of the following chart. Notice that removing one Ace or King significantly reduces the chances of being up against a monster hand by about

17%. If I have AK, that reduction is 33%. For example, if I'm facing a three-bet from a guy who I think is making this play 5% of the time and I have JJ (no Ace, no King), I will be up against QQ+ 30% of the time. If I held A♠5♠, I'd only be up against QQ+ 25% of the time. Simply having an Ace or a King in my hand reduces the number of combinations of huge hands my opponent can have.

3 Bet %	Raw Combos	My Opponent has AA, KK, QQ		
		No AK	1 A/K	AK
2%	25	72%	60%	48%
3%	37	48%	40%	32%
4%	49	37%	31%	25%
5%	61	30%	25%	20%
6%	74	24%	20%	16%
7%	86	21%	17%	14%
10%	123	15%	12%	10%
15%	184	10%	8%	6%

Note: Tight three-bettors have the nuts more often than not. A player that is only three-betting 3% of his hands has thirty-seven combinations in his range. 6 AA, 6 KK, 6 QQ, 16 AK = thirty-four combinations—sprinkle in a few "loose" JJ combos, and that is it.

——TOP 40% RULE——

If a player is all-in pre-flop with a known range of hands, approximately the top 40% of hands within that range are profitable against his entire range. For example, if a player moves all-in with the top 6% of hands, that equates to around 74 combinations (1,225 x 6%). There are approximately 40% x 74 combinations that are profitable all-in against that range, or 30 combinations (JJ+, AKs = 28 combos).

Another example: Against a 15% all-in range (184 combinations), approximately 6% of hands (73 combos) are profitable: 88+, AJs+, AQ+ = 78 combinations. These are the only hands profitable against a 15% all-in range.

	A	K	Q	J	T	9	8	7	6	5	4	3	2
A	84	61	57	52	49	45	44	42	41	41	40	40	40
K	59	73	45	42	41	39	37	36	36	35	35	34	34
Q	55	42	68	40	39	37	36	35	34	34	33	33	33
J	50	39	37	63	39	37	36	35	33	33	33	32	32
T	46	38	36	36	59	38	36	35	34	32	32	31	31
9	42	35	34	34	34	54	37	36	35	33	32	32	31
8	40	33	32	33	33	34	52	36	35	34	32	31	31
7	39	33	31	31	32	33	33	49	36	34	33	31	30
6	37	32	31	30	30	31	32	32	47	35	34	32	31
5	38	32	30	29	28	29	30	31	31	44	34	33	31
4	37	31	30	29	28	28	29	29	30	31	43	32	31
3	37	31	29	28	28	28	27	28	29	29	29	42	31
2	36	30	29	28	27	27	27	26	27	28	27	27	41

Last example: A player moves all-in without looking from the small blind (a 100% range). Approximately the top 40% of hands will be profitable against that shove.

——GIVING UP——

There is no shame in folding to a three-bet. Some of the best players in poker fold to three-bets as much as 70% of the time! I don't feel the least bit bad about throwing away hands that are pretty and play well post-flop but are significantly behind my opponent's three-betting range.

When I get three-bet by a player that has position, I fold a lot. Even against the most aggressive players, if I'm opening 25% of hands from the cutoff, I'm going to be folding more than half the time. There are plenty of hands that are "automatic" late position openers that should always fold to a three-bet. Trash hands like JTo or 86s (particularly hands without blockers) should immediately hit the muck.

If my hand is easily dominated by my opponent's three-betting range, most of the time I just give up and fold. I simply don't want to create an enormous pot when I'm dominated. If I open KTs from the cutoff and I get three-bet, I will fold.

Most hands at the bottom of my range are easy folds. I usually fold small pairs 22–66 unless we are playing extremely deep (150 big blinds or so) and I have a good idea that I can get my opponent to stack off with AA or KK on a Q-6-2 board after flopping a set. Playing small pairs out of position in a three-bet pot without getting at least 15 to 1 implied odds is a long-term losing proposition.

At this point in the hand, I only have 2 or 3 blinds invested, and giving up is the most prudent, sensible action. Getting involved entails substantial risk, so I proceed cautiously. Against tight three-bettors, folding all but the best of the best hands is usually the wisest course.

Against a polarized 6% range—TT+, AQs+, AK, JTs, T9s, 98s, 87s, 76s, 65s—the only hands with all-in positive EV are JJ+, AK. That's it.

	A	K	Q	J	T	9
A	81	53	47	44	43	42
K	50	72	44	42	41	39
Q	44	41	62	43	41	40
J	41	39	39	56	41	38
T	40	38	38	37	49	37
9	38	36	36	35	34	45

All-in equity vs. TT+, AK, JTs, T9s, 87s, 76s, 65s

Taking a Flop

If my hand has good value against my opponent's three-betting range and I'm not comfortable four-betting and potentially stacking off, calling the three-bet and taking a flop is my preferred move. With effective stack sizes of 100 big blinds, I'm not really interested in getting all-in with AK against the hands that would willingly get the money all-in (AA, KK, QQ). At that stack size, I just call the three-bet and take a flop. If the effective stack sizes were around 50 big blinds, I'd just shove all-in with AK and take my chances.

If I open with medium pocket pairs like 88–TT from middle or late position, it is too tough to fold and not really prudent to four-bet in most cases.* When I take a flop with these hands, *I'm not playing them solely for the value of flopping a set.* I will reevaluate my hand after the flop and try to make an intelligent play. With TT on a K-6-2 flop, I can play on against most continuation-bets. On an A-K-4 flop, I can get away. On a dry 9-9-2 board, I can check-raise or just check-call and try to get to a showdown.

Against competent opponents, there are very few hands that I want to take a flop with if I'm out of position. It is too difficult to win money, and I'm likely to find myself in some very tricky, marginal spots post-flop. Of course, incompetent opponents are another story altogether. Unfortunately, most unskilled players three-bet a very, very tight range, so getting involved with them is dangerous. Only the unskilled, aggressive three-bettors with a wide range can tempt me into playing a three-bet pot out of position.

---

* Against a pot-committed three-bettor playing a 14% range or more, get the 88+ all-in.

Four-Betting

The most effective defense against the relentless onslaught of three-bets is a four-bet. Four-betting is more popular than ever, but many of the players employing this technique do it for the wrong reasons, against the wrong opponents, and with the wrong hands.

With stack sizes of less than 100 big blinds, it is very difficult to four-bet and then fold to a five-bet shove—the pot odds are just going to be too good.* For that reason, I usually only four-bet with premium hands with 100 big blinds or less.

When stacks start to climb up near 120 big blinds or greater, I can start four-betting as a bluff when my opponents are three-betting frequently. Mostly, I'll be using my weak, suited aces to bluff—hands like A4s, A5s. Having an Ace in my hand when four-bet-bluffing is very valuable, as it reduces the number of combinations and probability that my opponent has AA, AK.

With a good four-bet-bluffing hand like A5s, it is easy to calculate a four-bet size that will have me committed to the pot against a tight five-bet-shove range of QQ+, AK.

Example: I hold A5s and open to 3 BB. My opponent three-bets to 10 BB. I decide to four-bet.

---

* If my four-bet is to 25 big blinds and my opponent five-bets with 100 big blinds or less, I will always be getting more than 1.5-to-1 pot odds.

My Four-Bet Size	Pot-Committed to Five-Bet Stack Size
23	60
26	68
28	74

This table shows that if the effective stack size is 60 big blinds or less and I four-bet-bluff with A5s to 23 big blinds, I will be getting the right odds to call a five-bet-shove range of QQ+, AK. When I'm playing in a tournament with a shallower stack, I might be able to pull off some four-bet bluffs that I wouldn't be able to get away with in a cash game: fold equities will be higher in tournaments than in cash games. Many tight players are willing to fold QQ and AK in a tournament when faced with a four-bet.

If my opponent three-bets and I believe that he is pot-committed, the decision to four-bet is much, much easier. As I've shown with the Top 40% Rule, it is just fine to get the money in with a four-bet with a hand in the top 40% of my opponent's three-betting range. Beware, however, that many opponents who are pot-committed against a four-bet that don't shove all-in pre-flop have a much higher chance than normal to have a monster.

For example, if I open from the cutoff for 3 big blinds and a player with 23 big blinds just raises to 8 blinds behind me, I know he is pot-committed, but then I have to ask: why didn't he just shove in? Probably, he wants action with a monster like QQ+ and is scared that a 23 blind shove would scare me out.

——COLD FOUR-BETS——

If there is an opening raise and a three-bet and the action is to me, let's face it, most of the time I need an absolute monster hand to get involved. We're talking a minimum of QQ. If I'm fortunate enough to wake up to one of these premium hands, I am very likely to four-bet, and in 95% of the cases, that is the correct play. I'm not going to spend a bunch of effort analyzing how to play AA and KK when there is a raise and a re-raise in front—only one play makes sense; move all-in.

When I cold four-bet, my opponents are going to give my hand tons of respect. Well, if they are going to give me that much credit, might it make sense to look for opportunities to throw a few cold four-bet bluffs into the picture just to spice things up a bit? Of course it does, but only if certain criteria are met:

♦ A very aggressive opener who is opening more than a 30% range.
♦ A loose, aggressive three-bettor who has noticed that the aggressive opener has been opening too many hands and is likely to be three-betting a wide range.

♦ A minimum stack size of 55 big blinds for my stack and the three-bettor. I need the three-bettor to have room to fold to a four-bet.

♦ A stack size of less than 20 big blinds or more than 55 big blinds for the opener. I don't care much about losing 20 big blinds, but I really don't want them in there with 40 big blinds. If they have more than 55 big blinds, I'll have lots of fold equity.

A cold four-bet gets a lot of respect because so few players are capable of making these bets as bluffs.

Ideal 4-Bet-Bluff Setup

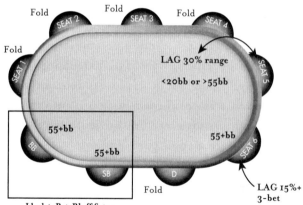

Ideal 4-Bet-Bluff Setup

When I cold-four-bet-bluff, I will raise to between 2.3 and 2.7 times whatever the three-bet was. I simply don't have to over-raise. My hand is going to get tons of respect—

they'll have AA, KK, QQ, AK or they won't, and the size of my raise won't change that at all.

Now, how often will this play succeed, and how profitable will it be assuming that my opponents play-back only with QQ+, AK? Let's look at a typical example, using the table below for the opening range and three-betting frequency:

	Range	Combos	QQ+AK (34 combos)	Folds
Aggressive Opener	30%	367	9.3%	90.7%
LAG 3-Bettor	15%	184	18.5%	81.5%

Both Fold = 90.7% × 81.5% = 74%

The combined probability of this play working is 74%. That is, 74% of the time, neither the opener nor the three-bettor will have QQ, AK+ and will fold to my four-bet bluff.

With an opening raise of 3 big blinds and a three-bet to 9 big blinds, there are 12 blinds currently in the pot (ignoring blinds and antes). Given the above assumptions, the expected value of a 23 blind four-bet bluff is:

74% × +12 blinds = +8.88 blinds ← 4-bet bluff works
26% × −23 blinds = −5.98 blinds ← 4-bet bluff runs into nuts
EV = +2.90 blinds

With all of these assumptions, I calculate that this play will profit almost 3 big blinds per effort, though with tremendous variance and risk. Big risk, big reward—apply this technique at your own risk. Remember that if you start four-betting like a crazy monkey against opponents with this profile, about 1 out of 4 times you'll run into the nuts.

I am extremely wary about making this four-bet bluff against a three-bettor with a range of 9% or less—that seems to be the drop-off-the-ledge point where I simply can't make a profitable four-bet bluff no matter how light the initial raiser. In fact, even against a 50% opener, four-bet bluffing against a three-bettor with a 9% range has a slight negative expectation.

Bluff-4-Bet-EV

Opener (3)	3-Bettor (9)	(23)
50%	25%	6.4
50%	15%	3.9
50%	9.1%	0
50%	5%	-8.3
40%	20%	5
40%	15%	3.5
40%	10%	0.5
30%	15%	2.9
30%	10%	0
20%	15%	1.6
20%	10%	-1.2
15%	10%	-2.4

EV of a 23 big blind bluff four-bet versus 3 big blind opening raise range and 9 big blind three-betting range, ignoring blinds and antes, and assuming opponent will play-back only with QQ+, AK and I fold to a five-bet.

When the stars align, I might just choose to make a cold four-bet bluff. If I can get some reads and time my spots perfectly, this play has a good chance of working and adding significant chips to my stack.

——FIVE-BETTING——

I am almost always holding KK or AA when choosing to five-bet pre-flop; hand ranges are extremely narrow. I'm not going to be able to fool anyone—when I five-bet, I might as well turn my hand faceup.

In some cases, I might consider simply flat-calling with AA in response to the four-bet instead of moving it in. My opponent will still suspect that I have a strong hand, but there will be a much stronger chance that I can convince him that I had AK and missed the flop. If my opponent has a high number of four-bet bluffs in his range, flatting is usually the correct play—I need to give him a chance to hang himself on the flop. Doing so will also slow him down in the future—he's less likely to four-bet-bluff in subsequent hands if he knows I can flat-call with AA. If there aren't many four-bet bluffs in his range and he only really four-bets for value, I just get it in—it will be very difficult for him to fold QQ+, AK.

In most cases, five-betting and getting it all-in with KK is going to be the correct play. If I run into AA, well, that's just too bad—maybe I'll get lucky and suck-out. If I start playing KK too tentatively in this spot, I'll lose more than I gain. I just close my eyes and get it in against all but the tightest, nittiest of opponents. Flatting with KK against a four-bet is not a recommended play—22% of the time you do this, you'll see an Ace on the flop and want to puke.*

—— SIX-BETTING——

Once upon a time, the fourth raise pre-flop meant Aces with virtual certainty. In Poker 2.0, the fourth raise could mean that your opponent has QQ+ or merely 8 high. At the 2010 World Series of Poker we witnessed some of the craziest action imaginable. With relentless aggression on the felt, on Day 6 a pre-flop seven-bet resulted in one opponent folding while the other flashed a 10. With millions on the line for first place and the best players in the world battling through the later stages, I guess you have to get creative.

The 2010 WSOP main event final table was headlined by one of the most heralded players in the game, Michael Mizrachi. "The Grinder" has an "anything goes" reputation and his tablemates had similar repertoires. None of the "November Nine" had any problem committing their chips with air if they felt they could get their opponents to fold.

Some major confrontations at the final table seemed inevitable. As nine dwindled down to the final three, the

* If an opponent doesn't have an Ace in the hand, an Ace will flop 22% of the time. If he does have an Ace (say, AQ), then an Ace will flop only 17% of the time.

poker world witnessed a hand that will be talked about for a very long time. It's a hand that exemplifies this new generation of aggression.

After nearly eight hours of play, Joseph Cheong held the chip lead over Jonathan Duhamel and John Racener. Cheong was in control and had played a nearly perfect final table from the start. Duhamel had entered the final table with the chip lead, lost most of his stack to the point where he was all-in and behind for his tournament life with five players to go, then rebounded back to within striking distance of Cheong. Racener was the short stack and had been playing a slow and patient game. He had all but abandoned the aggressive style that had gotten him this far and he was slowly being blinded away.

Table Diagram

Blinds: 600,000/1.2 million with a 200,000 ante

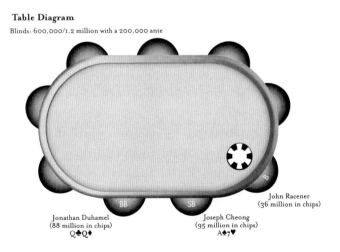

John Racener
(36 million in chips)

Jonathan Duhamel
(88 million in chips)
Q♣Q♦

Joseph Cheong
(95 million in chips)
A♠7♥

The action began with Racener folding his button. Now the action was on Cheong in the small blind, holding A♠7♥, who raised to 2.9 million. "Most of the time, I would be limping in because I didn't want to get into a raising war with a marginal hand. But I had been folding for the last couple orbits, so I decided to raise," said Cheong. "I wanted to take this one down pre-flop."

Duhamel, waking up with QQ in the big blind, had an easy first decision. "Three handed, Queens are like the nuts, especially in a game that aggressive, with Cheong in the lead,"* said Duhamel. "He raised, which is something he could do with any hand. He had a slight chip lead over me, so he could afford to be more aggressive than me. I think he's going to open raise 70–75% of his hands. I don't think he's going to call or fold much. As a general rule, I was waiting to play small pots versus Cheong in position there. But my hand was too strong. He opened to 2.9 million and there was no need to raise three times what he did, so I wanted to come in at a little over six—6.7 million felt about right. It was under 7 million and still a normal size for the three-bet."

Duhamel raised to 6.75 million and felt that Cheong would put him on just about anything from a good hand to suited connectors. Pretty straightforward, right? An

* One of the sources is the Duhamel interview published in Bluff Europe on Nov. 30, 2010; www.bluffeurope.com/interview/en/world-champion-Jonathan-Duhamel_9465.aspx.

Ace in the small blind opens and pocket Queens three-bet from the big blind. But here's where the hand started to get interesting.

"I'd expect him to call pretty much anything," said Cheong, regarding Duhamel's decision after he opened the pot. "He'd call with anything that's connected. He'd fold the worst of all hands, like 10-2 or 3-9, but everything else I'd expect him to call and play in position against me. He could also re-raise to try to take the pot down pre-flop."

Duhamel's raise didn't surprise Cheong. After all, this is a critical spot. That said, he wasn't too concerned about it either. "The raise didn't really mean much," he said. "It was the same as a call in my head. Since I already raised, I expected to get re-raised—and that's why I should've limped. But since I had open-raised, I didn't want to call and play a big hand out of position with a marginal hand. I decided to four-bet pretty big so that he could never just call, and instead would have to either fold or re-raise me."

Cheong four-bet to 14.25 million, something that, in retrospect, he felt he should have made around 20 million. Duhamel, going full-throttle with his Queens, thought Cheong's raise was simply a bullying technique. He analyzed the situation: "By raising to 14.2 million, he still could have anything because Racener was so short-stacked. Cheong's going to be playing a wide range in that spot. I knew he was going to play light, so I was trying to play small-ball against him. I tried to make it look like I was on a bluff.

109

I had already folded to his four-bet a couple of times during the final table, so he knew that the four-bet was going to work most of the time. He thought I could five-bet-light at some point during the game. He still thinks I'm going to five-bet-light, so I thought it was a good spot to make a small five-bet to make it look like a five-bet bluff and I'd fold if he shoved."

Duhamel five-bet to 22.75 million and Cheong spent a lot of time thinking about Duhamel's range of hands before making the next move. "When I four-bet him, I kind of expected him to call me with a lot of hands," said Cheong. "He didn't want to re-raise and have to fold, which he'd basically do with hands that are suited and connected, Jacks and below, and maybe AQ. Those kinds of hands, I expect him to call my four-bet. He had been trying to three-bet me a few times and I had been four-betting him, so I expected him to play a lot of pots with me, in position. His five-bet is polarized. He could have AA, KK, QQ, or AK, but also something like K-5 offsuit. It was a relatively small raise compared to how we'd been raising, but it was still 9 million more. It's big enough for me to fold a lot of hands. A lot of online players three-bet small. They don't care about sizing—it's all-in or fold. He didn't need to make the bet that much bigger. I noticed he had three quarters of his chips behind so he could've raised and folded. I thought I had some fold equity there."

Duhamel didn't think that Cheong would fold in this spot and he actively tried to get the aggressive chip leader to make a mistake and six-bet him. "Cheong four-bet me," he said. "It was the first time that I five-bet but, then again, because of the situation, I could've been five-betting light more than usual. In my head, I really didn't want to be involved in a big pot against him. Yes, in heads-up play, but not three-handed. The way everything went down over the last few hours, I would be five-betting light there, but I had been trying to play small pots as much as possible. It's very normal that he thought I could have been bluffing."

Cheong did feel that a bluff was a possibility but, being the chip leader, he knew that Duhamel would only put his tournament life on the line with the best of hands.

Meanwhile, Racener sat across the table watching in amazement. He knew that if the two locked horns, he could potentially make an additional $1.4 million for doing absolutely nothing. While that may seem like a lot, both Duhamel and Cheong claimed that the money factor had left their minds long ago and all they were focused on was the bracelet.

"At this point Racener is the happiest guy in the world," said Duhamel. "He was playing very small, very cautiously because he knows that Cheong and I were the most aggressive players at the final table and, at one point, something stupid would happen and he could fold his way to second place. He was right. He's never going to win with that theory, but he's going to take second place a lot of times. He doesn't care who is going to win the hand, as long as it wasn't a split pot."

Sitting at the table in front of the biggest audience a poker tournament has ever witnessed, Cheong contemplated his next move. "His calling range is really narrow—AA, KK, QQ, AK," said Cheong. "I never expected him to lay down Queens there. Jacks and below he could've flatted my four-bet. If I moved all-in he would fold enough of the time and when he does call, I have good equity against his calling range."*

Cheong moved all-in, which put Duhamel to the test. "Having Racener still at the table was definitely one of the reasons I made the move. Duhamel wasn't scared of busting, but it might have factored in a little bit."

Holding the Queens, Duhamel felt like the hand played itself. "When he shoved, I wasn't happy at all," said Duhamel. "When he six-bets, I'm going to call. I'm not going to five-bet and fold Queens. Just because of game theory and other considerations, he would be light much more often than usual. I know I have the best hand most of the time, so I have to call."

The board ran clean for Duhamel and he went on to become the 2010 WSOP main event champion. Many were left questioning Cheong's decision. But really, should they? His move was based on the idea that Duhamel would fold about 90% of the hands he could possibly be holding. Even when Duhamel calls, Cheong still wins the hand 30%

---

*A7o vs. AA, KK, QQ, AK has 25% equity. I'm not sure that qualifies as "good equity" with the championship on the line.

of the time and has a monstrous chip lead entering heads-up play. Neither player regrets any of their decisions during that hand. The way the hand played out simply demonstrates the aggressive nature of the game today.

"The game has evolved a lot," commented Duhamel. "It's not only much more aggressive, but there's a lot more raises—small raises. People don't open three times the big blind anymore; instead it's almost always smaller. The game features more aggression, but smaller jabs. Jab, jab, jab, jab all the time. Put the pressure on the other guy. Make yourself tough to play against."

Cheong echoes the champ's thoughts and attributes the shift to the advancement of online poker. "It's out of necessity [that the younger players have gotten more aggressive]," said Cheong. "Once people start raising more pre-flop with a bigger range, your only defense is to re-raise pre-flop with a bigger range. That in theory makes the loose opener open wider in general. Aggression raises variance and people get it in lighter, which makes the hand analysis more of a guessing game. That's what it takes to be good. I think the game is going to get tighter over time to offset all the aggression we see now and that it'll go in cycles."

No matter how the strategy of the game evolves, you don't have to have millions on the line to force yourself to work through situations as methodically as Cheong and Duhamel did. Always try to put yourself in your opponent's shoes and analyze what sort of range you are representing given your recent actions. But watch your step. Aggression's ultimate equalizer is more aggression. Try not to get caught with your hand in the cookie jar.

──SQUEEZES─FISH AND CHIP SANDWICH REVISITED──

When a player is opening a wide range and gets flat-called by a player with a wide range, this is an excellent time for a squeeze play. After the over-call (most often a weak, speculative hand), it can be very profitable to three-bet a very wide range of hands and try taking down the pot pre-flop. If the opening raiser folds, the over-caller won't have a hand that can withstand playing out of position in a big pot very often.

Squeeze

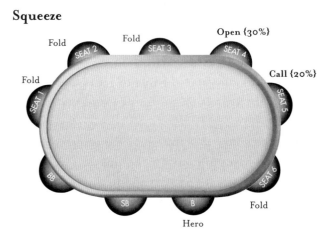

Much of the success of this play as a pure bluff rides on the tendencies of the opening raiser. If they don't give up very frequently to a three-bet, this play will be much less profitable over the long run. Once they call, the over-caller is likely to get in there as well, and you'll find yourself playing a multi-way pot with what is likely a weak hand. If the opening raiser responds to a three-bet in a normal or tight way, this play is much more effective and can be worth the risk.

If you try this play frequently, be aware that you might get set up for a reverse squeeze (see page 116). It doesn't happen all that frequently; I don't really worry about it unless I know that the over-caller is an excellent player and I've seen them make this play before.

If I'm squeezing and will be in position, I'll usually raise the pot to about 3 blinds less than a pot-sized raise. If I'm out of position and making this play from the small or big blind, I want to discourage action—I'll make it a pot-sized raise.

If I'm making this play with a somewhat short stack, it is important to understand when I'm pot-committed against a four-bet shove. For instance, if a player opens wide and gets called in two spots and I decide to squeeze with a raise to 14 big blinds, it's wrong to fold A5s against a four-bet range as tight as JJ+, AK when starting with 43 big blinds or less. Do some work with the simulators and you'll see that once there is that much money in the pot, you'll just have to call off the rest of it with lots of hands.

Note that squeezes work much better when there is

more than one caller in the pot. The first over-caller will have a fairly good hand range in most cases—the second over-caller, not so much. The payoff is better when there are more callers.

——REVERSE SQUEEZES——

Setting up and executing a reverse squeeze is one of the most satisfying plays to make in No Limit Hold'em, especially in tournaments. Here is the ideal setup:

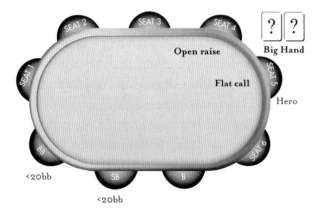

In this scenario, I flat-call the opening raise with a really big hand, like AA, KK. I am hoping that one of the short stacks sitting in the blinds will move all-in, creating a classic squeeze spot. Then, the opener might make an even bigger mistake and try to "isolate" the short stack with a mistimed four-bet. And I'll be ready to spring into action and can win an absolutely monster pot. I've seen opening raisers try to isolate for 100 big blinds with KQs in this spot by just moving it all-in over the top—and it didn't work out as expected.

I can also set up this type of reverse squeeze with weaker hands like 77–99 if there is a reasonable chance that the opening raiser will fold to the squeeze. Now, against an aggressive short-stack squeezer, I can go ahead and get it in. I might also be able to execute this same play when the button is a very aggressive three-bettor. But, when the action gets back to me, I just move it all-in—I don't want to play a big pot out of position.

The risk with this play is substantial—the blinds may not pick up a hand for a squeeze and I might end up playing KK or AA in a big multi-way pot without much clue as to my opponent's hand ranges. But, all is not lost: I still have a very premium, disguised hand, and they haven't beaten me yet.

In today's hyper-aggressive short-stack world, the reverse squeeze is a must-have play in the toolkit. The kids just can't help themselves when they see a wide opening range and a weak-looking over-call. They push quite frequently, and I'll be right there to sweep up the free money.

——EFFECT OF FOLDED HANDS ON BB HAND QUALITY——

As players fold around to late position, it is much, much more likely that an opponent will have a strong hand in the big blind. Barry Greenstein has run some simulations that show that if everyone at the table is playing a "standard" opening range and the action folds around to the small blind, it is around 65% more likely for the big blind to be sitting on AA than it was before the hand started—instead of 225 to 1, the chances are now about 132 to 1. By the same analysis, the player in the big blind will be dealt at least one Ace 20% more often than expected for a random hand.

——GORDON'S A-X RULE——

Using combined probability and combinatorics, I came up with a fairly straightforward formula that deals with A-X hands. It has limited utility, but is interesting nonetheless.

Count the number of players left to act behind you. If your kicker is greater than the number of players remaining, you are a favorite to have the best hand or be at worst a coin flip against an underpair. For example, with A5 and 4 players left to act, you're about 50/50 to not be dominated.

——GORDON'S PAIR PRINCIPLE——

Here is another quick combinatorics shortcut I find helpful:

C = Chance someone will have a higher pocket pair
H = Number of pairs higher than your pair
P = Number of players remaining

$C = H \times P \div 2$

Example 1:

You have 55 under the gun in a 6-handed game. There are five players left to act. There are 9 ranks higher than 5.

$$9 \times 5 \div 2 = 45 \div 2 = 22.5\%$$

There is a 22.5% chance someone at the table will have a higher pocket pair.

Example 2:

You have QQ on the button. There are two players left to act and two ranks higher than Queen.

$$2 \times 2 \div 2 = 2\%$$

There is a 2% chance that one of the blinds will have AA or KK.

Interestingly, this shows why pocket Jacks are so difficult to play under the gun in a full nine-handed game: There are 8 players left to act, 3 ranks higher.

$$8 \times 3 \div 2 = 12\%$$

There is a 12% chance someone will have QQ, KK, or AA—about one out of eight times you are dealt JJ under the gun, you're going to be in seriously bad shape.

FLOP PLAY

Playing well after the flop requires extensive range analysis. I examine how likely it is for my opponent to "hit" the flop, and I also consider how my perceived range connects as well. Only after this hard work is complete can I form a plan—a line of play—that will be the most exploitative and profitable.

——POST-FLOP QUESTIONS——

When the flop comes down, I try to run through a brief analysis of my opponent and his tendencies:

♦ What is my opponent's range?
♦ What is my perceived range?
♦ How likely is my opponent to have flopped a premium hand, a premium draw, a weak hand, or air?
♦ How likely will my opponent think that I've flopped a premium hand, a premium draw, a weak hand, or air?
♦ What are my opponent's tendencies when he has the betting lead? How often does he continuation-bet? How often does he slow-play? How often will he check-raise?
♦ If I have the betting lead, how often will my opponent expect me to make a continuation-bet? How does he like to play post-flop? Does he raise right away? Float frequently? Wait for the turn? Call the flop and fold-turn quite often?

——POST-FLOP RANGE ANALYSIS——

Range analysis is the first and most important skill in post-flop play. There are three steps in this process:

- Guess at my opponent's range based on their actions pre-flop.
- Estimate my perceived range based on my actions pre-flop.
- Analyze the flop with respect to those two ranges.

Let's say I'm playing a $5–$10 cash game, 6-handed. Everyone folds to me on the button and I raise to $30 playing about a somewhat loose 40% range. Small blind folds. I estimate that a typical player in the big blind will respond along these lines:

	A	K	Q	J	T	9	8	7	6	5	4	3	2
A	3	3	3	3	3	C	C	C	C	3	C	C	C
K	3	3	3	C	C	C							
Q	3	C	3	3	C	C							
J	C	C	C	3	3	C							
T	C	C	C	C	3	3	C						
9						C	3	C					
8						C	C	3	C				
7								C	3				
6									C	3			
5										C			
4											C		
3												C	
2													C

LEGEND: 3 = Three-Bet, C = Call, Empty = Fold

There are 108 combinations he will three-bet and 212 combinations that call. What does this action look like? When I open the pot, I expect to get three-bet 8% of the time and get called 16% of the time. I expect my opponent's three-bets to be polarized—very strong hands and some weak suited-connector-type hands as well.

My opponent calls my pre-flop raise and I narrow his range in my head.

The flop comes 7-4-2 rainbow.

I now analyze my opponent's range and place each of his potential combinations into a category: nuts, very good (top pair), some pair, premium draw, gut-shot, 2 good over-cards, no pair or draw.

Let's take a look at how this 7-4-2 flop intersects with my opponent's 16% calling range.

	A	K	Q	J	T	9	8	7	6	5	4	3	2
A						o	o	+	o	G	P	G	P
K				o	o	o							
Q		o			o	o							
J	o	o	o			o							
T	o	o	o	o			o						
9						+		P					
8							+		G				
7								N					
6								P					
5										P			
4											N		
3												P	
2													N

LEGEND	COMBOS	%
+ = Very good hand	15	8%
N = Nuts	9	5%
P = Paired, but not top pair	9	5%
G = Gut-shot draw	12	7%
o = No pair, no draw	136	75%

24 combinations (+, N) are "premium" hands that can withstand significant post-flop pressure and will fight back and play aggressively.

21 (P, G) combinations have a little something going for them, but aren't strong enough to stand significant pressure and might have to get very lucky to win (in the eyes of the defender).

136 (o) combinations have exactly nothing except high-card value and will probably have to fold to a continuation-bet.

	A	K	Q	J	T	9	8	7	6	5	4	3	2
A	N	2	2	2	2	2	2	P	o	G	P	G	P
K	2	N	2	2	2	2	2	P	o	o	P	o	P
Q	2	2	N	2	2	2	2	P	o	o			
J	2	2	2	N	2	2	2	P					
T	2	2	2	2	N	o	o	P					
9	2	2	2	2		+	2	P					
8	2	2				+	P						
7	P	P						N					
6	o	o							P				
5	G	o								P			
4	P										N		
3	G											P	
2	P												N

LEGEND	COMBOS	%
N = Nuts	39	7.2%
+ = Very Good, Top Pair	96	17.8%
P = Some Pair	66	12.3%
G = Gut-shot	32	5.9%
D = Premium Draw	o	0%
2 = 2 Good Over-cards	241	44.7%
o = No Pair, No Draw	64	11.8%

Now, I also examine how my perceived range intersects with the flop in an attempt to understand how my opponent will view the quality of my hand post-flop.*

How does this flop intersect with my pre-flop raising range (40.6%, 538 combinations)?

If my opponent is doing a range analysis on my hand, he'll see that I'll have a great hand on this flop about 25% of the time, and at least a pair about 37% or so. Almost 55% of the time, however, I don't hit this flop.

Doing this analysis makes it completely clear that a continuation-bet is the right play with my entire pre-flop range: my range is much more likely to have hit this flop than my opponent's range. There are very few "nut" combinations in my opponent's range as well. I expect a continuation-bet to be an immediate success quite often.

Let's look at another hand example. Same pre-flop action. I raise on the button and get called from a player in the big blind playing a typical (16%) range. Now the flop is:

Flop: J♠ T♠ 4♥

<hr>

* This step is only really required against thinking opponents who are actually analyzing my range. If they aren't thinking much about my hand, then I don't spend too much effort on perceived range analysis. Interestingly, these are exactly the types of opponent I'm often targeting, so I end up in many pots against them.

	A	K	Q	J	T	9	8	7	6	5	4	3	2
A						D	D	D	D	D	D	D	D
K				+	P	G							
Q		D			P	D							
J	+	+	+			+							
T	P	P	P	N			P						
9						o		G					
8							o		D				
7								o					
6									o				
5										o			
4											N		
3												o	
2													o

LEGEND	COMBOS	%
N = Nuts	9	6%
+ = Top Pair	41	26%
D = Premium Draw	22	14%
P = Middle, Bottom Pair	45	28%
G = Gut-shot	8	5%
o = Nothing	42	26%

On this flop, my opponent only whiffs with 26% of his hands! His range intersects with this flop in some capacity a remarkable 74% of the time. A continuation-bet is very unlikely to get my opponent to fold. Even worse, further analysis shows that my 40% range doesn't hit this flop very hard at all.

Doing this exercise with various pre-flop calling ranges and flop textures is very instructive. I'll save you a little effort, though, and show you some of my findings:

	A	K	Q	J	T	9	8	7	6	5	4	3	2
A	AA	AKs	AQs	AJs	ATs	A9s	A8s	A7s	A6s	A5s	A4s	A3s	A2s
K	AK	KK	KQs	KJs	KTs	K9s	K8s	K7s	K6s	K5s	K4s	K3s	K2s
Q	AQ	KQ	QQ	QJs	QTs	Q9s	Q8s	Q7s	Q6s	Q5s	Q4s	Q3s	Q2s
J	AJ	KJ	QJ	JJ	JTs	J9s	J8s	J7s	J6s	J5s	J4s	J3s	J2s
T	AT	KT	QT	JT	TT	T9s	T8s	T7s	T6s	T5s	T4s	T3s	T2s
9	A9	K9	Q9	J9	T9	99	98s	97s	96s	95s	94s	93s	92s
8	A8	K8	Q8	J8	T8	98	88	87s	86s	85s	84s	83s	82s
7	A7	K7	Q7	J7	T7	97	87	77	76s	75s	74s	73s	72s
6	A6	K6	Q6	J6	T6	96	86	76	66	65s	64s	63s	62s
5	A5	K5	Q5	J5	T5	95	85	75	65	55	54s	53s	52s
4	A4	K4	Q4	J4	T4	94	84	74	64	54	44	43s	42s
3	A3	K3	Q3	J3	T3	93	83	73	63	53	43	33	32s
2	A2	K2	Q2	J2	T2	92	82	72	62	52	42	32	22

5% Calling Range
77-TT AQ AJ ATs KQs KJs

	Nut	Exc	Pair	Draw	Gut	Zero		Flush Draw	Flush
J-8-3	5%	24%	31%	0%	0%	41%		7%	5%
Q-9-2	5%	24%	31%	0%	7%	34%		7%	5%
K-9-4	5%	10%	29%	0%	0%	57%		6%	5%
Q-Q-4	17%	0%	41%	0%	0%	41%		5%	0%
Q-Q-T	24%	6%	33%	7%	30%	0%		4%	0%
T-T-6	5%	0%	30%	0%	0%	66%		7%	0%
A-9-8	10%	56%	10%	0%	0%	24%		7%	3%
J-T-9	18%	27%	5%	39%	11%	0%		9%	4%
J-9-6	5%	24%	31%	0%	7%	34%		7%	5%
3-4-5	0%	35%	0%	0%	53%	12%		7%	7%
A-K-J	7%	33%	7%	0%	13%	40%		9%	0%
A-Q-8	9%	56%	6%	0%	7%	22%		6%	2%
A-T-3	9%	44%	33%	0%	15%	0%		5%	4%
K-Q-9	10%	5%	20%	0%	44%	20%		7%	3%
Q-T-8	11%	27%	5%	36%	11%	11%		5%	4%
A-5-5	0%	46%	41%	0%	0%	14%		3%	0%
7-8-T	16%	5%	0%	10%	34%	34%		9%	9%

126

	A	K	Q	J	T	9	8	7	6	5	4	3	2
A	AA	AKs	AQs	AJs	ATs	A9s	A8s	A7s	A6s	A5s	A4s	A3s	A2s
K	AK	KK	KQs	KJs	KTs	K9s	K8s	K7s	K6s	K5s	K4s	K3s	K2s
Q	AQ	KQ	QQ	QJs	QTs	Q9s	Q8s	Q7s	Q6s	Q5s	Q4s	Q3s	Q2s
J	AJ	KJ	QJ	JJ	JTs	J9s	J8s	J7s	J6s	J5s	J4s	J3s	J2s
T	AT	KT	QT	JT	TT	T9s	T8s	T7s	T6s	T5s	T4s	T3s	T2s
9	A9	K9	Q9	J9	T9	99	98s	97s	96s	95s	94s	93s	92s
8	A8	K8	Q8	J8	T8	98	88	87s	86s	85s	84s	83s	82s
7	A7	K7	Q7	J7	T7	97	87	77	76s	75s	74s	73s	72s
6	A6	K6	Q6	J6	T6	96	86	76	66	65s	64s	63s	62s
5	A5	K5	Q5	J5	T5	95	85	75	65	55	54s	53s	52s
4	A4	K4	Q4	J4	T4	94	84	74	64	54	44	43s	42s
3	A3	K3	Q3	J3	T3	93	83	73	63	53	43	33	32s
2	A2	K2	Q2	J2	T2	92	82	72	62	52	42	32	22

10% Calling Range									
22-TT A9s-AQs KTs-KQs QJs ATo-AQo KQo									
	Nut	Exc	Pair	Draw	Gut	Zero		Flush Draw	Flush
J-8-3	5%	15%	30%	0%	0%	51%		3%	3%
Q-9-2	5%	23%	38%	0%	7%	27%		3%	3%
K-9-4	5%	15%	25%	2%	3%	50%		4%	3%
Q-Q-4	16%	0%	33%	0%	0%	51%		5%	0%
Q-Q-T	19%	11%	3%	4%	15%	48%		4%	0%
T-T-6	12%	0%	16%	0%	0%	72%		5%	0%
A-9-8	7%	32%	5%	0%	4%	53%		4%	4%
J-T-9	19%	16%	16%	13%	0%	37%		3%	2%
J-9-6	5%	18%	18%	0%	10%	48%		4%	3%
3-4-5	7%	19%	0%	10%	42%	22%		6%	6%
A-K-J	8%	27%	16%	0%	5%	43%		2%	0%
A-Q-8	10%	27%	24%	0%	7%	32%		3%	2%
A-T-3	7%	30%	3%	0%	22%	38%		4%	3%
K-Q-9	10%	5%	21%	0%	28%	37%		3%	2%
Q-T-8	13%	16%	18%	18%	4%	32%		4%	3%
A-5-5	1%	34%	26%	0%	0%	40%		1%	0%
7-8-T	7%	12%	0%	10%	24%	46%		6%	5%

	A	K	Q	J	T	9	8	7	6	5	4	3	2
A	AA	AKs	AQs	AJs	ATs	A9s	A8s	A7s	A6s	A5s	A4s	A3s	A2s
K	AK	KK	KQs	KJs	KTs	K9s	K8s	K7s	K6s	K5s	K4s	K3s	K2s
Q	AQ	KQ	QQ	QJs	QTs	Q9s	Q8s	Q7s	Q6s	Q5s	Q4s	Q3s	Q2s
J	AJ	KJ	QJ	JJ	JTs	J9s	J8s	J7s	J6s	J5s	J4s	J3s	J2s
T	AT	KT	QT	JT	TT	T9s	T8s	T7s	T6s	T5s	T4s	T3s	T2s
9	A9	K9	Q9	J9	T9	99	98s	97s	96s	95s	94s	93s	92s
8	A8	K8	Q8	J8	T8	98	88	87s	86s	85s	84s	83s	82s
7	A7	K7	Q7	J7	T7	97	87	77	76s	75s	74s	73s	72s
6	A6	K6	Q6	J6	T6	96	86	76	66	65s	64s	63s	62s
5	A5	K5	Q5	J5	T5	95	85	75	65	55	54s	53s	52s
4	A4	K4	Q4	J4	T4	94	84	74	64	54	44	43s	42s
3	A3	K3	Q3	J3	T3	93	83	73	63	53	43	33	32s
2	A2	K2	Q2	J2	T2	92	82	72	62	52	42	32	22

16% Calling Range
22-99 A2s-A9s K9s-KJs Q9s QTs J9s T8s 97s 86s
ATo AJo KT-KQo QTo QJo JTo

	Nut	Exc	Pair	Draw	Gut	Zero	Flush Draw	Flush
J-8-3	3%	22%	22%	0%	13%	39%	7%	6%
Q-9-2	4%	16%	27%	6%	19%	28%	6%	5%
K-9-4	4%	18%	21%	0%	21%	36%	5%	5%
Q-Q-4	13%	0%	24%	0%	0%	62%	8%	0%
Q-Q-T	11%	11%	16%	11%	9%	42%	7%	0%
T-T-6	19%	0%	12%	0%	2%	67%	7%	0%
A-9-8	5%	20%	10%	7%	15%	43%	4%	2%
J-T-9	9%	32%	17%	0%	7%	34%	5%	5%
J-9-6	4%	21%	16%	11%	15%	32%	7%	6%
3-4-5	7%	2%	9%	13%	20%	50%	8%	7%
A-K-J	14%	23%	26%	0%	4%	33%	4%	2%
A-Q-8	2%	12%	6%	8%	24%	48%	5%	3%
A-T-3	6%	17%	40%	0%	22%	15%	4%	3%
K-Q-9	13%	16%	15%	0%	15%	40%	7%	5%
Q-T-8	8%	13%	20%	18%	8%	33%	7%	6%
A-5-5	11%	11%	13%	0%	0%	66%	5%	0%
7-8-T	7%	26%	6%	6%	21%	33%	6%	5%

128

Opponents who are aware of the Gap Principle have a tighter range than my pre-flop raising range—often significantly tighter, especially if the opponent is out of position and calling my raise from the blinds.

—— OPPONENT ANALYSIS ——

After my range analysis, I try to piece together everything I know about my opponent:

- ◆ Is my opponent almost always either raising or folding, or is he more creative?
- ◆ How often do I expect my opponent to float?
- ◆ Does my opponent raise his good hands right away or wait for the turn?
- ◆ How often does my opponent make a continuation-bet? Does he have any exploitable continuation-betting tendencies?
- ◆ How often does my opponent check-raise?
- ◆ How aggressively does he play his flush and straight draws?

In the online world, many of these questions are easily answered by looking at the stats in my Heads Up Display (see HUD section). At a live table, I rely on experience and intuition and make my best guess.

——MAKE A PLAN——

Armed with the range and opponent analyses, it is time to make a plan. My goal is to integrate all of this information and make the highest EV, most exploitative post-flop play possible.

There aren't many situations that are 100% clear-cut post-flop. If a decision is close between an aggressive or passive course, I choose the aggressive action.

——CONTINUATION-BETS——

When I have the betting lead post-flop, my thoughts are focused on one central question: should I make a continuation-bet?

Continuation-bets have four main functions:

♦ Extract Value: to get worse hands to call
♦ Protect: to price out draws
♦ Bluff: to get better hands to fold
♦ Semi-Bluff: a bet that might get a better hand to fold or has the possibility of making the best hand on the turn

A continuation-bet that doesn't have a high probability of accomplishing at least one of these purposes is most likely incorrect. If I can't get better hands to fold, I can't get worse hands to call, I can't price out draws, and my hand is unlikely to improve, continuation betting has very little going for it.

In the old days, many players ignored the Gap Principle and called pre-flop raises with a very wide range. They also played a fit-or-fold style post-flop. Against these opponents, the "automatic" continuation-bet was a winner. In today's game, most obey the Gap Principle and are much better pre-flop players. As a result, post-flop continuation-bets have less going for them now.

Continuation-Bet Sizing

When continuation betting, I size my bet based on the texture of the board. On very dry boards (7-4-2 rainbow), I bet 1/2 the pot or so. On damp boards (J-8-6 two-tone), I bet 2/3 of the pot. On wet boards (K♠ J♠ 7♣), I bet somewhere around 3/4 of the pot. On monsoon flops (K♠ Q♠ J♠), I bet the full pot.

If I vary the size of the continuation-bet with the strength of my hand, I give away too much information. Therefore, *I do not vary the size of my post-flop bets based on the strength of my hand.* If I'm bluffing with air or flop the immortal nuts, I make the same bet.

Remember, one purpose a continuation-bet serves is to price out draws. By increasing the size of my continuation-bet as the board gets wetter, I reduce the expectation of drawing hands.

In three-bet pots, ranges are narrower and obviously the pot is much bigger. I find that small continuation-bets can be effective. There will usually be around 18 to 20 big blinds in the pot pre-flop.

	Dry	Damp	Wet	Monsoon
Standard Open Call (6.5-9 blinds)	½	⅔	¾	**Pot**
Three-Bet Pots (16-20 blinds)	⅓	½	⅔	¾

Continuation-Bets for Bluffs

When I bet or raise as a bluff post-flop, I realize that the only way for this bet to be profitable is if my action will result in the required number of folds. A 1/2-pot pure bluff needs to elicit a fold 33% of the time to be profitable. A full-pot bluff needs to work 50% of the time. If after analyzing my opponent's range it is clear that my bet won't produce enough folds, I simply won't bluff.

Against typical pre-flop calling ranges, bluff continuation-bets are most likely to work on King-high dry flops—there just aren't very many combinations of Kings in most calling ranges. Dry Ace-high and Queen-high boards are decent as well. Dry Jack- and Ten-high boards are very dangerous—as we've seen, those kinds of flops hit a pre-flop caller pretty hard.

Low, Paired Boards

Against a tight pre-flop calling range of 10% or less, paired, low, dry boards (3-3-8 rainbow) are dangerous to continuation-bet. An opponent that is flatting my opening raise with a 10% range that includes 22—99 has a pair more than 1/3 of the time. Conversely, an opening range of 25% that includes all pocket pairs will only be paired in 1/4 of the combinations. If I continuation-bet on these low, paired boards, I expect significant resistance and I must be ready to fire multiple bullets. It is pretty bad to continuation-bet with hands that will fold to a check-raise but have significant chance to catch up on the turn or have good showdown value. For instance, on a 2-2-9 board, continuation betting from late position with A-T against a 10% pre-flop calling range is likely incorrect—I'll have to fold to a check-raise, I have a reasonable chance of catching a Ten or Ace on the turn, and if I so choose, I could just call a turn and river-bet for showdown value.

If I've raised from early or middle position, I make continuation-bets on almost all Ace-high, King-high, and Queen-high boards. My opening range from early and middle position hit this type of flop much harder than my opponent's pre-flop calling range.

Monotone Boards

Monotone boards (all cards the same suit) hit most opening ranges harder than most pre-flop calling ranges. There are more flopped flushes and nut-flush draws in a wide opening range than there are in a tighter pre-flop calling range.

Example Monotone Flop: J♠8♠4♠

	A	K	Q	J	T	9	8	7	6	5	4	3	2
A	AA	AKs	AQs	AJs	ATs	A9s	A8s	A7s	A6s	A5s	A4s	A3s	A2s
K	AK	KK	KQs	KJs	KTs	K9s	K8s	K7s	K6s	K5s	K4s	K3s	K2s
Q	AQ	KQ	QQ	QJs	QTs	Q9s	Q8s	Q7s	Q6s	Q5s	Q4s	Q3s	Q2s
J	AJ	KJ	QJ	JJ	JTs	J9s	J8s	J7s	J6s	J5s	J4s	J3s	J2s
T	AT	KT	QT	JT	TT	T9s	T8s	T7s	T6s	T5s	T4s	T3s	T2s
9	A9	K9	Q9	J9	T9	99	98s	97s	96s	95s	94s	93s	92s
8	A8	K8	Q8	J8	T8	98	88	87s	86s	85s	84s	83s	82s
7	A7	K7	Q7	J7	T7	97	87	77	76s	75s	74s	73s	72s
6	A6	K6	Q6	J6	T6	96	86	76	66	65s	64s	63s	62s
5	A5	K5	Q5	J5	T5	95	85	75	65	55	54s	53s	52s
4	A4	K4	Q4	J4	T4	94	84	74	64	54	44	43s	42s
3	A3	K3	Q3	J3	T3	93	83	73	63	53	43	33	32s
2	A2	K2	Q2	J2	T2	92	82	72	62	52	42	32	22

	A	K	Q	J	T	9	8	7	6	5	4	3	2
A	AA	AKs	AQs	AJs	ATs	A9s	A8s	A7s	A6s	A5s	A4s	A3s	A2s
K	AK	KK	KQs	KJs	KTs	K9s	K8s	K7s	K6s	K5s	K4s	K3s	K2s
Q	AQ	KQ	QQ	QJs	QTs	Q9s	Q8s	Q7s	Q6s	Q5s	Q4s	Q3s	Q2s
J	AJ	KJ	QJ	JJ	JTs	J9s	J8s	J7s	J6s	J5s	J4s	J3s	J2s
T	AT	KT	QT	JT	TT	T9s	T8s	T7s	T6s	T5s	T4s	T3s	T2s
9	A9	K9	Q9	J9	T9	99	98s	97s	96s	95s	94s	93s	92s
8	A8	K8	Q8	J8	T8	98	88	87s	86s	85s	84s	83s	82s
7	A7	K7	Q7	J7	T7	97	87	77	76s	75s	74s	73s	72s
6	A6	K6	Q6	J6	T6	96	86	76	66	65s	64s	63s	62s
5	A5	K5	Q5	J5	T5	95	85	75	65	55	54s	53s	52s
4	A4	K4	Q4	J4	T4	94	84	74	64	54	44	43s	42s
3	A3	K3	Q3	J3	T3	93	83	73	63	53	43	33	32s
2	A2	K2	Q2	J2	T2	92	82	72	62	52	42	32	22

	A	K	Q	J	T	9	8	7	6	5	4	3	2
A	AA	AKs	AQs	AJs	ATs	A9s	A8s	A7s	A6s	A5s	A4s	A3s	A2s
K	AK	KK	KQs	KJs	KTs	K9s	K8s	K7s	K6s	K5s	K4s	K3s	K2s
Q	AQ	KQ	QQ	QJs	QTs	Q9s	Q8s	Q7s	Q6s	Q5s	Q4s	Q3s	Q2s
J	AJ	KJ	QJ	JJ	JTs	J9s	J8s	J7s	J6s	J5s	J4s	J3s	J2s
T	AT	KT	QT	JT	TT	T9s	T8s	T7s	T6s	T5s	T4s	T3s	T2s
9	A9	K9	Q9	J9	T9	99	98s	97s	96s	95s	94s	93s	92s
8	A8	K8	Q8	J8	T8	98	88	87s	86s	85s	84s	83s	82s
7	A7	K7	Q7	J7	T7	97	87	77	76s	75s	74s	73s	72s
6	A6	K6	Q6	J6	T6	96	86	76	66	65s	64s	63s	62s
5	A5	K5	Q5	J5	T5	95	85	75	65	55	54s	53s	52s
4	A4	K4	Q4	J4	T4	94	84	74	64	54	44	43s	42s
3	A3	K3	Q3	J3	T3	93	83	73	63	53	43	33	32s
2	A2	K2	Q2	J2	T2	92	82	72	62	52	42	32	22

	6% Call	10% Call	30% Opening
Total Combinations	76	118	390
Flopped Flush	3	5	15
A-High Flush Draw	7	11	36
K-High Flush Draw	0	4	11
Total Nut/Draw Combos	10 (13%)	20 (17%)	62 (16%)

I tend to be more aggressive on monotone when I am the pre-flop raiser. I expect my opponent to float far less often and fold some quite strong hands when facing a continuation-bet on a monotone flop. Think about how you'd react if you called a pre-flop raise with 9s-9d and the flop came 8♥4♥3♥. You'd like the over-pair, but that hand is extremely vulnerable (and actually behind, equity wise) against almost every flush draw imaginable. Since I'm bluffing quite often on monotone boards, I must balance those bluffs by betting the nuts (flopped flushes).

On monotone boards, I rarely continuation-bet for thin value. These thin-value hands are better for checking back, controlling the size of the pot, and reevaluating on the turn. Hands like middle pair without a flush draw, or small pair with a small flush draw are best played conservatively in many instances.

——CHECK-RAISING——

Here are some factors that might lead me to go for a check-raise post-flop:

♦ My hand is very powerful and my opponent is likely to have hit the flop. Opponents who call most continuation-bets will also bet if they are checked to.

♦ My opponent will bet many of the combinations with little or no value if I check but won't call a continuation-bet. The only way to get him to put chips into the pot is to give him a little rope.

♦ My opponent won't check behind with many draws. Most opponents will bet premium draws (open-ended straight draws, flush draws) if I check, but won't bet the long shots (gut-shots, one over-card).

♦ If I check-raise and get called, I'll be able to narrow my opponent's range sufficiently such that I'll know what to do after most turn cards.

If a check-raise will leave me pot-committed, I simply check-raise all-in. Most often these situations come up in tournaments (or cash games) with an effective stack size of around 50 big blinds or less. At 50 blinds, if I raise pre-flop and get called, there is really no way to check-raise the flop with a premium draw without getting pot-committed:

	Pre-Flop	Flop	Check-Raise
Me 50bb	3	check 13	34 to call?
Opp 50bb	3	5	50 (All-in)

At this point in the betting, there are 24 blinds in the pot. If my opponent goes all-in, I'll be asked to call 34 to win a pot of 100 blinds. My Break Even Percentage is 34%—any flush draw or open-ended straight draw will give me the required pot odds to make the call. Since I'll be pot-committed anyway, I might as well check-raise all-in, apply maximum pressure, and realize the most fold equity possible.

Most knowledgeable opponents know this 50-blind threshold. So, if the effective stack sizes are around 50 big blinds and my opponent checks to me post-flop, I feel fairly confident that I will not be check-raised unless my opponent is check-raising all-in. Knowing that a check-raise is unlikely, I can bet the flop for thin value more often.

When playing online, I find the "Bets vs. Missed C-Bet" stat very helpful. Many opponents just can't help themselves and have an absurdly high propensity for betting against a missed continuation-bet. On dry boards, check-raising these maniacs is a very profitable play for value or as a bluff.

——CHECKING BACK——

In the old days, checking back* just wasn't a strategy that a winning player employed very often. If an opponent checked, it meant they were weak, and they were simply giving up. Against weak, predictable opponents, that is still the case. Against the new Internet whiz kids, I'm much more careful with my continuation-bets—checking back has become much more prevalent and correct.

There are five very good reasons to check-back on the flop:

♦ Trapping—giving an opponent a chance to catch up a little

---

* Checking the flop as the last player to act, either with the betting lead (I'm the pre-flop raiser) or without the betting lead (my opponent opened the pot and checked the flop).

- Pot Control—keep the pot small with a hand with decent showdown value
- Taking a Free Card—take a free shot at hitting a great hand
- Setting up a Bluff on the Turn or River—balance the trapping hands by playing aggressively on the turn and river with air
- Giving Up—save all the chips possible

Check-Back to Trap

I don't trap (slow-play) on the flop very often. With the betting lead and the nuts, I'm very likely to just bet the flop. I'll be betting the flop as a bluff often enough that I can balance by betting the nuts as well. For a slow-play to be considered, the following conditions must be met:

- Very dry flop very unlikely to have improved my opponent's range
- Straightforward fit-or-fold—type opponent (against creative opponents, betting is often better)
- Quite a few cards that can come on the turn that will give my opponent a decent enough hand to call a turn bet
- Very, very few turn cards that will give me the second-best hand
- Very few combinations that will call more than two streets of value; by slow-playing, I intend to attempt to extract value from the turn and river

Suppose I raise from the button and get called from the big blind playing the following range:

	A	K	Q	J	T	9	8
A	AA	AKs	AQs	AJs	ATs	A9s	A8s
K	AK	KK	KQs	KJs	KTs	K9s	K8s
Q	AQ	KQ	QQ	QJs	QTs	Q9s	Q8s
J	AJ	KJ	QJ	JJ	JTs	J9s	J8s
T	AT	KT	QT	JT	TT	T9s	T8s
9	A9	K9	Q9	J9	T9	99	98s
8	A8	K8	Q8	J8	T8	98	88

I have 88 and flop a set on a K-8-3 rainbow flop. My opponent, meanwhile, will not have that great a hand:

Top Pair	36 Combinations (24%)
Middle Pair (TT, 99)	12 Combinations (8%)
Ace High	40 Combinations (26%)
No Pair, No Ace	64 Combinations (42%)
Total Combinations	152 Combinations

Against a standard opponent playing this profile, I expect a fold with about 68% of my opponent's range. Betting is unlikely to produce much value. However, any Broadway (T,J,Q,A) on the turn will give my opponent a piece of the board quite often—a card that can help me extract value. For instance, if a Jack comes on the turn, every single combination in that range will have at least a gut-shot and many will have an open-ended straight draw one pair, or even two pair:

K-8-3-J	
Two Pair	9 Combinations (7%)
Top Pair	36 Combinations (28%)
Middle Pair (TT, 99, JX)	48 Combinations (37%)
Straight Draw	20 Combinations (16%)
Gut-Shot	16 Combinations (12%)
Nothing	0 Combinations (0%)
Total Combinations	129*

* Note that there are fewer combinations possible after the turn due to the effects of card removal.

Trapping is best against fit-or-fold–type players. In contrast, I don't slow-play against calling stations, super-aggressive LAGtards, and Internet geniuses. Against the aggressive players, I find that I get more value by just betting and inducing bluffs and floats.

Check-Back for Pot Control

There are many flops where it is hard to imagine an opponent paying off all three streets with a worse hand. For instance, if I have A9s and raise pre-flop and get called from the big blind and the flop comes A-8-2 rainbow, there just aren't many combinations in my opponent's range that will pay off a flop, turn, and river bet. This is a classic spot for checking back for pot-control purposes. I don't want to bet, get check-raised, and suddenly find myself guessing if the villain is on AJ or air in a big pot.

Checking back for pot control gives my opponent plenty of ways to go wrong: he can try to bluff the turn or he can call down on the turn and river with significantly weaker hands.

Against calling stations and players that aren't very tricky, checking back is seldom the preferred line. Against these types, I just bet and hope to get called.

Remember, for a bet to have value, I have to get a better hand to fold or a worse hand to call. If neither of these possibilities is likely, then eschewing the "automatic" continuation-bet and checking back has a lot going for it.

Check-Back to Take a Free Card

Against an aggressive opponent and in multi-way pots, checking back to take a free card with a gut-shot is a decent line of play. On a J-8-4 rainbow board, I'd likely check-back QT and hope to spike a nine (making a straight) or a Queen on the turn. My hand has little or no showdown value, can't call a check-raise, and is unlikely to get a better hand to fold.

In multi-way pots, checking back the nut-flush draw

or an open-ended straight draw can be very deceptive and profitable, particularly when playing shallow stacks because an Ace-high flush draw has showdown value on many boards—particularly against players that won't fire a turn AND a river bluff.*

Playing deep stacks, I think betting the nut-flush draw is better—I want to get more money in the pot in case my opponent is also on a flush draw. If I check-back on the flop, it is difficult to get 300 big blinds in the pot in what I hope will be a flush-over-flush setup. Against players with "suititis" (call a pre-flop raise with way too many suited combinations), this is particularly effective.

With the non–nut-flush draw in a multi-way pot, checking back on the flop is my preferred line of play.

Check-Back to Set up Turn/River Bluff

Because I can check-back for pot control with decent hands with value, I balance by checking back with air. In these spots, I'm hoping to pick up a pair on the turn, or be able to bluff the turn and river (representing a hand that checked back for pot control). For instance, on the same A-8-2 rainbow flop, I check-back with JT and then fire the turn and river for bluffing purposes. This keeps my opponent guessing.

---

* If I check-back the flop and call a turn bet (what I hope is a bluff), I can win with Ace-high on the river against an opponent unwilling to fire another bluff bet on the river.

Note that it is vital that these two lines of play are balanced in my range. If I'm always betting top pair for thin value, I can't credibly represent top pair after checking back the flop.

On a K-9-7 board, there are many combinations that I'd check-back on the flop with a gut-shot or double-gutter: QJ, QT, J8, and maybe JT. If a high card comes, I'll be able to credibly represent a straight and give my opponent a very hard time.

Check-Back to Give Up

There are many flops that hit my opponent's range so hard that continuation betting just isn't profitable. I just check-back and intend on giving up.

For instance, if I raise pre-flop and get called from the big blind, I check-back and give up all of these hands:

My Hand	Flop
22	T98, T97, JT9, JT8, JT7
KQ	987, 986, T86
A3	QJ6, QT9, JT9, T97

There is no point in making a continuation-bet that will be extremely unprofitable against a standard calling range. Save the chips for the next hand.

Without the Lead

If my opponent raised and I called in position, my opponent has the betting lead. If he checks the flop, checking back is my preferred line in certain situations:

♦ My opponent is tricky and aggressive and capable of check-raise bluffing
♦ The board hits my opponent's range harder than my range
♦ My opponent believes that I have a tendency to bet vs. missed continuation-bets frequently
♦ My opponent has a high continuation-bet frequency and suddenly checks a dry, paired board like AA8, KK3, or 88T. This smells very fishy—definitely a set, and potentially quads!
♦ With under-cards and a gut-shot straight draw, checking back seems right; for instance, I have Q8s on a J-T-4 board—I could easily be up against KQ and drawing to only 3 outs

Opponents that don't continuation-bet on a dry, Ace-high board are often slow-playing. Conversely, if they do bet a dry Ace-high board, they are often bluffing!

There are quite a few players that have a tendency to just check-fold if they miss the flop. Obviously, against these types of players, I bet with 100% of my range if they check the flop. Often, even small bets are sufficient against these fit-or-fold types.

——RESPONDING TO A CONTINUATION-BET——

Responding appropriately to post-flop continuation-bets is critical. There are many opportunities to "make plays" and apply tremendous pressure—especially if I'm in position. For players that make continuation-bets with a very high percentage of their range, realize that the flop actually didn't change anything about the hand—if your range was ahead of his range pre-flop, it is still ahead of his range post-flop. There is no "new information" presented if the opponent makes an "automatic" continuation-bet—all you really know is that they haven't gone to sleep or passed out.

There are many instances where my range will be much stronger than my opponent's range. Because I employ the Gap Principle, any time my opponent opens in late position and I call, my range will be well ahead. I can take advantage of this and be very aggressive on two-tone flops with two Broadway cards:

K♠ Q♠ 4♦   Q♦ J♦ 7♣   Q♥ T♠ 6♠   J♦ T♥ 2♦

These types of flops hit my range much harder than they hit my opponent's opening range. With a flush draw on the board, my opponent will have to give me some serious credit if I go barreling off on the turn and the river if the flush completes. When I'm aggressive on these flops in position, my opponent will usually tip their hand right away and won't be inclined to slow-play—there are too many draws and too many outs—they'll want to protect, especially if they are out of position. So, if they don't play-back, I can be fairly confident that a triple-barrel has a great shot at working. But, make sure that the stack sizes are right for this kind of play—if I can't set up the stacks so that I'm making decent 2/3-or-so-sized bets on each street, this line will be ineffective. Raising a continuation-bet and barreling off on the turn with some equity (gut-shot, straight draw) is very powerful.

Against fit-or-fold types, I'm more careful about calling continuation-bets. There are some opponents that are just transparent—you know for sure that when they make that bet, they hit the flop. If I'm getting the right pot odds and implied odds, I'll continue on, of course, but I won't be raising these types of continuation-bets very often.

I will call a continuation-bet in an attempt to "trap" my opponents if I flop a truly great hand (set, nuts, etc.). These calls balance the times that I call with a float-type hand. Balance is very important in these spots—the more that I float, the more trappy I have to play with the made hands.

I'm much more likely to float on an Ace-high flop than King- or Queen-high flops. Most opponents will fire a continuation-bet on almost every Ace-high flop, but they'll shut down and give up if they get called. On a King- or Queen-high flop, I'm not floating very often, so I don't trap very often. On these boards, I just raise with my big hands (small sets, two pair, etc.). I can't really represent much of a hand in these spots, and I find that my opponents will radically overvalue top-pair top hands or make some crazy pure bluffs trying to get me off what they believe is King-Queen. For example, say my opponent raises from the Hi-Jack (23% opening range) and I call on the button. The flop is K♠ T♥ 7♣. My opponent continuation-bets. If I flop a set here, it is much better to just raise—bad players will ship A-K all-in trying to protect against the straight draws. Getting an opponent to call off three streets of value on boards like this is quite possible.

If I call a continuation-bet with middle pair on a two-tone board and the flush comes in, I play very aggressively—I will often try to represent the flush and force my opponent to fold what is likely a better hand. For instance, my opponent raises from the cutoff (30%) and I call from the big blind with J♠ T♠. The flop comes A♥ J♣ 4♥. I check and call my opponent's continuation-bet. The turn brings the 8♥. This is a great time to barrel off and donk the turn— I'm representing the flush, I have a great chance of getting my opponent to fold a better hand, and even if I'm called, I probably have a few outs on the river.

Floating

If my opponent has the lead and I decide to call a continuation-bet without much of a hand, that is called "floating" the flop. Essentially, this line of play dares my opponent to fire another bullet on the turn. Against opponents that will rarely fire the turn without a "real" hand, this line is a cheaper way to find out if they hit the flop. For instance, my opponent raises from the cutoff and I call from the button. He fires a pot-sized bet on a dry A♣ 7♦ 4♠ flop. I expect that he'll be continuation betting with his entire range on a dry Ace-high flop. I have K♠ Q♠. I call. He'll have to suspect that I have a hand like AJ or AT, or perhaps I'm even slow-playing a set. Without AK, AQ, AJ, two pair, or a set, he'll likely check the turn and give up to a small bet. Notice that this line of play risks far fewer chips than raising the continuation-bet. With the float, I'm only calling the flop bet and then betting between 1/3 to 1/2 the pot on the turn if my opponent checks. If I raise the flop bet, I'll have to commit more of my stack right away.

Dry boards are the best for floating: AXX, KXX, Q52, 882. Floating on wet boards is not recommended—an opponent can put you on a draw and might keep barreling in an attempt to price out the draw and win the pot. I also like to have some backdoor potential that could give me some equity on the turn. Backdoor-flush draws are valuable, as are gut-shots and backdoor straight potential. I win some really massive pots when I hit a runner-runner perfect turn and river and my opponent never saw it coming and can't easily read my hand.

If I'm playing against an opponent that makes frequent continuation-bets and follows that up with very frequent bets on the turn, floating is not a recommended line of play—raising the turn will be more profitable, but it will also be incredibly expensive when it is wrong. Against these types, I find it is better to just bluff-raise the flop.

Players that frequently float the flop also have to call with their top-pair hands more often for balance. This is the "normal" line of play with these hands anyway, so in a way, the floats are balancing the made hands.

Floating out of position should be called sinking—I never do it. If I check-call a flop continuation-bet, I have a real hand or a real draw. I've seen a lot of the new whiz kids try to make this play recently and I'm still flabbergasted by it—my guess is that this is a not-so-rare case of the deadly Fancy Play Syndrome.

Here is a recap of the ideal, judicious setup for floating:

♦ I'm in position
♦ My opponent makes very frequent continuation-bets
♦ The flop is very dry—no flush draws or obvious straight draws possible
♦ I have some backdoor potential (backdoor-flush draw, gut-shot straight draw, etc.) that can give me equity on the turn

- Opener will infrequently fire a second bullet on the turn—they give up if they get called and don't have top pair
- There are few cards that can improve my opponent's range on the turn

——DONK BETTING——

Don't let the name fool you. Donk betting is a tremendously valuable tool to have in your arsenal. What's a donk bet? Simple. When an opponent opens and you call from the blinds, you are first to bet after the flop. If you lead right out after the flop, that is called a donk bet.

There are quite a few good reasons you might consider making one of these donk bets:

Donk Bet to Extract Value

Some of your weak-tight opponents won't continuation-bet often enough after the flop to make going for a check-raise a good play. Against this type of opponent, donk—if they call, you'll get good value from your made hands, and if they fold you'll have likely protected a vulnerable hand. Many weak-tight opponents described above will "take one off" and see a turn card, even if they aren't getting the right odds to do so.

Cheap Bluff

Against straightforward opponents that will fold if they missed the flop and bet or raise if they hit it, a great play is a 1/2-pot donk bet on most uncoordinated boards. This bluff only has to work 1/3 of the time to be profitable. As your opponent is going to miss the flop about 2/3 of the time when he is unpaired, this is a very effective play. Use this play against competent opponents who make their fair share (a high percentage) of continuation-bets but won't creatively raise with air on the flop if you donk into them.

Donk to Define Your Opponent's Hand Range

Very often, a donk bet will get you tons of information that you would never get if you just checked to the pre-flop raiser. Their "call" and "raise" range actions on the flop will be very telling.

Donk to Tilt Your Opponent

So many players tilt when you consistently donk into them. You can almost hear them yelling at their computers: "Don't you know you're supposed to check to the pre-flop raiser, you moron?" Well, if your small post-flop donk bets are going to tilt them, so be it—that is probably a good enough reason in and of itself.

Donk Against Multi-Tablers

If a guy is playing 8 tables at once,* donk bet more often. They'll be so distracted by all the other action, they will give up more frequently and won't really have time to consider all the consequences and implications of your donks.

Donk Against Super-Agro Players

Against super-aggressive players that will try to move you off your hand, donk into them with excellent hands and expect them to raise. You'll often extract more value from this line than from a typical check-raise line. If you check-raise, they're good enough to fold, but if you make a weak-looking donk bet, they can't help themselves—they'll have to try to put you to the test, a test you aren't going to fail.

Donk the Right Boards

Donk on very wet boards that hit your perceived range and will likely not receive a continuation-bet. For instance, say a typical late-position opener (40%) raises and you call from the big blind. The flop comes J-T-4 two-tone. This is a decent board to donk with value hands (TT, 44, JT,

---

* Quickly scan the lobby for other games at the same stake and see how many tables your opponents are playing. Most sites also have a "Find a Player" function to determine total number of tables a player is seated at.

straight flush draws) and total bluff hands (A9, A5, 33, 45, 99). Note that your donk bets will be very polarized—you'll either have something really, really good, or you'll have complete air. Opponents will be very hard-pressed to raise your donk bet on a board like this, and you'll be able to barrel off quite effectively against a weak call.

Donking Requires Adjustments

There are many players who almost never donk bet, and they are winning, effective players. Remember, adding donk betting to your arsenal will force you to change the way you play almost every aspect of the game if you're going to be balanced and effective. If you donk regularly, it will change the ranges of your flop check-raises, check-calls, and check-folds. If you are new to the game, I'd suggest just never donking until you get a few hundred thousand hands under your belt.

TURN PLAY

In No Limit Hold'em, the turn is the place where great players crush their opponents and the worst players lose the most. Mistakes are easy to make on the turn and avoiding them is exceptionally difficult.

Betting on the turn with a very strong hand isn't very difficult—the pot is usually quite big at this point, and there is only a small chance an opponent can suck-out on the river. Usually, a reasonably sized bet is good enough to extract value and protect the best hand. However, aggressive players who open a fairly wide range, three-bet as recommended, and make post-flop continuation-bets rarely get to the turn with an extremely strong hand. Playing these weak and marginal strength hands differentiate high-caliber players from the field.

I try to always take my time with decisions on the turn, the most critical street in Hold'em. While my pre-flop plays are nearly automatic, and correct post-flop play rarely will take more than 20–30 seconds to work out, it is not uncommon for me to spend a minute or more figuring out the best play on the turn.

——RANGES NARROW——

After the action on the flop and the revelation of the turn card, my perceived range and my opponent's range have narrowed. Even "check-check" on the flop requires range reevaluation.

In most cases, the turn card itself won't change much about the hand at all—if I was in the lead after the flop, I'm still likely in the lead after the turn, and vice versa. But, there are "action" turn cards—cards that complete potential straight, flush draws, cards that pair the board, over-cards to the board—and they are the most difficult to assess.

——TURN BETS——

Bets on the turn serve the same purpose as bets on the flop. I'll repeat them because they are important:

♦ Extract Value: to get worse hands to call
♦ Protect: to price out draws
♦ Bluff: to get better hands to fold
♦ Semi-Bluff: a bet that might get a better hand to fold or has the possibility of making the best hand on the river

If betting on the turn can't accomplish at least one of these goals against an opponent's range, that bet has little or no value.

On the turn, my bet sizing will take into account the texture of the board, but will also try to factor in stack sizes at the river. Ideally, I try to size my turn bet so that I'll be left with a pot-sized bet on the river, since pot-sized river bets are the most effective for extracting further value and/or bluffing. This is the formula to calculate the exact turn bet size I need to make:

Turn Bet Size = (Effective Stack Size—Current Pot Size) ÷ 3

For instance, say I have $500 and my opponent has $370 remaining. There is $100 in the pot. What turn bet size will set up the stacks so that I have exactly a pot-sized bet remaining on after the river is dealt?

> Effective Stack Size = 370 (the smallest of the two stacks)
>
> Current Pot Size = 100
>
> Turn Bet Size = (370 − 100) ÷ 3 = 270 ÷ 3 = 90
>
> If I bet $90 on the turn and get called, the pot will swell to:
>
> $100 + $90 + $90 = $280

After calling my $90 bet, my opponent will be left with exactly $280. Perfect.

——TURN QUESTIONS——

There are a million questions racing through my mind after the turn is dealt, and there is no prescriptive formula that will lead to the right play. All I can do is ask the right questions, perform the analysis to the best of my ability, then act and see what happens.

Perceived Range Questions:

♦ What is my perceived range?
♦ Did the turn card help or hurt my perceived range?
♦ How many combinations of strong value, weak value, premium draws, weak draws, and air will my opponent put me on?

Opponent's Range Questions:

♦ What range of hands is my opponent playing?
♦ Did the turn card help or hurt my opponent's range?
♦ How many combinations of strong value, weak value, premium draws, weak draws, and air will my opponent have in his range?
♦ Are there any combinations in my opponent's range before I saw the turn card that are no longer possible after?*

With the Betting Lead:

♦ If I bet, can I get better hands to fold or worse hands to call?
♦ How likely is my opponent to check-raise me off a winning hand if I bet?
♦ Does my opponent expect me to bet, and, if so, with what hands?
♦ Can my hand stand a check-raise?
♦ Can I credibly represent strong hands?
♦ Are there more strong-value hands in my opponent's range than in my range?

---

* The most likely candidate for this dynamic is on a flop like Q♠ 9♠ 4♦, when the A♠ hits the turn. If I bet that flop and got called, I'd give my opponent quite a few A-high flush draws in his range—after the turn, those combinations are no longer possible.

- If I bluff the turn and get called, am I prepared to fire another bigger bullet on the river?
- How often does my opponent call a turn bet and then fold the river with weak-value combinations? Does he call down light, or does he make tight folds to big river bets?
- How much would I bet if my opponent turned their hand over and showed me an open-ended straight draw or a flush draw?

Without the Betting Lead, Opponent Bets:

- If I just call with what I believe is the best hand, how likely is my opponent to continue barreling on the river?
- Is my opponent pot-committed?
- Does my opponent double-barrel with drawing hands, or will he bet the flop and then try to check-call the turn?
- What combinations in my range does my opponent think I will slow-play post-flop?

——PARCHED BOARDS——

Parched boards are super dry, rainbow, disconnected, low boards. Flops like these qualify for this designation:

Flop: 2♥2♦4♦
Flop: 7♥4♣2♦
Flop: 9♣3♦5♥

This board texture offers no real draws against normal ranges. In late position battles (cutoff raise or Hi-Jack raise, button or blinds call), these flops and the ensuing action are quite dynamic and interesting. Pre-flop ranges with wide boards like this are unlikely to have hit either hand. As the pre-flop raiser, I continuation-bet these flops with almost my entire range, and I expect to get called quite frequently, often by a range that includes many very weak-value hands and many floats.

If a non-Ace over-card comes on the turn that improves my equity by giving me a straight (even a gut-shot) or a flush draw, I will frequently fire a second bullet. If I happen to make a top pair on the turn, I'm betting, of course.

If I have an over-pair on a parched flop and I've made a continuation-bet, I'll keep on firing on all non-Ace turns with pairs 88+. For instance, with 99 or TT on a 7-4-2 rainbow flop, I'll fire a turn bet on all turn cards except an Ace. Because I'm firing so often on the turn with weak hands, I balance these spots by continuing to fire with strong hands like sets and two pair.

On dry boards, I bet when I have the goods and bet when I don't. Continuous pressure on the flop and turn is the key to success against most players—they will get to the turn quite light and won't be able to stand a turn bet very often. Now, if an Ace hits the turn on a parched flop, everything changes. If I bet the flop and my opponent calls, very often they've floated with hands like AJ, AT, trapped with very strong hands, like sets, or called for value with small pocket pairs. It is very difficult to judge which of these three hand-types my opponent holds.

If I got lucky and spiked an Ace with a hand like AQ and I bet the turn, I don't expect a player on 88–TT to be able to call on the turn and on the river—I'll get only one more street of value at the most. But, if I check, he's likely to fire a bullet and I have an easy call. Betting against these hands wins the same money as checking. But, if my opponent has a very strong hand, check-calling can save money. If I bet, I put myself in a very awkward situation and put my stack in jeopardy.

I raise with A♦T♠ pre-flop from the cutoff. Button calls with about a 9% range.

	A	K	Q	J	T	9	8	7	6	5	4	3	2
A	AA	AKs	AQs	AJs	ATs	A9s	A8s	A7s	A6s	A5s	A4s	A3s	A2s
K	AK	KK	KQs	KJs	KTs	K9s	K8s	K7s	K6s	K5s	K4s	K3s	K2s
Q	AQ	KQ	QQ	QJs	QTs	Q9s	Q8s	Q7s	Q6s	Q5s	Q4s	Q3s	Q2s
J	AJ	KJ	QJ	JJ	JTs	J9s	J8s	J7s	J6s	J5s	J4s	J3s	J2s
T	AT	KT	QT	JT	TT	T9s	T8s	T7s	T6s	T5s	T4s	T3s	T2s
9	A9	K9	Q9	J9	T9	99	98s	97s	96s	95s	94s	93s	92s
8	A8	K8	Q8	J8	T8	98	88	87s	86s	85s	84s	83s	82s
7	A7	K7	Q7	J7	T7	97	87	77	76s	75s	74s	73s	72s
6	A6	K6	Q6	J6	T6	96	86	76	66	65s	64s	63s	62s
5	A5	K5	Q5	J5	T5	95	85	75	65	55	54s	53s	52s
4	A4	K4	Q4	J4	T4	94	84	74	64	54	44	43s	42s
3	A3	K3	Q3	J3	T3	93	83	73	63	53	43	33	32s
2	A2	K2	Q2	J2	T2	92	82	72	62	52	42	32	22

Flop is 8♠4♦2♣.

I fire a 3/4-pot continuation-bet and my opponent calls.

Turn comes A♣.

If I fire and my opponent raises, I'll have no idea what to do. He could be on a set, could have me crushed with AQ or AJ, or could be semi-bluffing. I'm in a really bad spot.

I check, my opponent bets, I call. River is the J♦. I check, my opponent bets, I call. He turns over K♣ T♣ and gets caught bluffing. On the flop, he floated, then he picked up a flush draw on the turn and semi-bluffed after I checked. On the river, he felt he had to take a stab at the pot because he couldn't win at showdown.

When I'm in the small or big blind and I've called a pre-flop raise and then check-called a continuation-bet on a very dry flop, I'm often getting to the turn with hands like ATs, AJs, 88, 99, TT, and slow-played sets.

	Floats	Value	Sets
Flop: 7-4-2 rainbow	ATs, AJs	88, 99, TT	22, 44, 77
Flop: 9-6-3 rainbow	ATs, AJs	77, 88, TT	33, 66, 99
Flop: 8-5-4 rainbow	ATs, AJs	77, 99, TT	44, 55, 88

All of these examples are consistent with good pre-flop hand selection and post-flop action. In hands like this, when the turn gives me a flush draw, I will often go for a semi-bluff check-raise. Of course, in balance, I'll also be going for a check-raise with my sets. My opponent will be put to a tough test. Beware, however: check-raising this flush draw against a calling station is not likely to work—more often than not, a calling station that fires a second shell on the turn will have a strong enough hand to call and go to showdown.

Against most opponents with a wide opening range and a high propensity for continuation betting, I won't let over-cards discourage me from check-calling the turn. My opponents will likely be betting a wide range of hands on the turn as bluffs. If I call the flop and the turn bet, and my opponent fires a third shell on the river, well, against all but the trickiest opponents, I'll probably give it up. Not many players are capable of firing three bullets as bluffs.

In multi-way pots and a parched flop, if my continuation-bet got called by an opponent with players left to act behind him, he is much more likely to have a hand that he will be unwilling to fold to a turn bet. I don't fire a second barrel bluff often in these spots. If he called after the other player in the hand folded, it is much more likely that he's floating or has a weak hand that can give up when facing aggression. My perceived range will be much stronger in these hands because I bet into a multi-way pot. This leads me to bluff more frequently and value-bet fewer of my combinations in hands like this.

——HIGH AND DRY BOARDS——

Dry, uncoordinated boards with one Broadway card (A-T) share many qualities with their parched board cousins. But, on these high and dry boards, bluffing on the turn is much less frequent. Due to the high card, my perceived range and my opponent's range will be much stronger if we get to the turn after putting in some action on the flop.

Flops that are high and dry look like this:

Flop: A♣ 9♦ 4♠
Flop: K♦ 7♥ 3♠
Flop: Q♠ 9♦ 7♥

Opponents who call a flop and turn bet on boards like these will generally have top pair or a middle pocket pair. Getting a guy to hero fold a top pair by firing a third barrel on the river is not usually productive. After betting the flop and getting called, there just aren't that many good cards (if any) to fire a second barrel as a bluff.

Against weak opponents, firing that second shell when an over-card hits the turn can be a good play (Flop J-7-2, Turn K or A). But, again, trying to get a weak player to fold top pair isn't likely to produce the desired result. They are incapable of folding. Bluffs don't work against players who can't fold. Even if the turn card improves my equity (by turning a straight or flush draw) it is usually correct to just check/call against weak opponents and hope to see a cheap or free river card.

Against strong opponents and high-card dry boards, it is, at times, difficult to represent a very strong hand. My perceived range post-flop will be comprised of many weak hands. Strong opponents are suspicious on flops like this and will often call a flop and turn bet quite light. A proper counterstrategy requires that I don't bluff very frequently on the turn. However, if the turn significantly improved my hand, I will fire a second barrel.

Check-raising the turn with my very strong hands (two pair, sets), as well as with some weak semi-bluffs (gut-shot straight draw and an over-card, low end of a straight draw) is correct. My range is polarized and will be tough for my opponent to combat. If the turn pairs the board, I will rarely bet. If I have trips, I go for a check-raise or check-call. I'm also capable of check-raising with air. Betting after the board pairs, there aren't going to be many combinations of hands that make trips. It is nearly impossible to be balanced when betting all turn cards that pair the board. Players who continue to barrel on paired turns are highly exploitable.

——WET BOARDS, BOARDS WITH DRAWS——

Draw-heavy boards are very difficult to play against aggressive opponents. Wet boards are relentlessly attacked by tough players with thin value bets and semi-bluffs. There are many varieties of wet boards, and a lot of guesswork to be done—let's break them down by example.

Low/Low/Low and Wet

Flop: 8♣5♦4♥
Flop: 9♣8♣5♦
Flop: 7♠6♠5♣

On low, wet boards, there are likely to be many draws in my opponent's range. I expect a flop bet to get called quite frequently. Barreling on many turn cards is correct if I believe I can get my opponent to lay down a weak draw. I'm also firing away with all my strong hands—I have to protect my hand against the draw.

If the turn is a Broadway card, I bluff more often than if the turn card is a small card. The high cards are better because I am more likely to get my opponent to fold middle pair hands.

On low cards, I expect to get looked up and may need to fire a third river barrel to win the pot (expensive!). For example: I raise pre-flop with QTs from the cutoff. Opponent calls from button. Flop is 8♣5♦4♥. I bet the flop and he calls. Turn is K♣. I fire again and expect him to fold 77, 66, 98♠, AT, AJ fairly often. However, if the turn was a 3, I don't think I can get any of those hands to fold often enough for my bet to be profitable.

If my opponent had the betting lead and I called a

post-flop continuation-bet, I am very suspicious if they fire away on the turn. I will bluff-raise quite frequently with flush draws in these situations. Of course, that is balanced by the monsters that I've slow-played on the flop (sets, two pair). It is vital to raise on the turn with these monster hands—a player barreling the turn on boards like this very often has draws that can come in. I make them pay dearly for that draw.

High/Low/Low and Wet

Flop: Q♠8♥6♠
Flop: K♠9♥8♠
Flop: A♥8♥7♦

On High/Low/Low wet boards, it is very common to see a flop continuation-bet and a call. The range of hands that will call a continuation-bet on a board like this is fairly constrained for most players. After a post-flop continu-ation-bet and call, when the turn completes a flush draw and the pre-flop raiser bets again, they are representing an extremely narrow range of hands:

Pre-flop Opening Range: 20%—22+, A2s+, AT+, K9s+, KJ+, QTs+, QJ, J9s+, JT, 98s, 87s, 76s, 65s

Flop: K♥ 8♥ 7♦

Post-flop continuation-betting range: 22+, A2s+, AT+, K9s+, KJ+, QTs+, QJ, J9s+, JT, 98s, 87s, 76s, 65s— the same as the pre-flop range—it is commonly correct to continuation-bet on King high boards.

Turn: Q♥

At this point in the hand there are only 14 combinations in the 20% range that made a flush: A♥2♥, A♥3♥, A♥4♥, A♥5♥, A♥6♥, A♥7♥, A♥9♥, A♥T♥, A♥J♥, J♥T♥, J♥9♥, T♥9♥, 7♥6♥, 6♥5♥. Those suited hands represent less than 2% of the entire range. Checking the turn with a made flush with the intent of check-raising is often the correct line of play. After all, in many cases where I fire a single bullet on the flop as a bluff, I'll be checking to give up on the turn.

Opponents will often bet this turn if checked to—they'll be very afraid of giving a "free card" and won't check top or middle pair hands. They will also be very suspicious of the check-raise and frequently call down with weak hands. I expect them to bet just about every hand that would have called a turn bet if I had checked instead.

With medium-strength hands on wet boards, my opponent's profile is extremely important.

Loose-Passive	Bet thinly for value and give up quickly if they raise.
Aggressive, Well Balanced	Rarely bet for thin value—they will put me in marginal spots with some speculative bluffs and raises.
Aggressive, Unbalanced	Bet for thin value and reevaluate if raised, with a propensity for calling down.
Tight, Passive	Rare bluffing and don't turn hands without showdown value into semi-bluffs. Absolutely **never** triple-barreling.

Sopping Wet

Sopping wet boards typically contain two Broadway cards and a two-card flush. These are "action" flops—this type of board is very likely to hit a pre-flop raising range *and* the types of hands that call a pre-flop raise.

Flop: J♥T♥5♣
Flop: A♦J♦8♥
Flop: K♥Q♥9♠

On the wet JT flop, I rarely make a continuation-bet without good value. As we've seen in the post-flop section, this type of flop connects with my opponent's calling range quite often. So, when the turn "bricks" with a low card (2-6) that doesn't complete the flush, I will bet most of the time. I bet here for thin value with top or middle pair hands with a decent kicker: J9, KT, QT, etc. Of course, I'll also continue to barrel with my premium flush and straight draws as well—these turn continuation-bets are in balance.

Against LAGs, check-raising the turn with my monsters and some draws (again, in balance) can be a great play as well. If I'm not in the betting lead and out of position (I called a pre-flop raise from the blinds), this is exactly the type of board that I might donk bet on the flop (either as a bluff or for value). I donk bet on this flop because a thinking opponent won't be making many continuation-bets, and check-raising might be too expensive. Once I donk the flop and get called, I'll barrel on the turn with my entire range if the board doesn't pair. If the board pairs, however, I'll check-fold all my donk-bluff hands.

On a flop of A♦ J♦ 8♥ and I have the betting lead, made a continuation-bet, and got called, any high card on the turn is a good card to barrel. Checking Broadway turn cards on this flop is a recipe for getting bluffed and put in some very marginal spots. The Broadway cards are likely to hit my range harder than my opponent's range. These "scare" cards make my range so much stronger that I can turn even the weakest of my value hands into a bluff and barrel them as well.

——PAIRED TURNS——

When the board pairs on the turn, I routinely check to my opponent. Paired boards are terrible to barrel—opponents will pick up on that quickly and start exploiting me. By checking on most paired turns, I can check-raise my monsters and check-fold air. I'll also check with the intention of giving up on a lot of my draws. There is nothing worse than chasing a flush draw on a paired board, making it, and then finding out I was drawing dead when the turn made my opponent a full house.

RIVER PLAY

By the time I get to the river, ranges have narrowed. I should have a pretty good idea of my opponent's range. My perceived range is also tighter—my opponent probably knows the types of hands I'm holding.

There really are only three rules necessary for playing well on the river:

♦ I base my actions on my perceived range, not on my actual hand.
♦ I base my actions on my opponent's range, not any individual hand within that range.
♦ I base my actions on my opponent's playing tendencies and characteristics.

At the river, hands within the ranges can be categorized into four distinct bins:

♦ Missed Draws (no value)
♦ Bluff-catchers (weak hands that can beat a bluff)
♦ Thin Value Hands (moderate-strength hands)
♦ Strong Value Hands (nuts, near nuts, clearly best hand)

At the river, I do some hard work. I essentially count the number of combinations for my perceived range and for my opponent's range and fit them into the four bins above. After that is done, I feel like I'm in a position to make some good plays on the river. I try to visualize my perceived range and my opponent's range in a continuum:

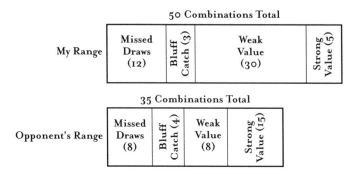

At the river, there are only two reasons to bet or raise: for value or as a bluff. If my opponent bets, there is only one valid reason for calling that bet—I am getting the right pot odds to call based on the number of combinations my opponent will bet that my hand can beat.

——CALLING A RIVER BET——

Making good calls on the river is rather straightforward:

1) Count or estimate the total number of combinations my opponent is likely to bet.

2) Figure out how many of those combinations I can beat.

3) Examine the size of the river bet and determine if I am getting the correct price to call.

Let C = Number of combinations my opponent will bet

Let W = Number of Value Combinations my hand beats

Let P = Size of the Pot Before the River Bet

Let S = River Bet Size

A call on the river will be profitable when:

EV(Call and Win) > EV(Call and Lose)

$$EV(\text{Call and Win}) = (W \div C) \times (P + S)$$

$$EV(\text{Call and Lose}) = ((C-W)/C) \times S$$

Now, after doing some algebra, I find calling is profitable when:

$$W \div (C - W) >= S \div (P+S)$$

That is to say, when the ratio of winning hands I have against my opponent's entire betting range is equal to or greater than the ratio of the bet size to the pot after the bet, calling is profitable.

This formula makes it seem much harder than it really is. Let's take a look at a quick example.

Example 1:

Opponent has 50 combinations in his range (C = 50). I beat 10 (W = 10). He bets 75 (S = 75) into a pot of 100 (P = 100). Should I call?

10 ÷ (50−10) >= 75 / (100 + 75)?

10 ÷ 40 >= 75 ÷ 175?

0.25 >= 0.428

In this case, calling is not profitable.

Example 2:

Opponent has 100 combinations in his range (C=100). I beat 40 (W=40). He bets 200 (S=200) into a pot of 250 (P=250). Should I call?

40 ÷ (100 − 40) >= 200 ÷ (200 + 250)?

40 ÷ 60 >= 200 ÷ 450?

0.66 >=0.44? Yes! Calling is profitable.

Example 3:

You are playing against an aggressive opponent. You've narrowed the range of hands he's playing to AA, KK, QQ, A♣2♣+ (all suited aces), K♣Q♣, K♣J♣, Q♣J♣. Board is T♣9♣4♠5♦7♠. He bets 1,000 into a pot of 3,000. You have J♦J♠. Should you call?

Opponent Combinations:

AA, KK, QQ = 18

Suited Aces = 1 × 12 = 12

K♣Q♣, K♣J♣, Q♣J♣ = 3

Total Combinations = 18 + 12 + 3 = 33

Combinations I beat with JJ = 12 + 3 = 15

15 ÷ 33−15 >= 3000 ÷ (3,000 + 1,000) ?

15 ÷ 18 >= 3000 ÷ 4,000?

0.83 >= 0.75? Yes! Calling is profitable.

If the number of combinations my hand beats is greater than the number of combinations my hand will lose to, I can call a bet of any size on the river. In that case, W/(C - W) will be greater than 1.0 while S/(P + S) can never be greater than 1.0. Another way to look at this: If I'm going to have the best hand more than 50% of the time, I should always call no matter how big the river bet is.

Adjustments Based on My Range

If I bet the river, a thinking opponent will be doing exactly the same thing I do when considering a call. My opponent will be going through my entire range, figuring out how often I'm bluffing, how often his hand beats my value hands, and making an intelligent decision about calling my river bet.

When my perceived range has many combinations of missed draws, my opponent will call a river bet with bluff-catchers and very low-strength hands. To effectively counter that strategy, I will bluff less frequently and bet some of my more marginal holdings for thin value.

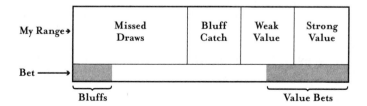

When my perceived range has many value combinations, I bluff more frequently, and I will rarely make thin-value bets. Essentially, my betting will be polarized—I'll either have a great hand, or I'll have air. In other words, don't bet medium-strength hands on the river. Bet weak and strong hands.

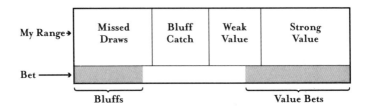

When my perceived range has very few missed draws and many combinations that have strong value, I bet more frequently as a bluff and less frequently for value. I'll also turn the worst of my value hands into bluffs. I'm going to get tons of respect and don't expect to get paid off much.

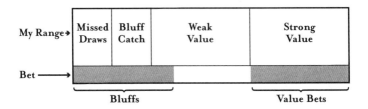

When my perceived range has many combinations of bluff-catchers, I bluff less frequently and check to my opponent more often. I also reduce my check-raise frequency.

Adjustments Based on My Opponent's Range

If my opponent has many missed draws in his range, I will bluff more frequently with my missed draws, check more of my weak and medium-strength hands, and call his bets and raises with weaker hands.

If my opponent has many bluff-catchers in his range, I bluff less frequently, value bet a wider range, and check-raise much less frequently.

If my opponent has many weak-value combinations, I bet less frequently as a bluff, do very little bluff-catching, and bluff-check-raise the river more frequently.

If my opponent has many combinations of very strong, made hands, I will definitely bluff less frequently and call with fewer of my made hands.

Adjustments Based on My Opponent's Style

If my opponent rarely if ever bluffs on the river, I tighten up my calling requirements and only call with hands that beat an appropriate number of his value combinations to be getting the right pot odds.

Some opponents just can't help themselves—they will definitely try to steal on the river with almost all of their missed draws. If my guy is one of these maniacs and he has lots of missed draws in his range, I'll check to him and let him hang himself—I'll be calling very, very light.

Many opponents don't know how to react to large

over-bets of the pot on the river and can't make appropriate adjustments. With good timing and a compelling story, I can get some really big hands to fold. I can also get some very light calls if I make my over-bet look like I'm trying to steal with a missed draw. I try to figure out how my opponent will react to a two- or three-times-pot bet on the river. With the nuts or very strong value hands, I will look for the highest pain tolerance I can inflict, regardless of the bet size, and stick it in.

——EMPTY THE CLIP——

Everyone that's seen me play on TV knows that I'm not afraid to look like an idiot. If I believe a triple-barrel bluff is the correct play and is positive expectation, my chips will be going in. There are many players that can fire two bullets, but very few can fire three. I do not empty the clip against calling stations that play a trappy game. However, calling stations that rarely, if ever, trap are good triple-barrel targets. This type of player will call flop and turn bets with weak and moderate-strength hands, but then give up on the river. If I'm caught in one of these plays, I know that my opponents will be looking for more bluffs in the future. I can bet more hands for thin value in subsequent hands and hopefully regain some of the chips I spewed with the unsuccessful bluff.

POT LIMIT OMAHA 1.0

Pot Limit Omaha (PLO) is the new game of choice among the action junkies. As the NLH games got tougher, players branched out and looked for weaker spots. They found them at the PLO tables, and ever since, the game has grown steadily in popularity. Many of the skills that make you a winning No Limit Hold'em player translate well into your PLO game.

However, there are many important, nonintuitive differences. See, PLO is still in its infancy, much like NLH was ten years ago. So the fundamentals in this section should give you the tools to beat a $5–$10 game. At stakes higher than that, you'll have to wait for Galfond or Dwan to write a book—I'm waiting for that myself.

PLO BASICS

Among popular poker variants, PLO is the most fun and action packed. The game is played in the same sequence as Hold'em. Hole cards dealt, round of betting. Three-card flop, round of betting. Turn, bet. River, bet. Showdown. There are two essential differences between No Limit Hold'em and PLO:

- Each player gets four hole cards and has to use two, and exactly two, of those four—three from the board, two from the hand.
- Pot Limit Omaha is "Pot Limit," not "No Limit." Players are limited to the size of the pot with each raise.

Having two more hole cards in each hand drives action to an unprecedented level by effectively giving players six different Hold'em hands to play at the same time. As a result, pre-flop hand values are much closer in Omaha than in Hold'em. Many more hands are playable in Omaha, leading to tons of multi-way pots. With so many possibilities and close hand values, the variance for PLO skyrockets. If you have a hard time handling the swings of NLH, stay away from PLO.

In Pot-Limit betting, if you're going to raise, that raise is limited to the size of the pot. For example, in a

$5–$10 game with a $5 small blind and a $10 big blind, a "pot-size raise" is to $35:

    $5 small blind
    $10 big blind
    $10 my "call" of the big blind
    $25 subtotal size of pot before I raise
    $25 raise
    $35 maximum pot-size raise

Now, say my opponent raises the pot and the action is folded to my big blind and I want to raise the maximum:

    $5 small blind
    $10 my big blind
    $35 my opponent opens for a pot-size raise
    $25 I call his raise
    $75 total pot after I call the raise, and new maximum
        pot raise

I make it $110 to go ($25 + $75)

In PLO, I can't simply go all-in and blow my opponents out of the hand like I can in NLH.

COMBINATORIAL
EXPLOSION

With four hole cards, there are six two-card combinations for a player to combine with the five community cards. As we've seen, in Hold'em there are 1,326 possible starting hands. In PLO, there are a staggering 270,725 possible starting hands (52 x 51 x 50 x 49 ÷ 24), about 200 times more than Hold'em.

Although the number of combinations has soared, the method of calculating the combinations is the same as in Hold'em. Let's try a few examples:

Example 1:

What are the chances of being dealt AAXX in Omaha?

6 ways to choose AA × (50 cards × 49 ÷ 2) = 7,350

7,350 ÷ 270,725 = 2.7%

Example 2:

What are the chances of being dealt a hand with the A♠ and the 5♠ and two other cards?

(50 × 49 ÷ 2) ÷ 270,725 = 0.0045 = 0.45%

Example 3:

How many combinations and probability of being dealt JT98 double-suited?

JTs 98s = 4 × 4 = 16
J9s T8s = 4 × 4 = 16
J8s T9s = 4 × 4 = 16
= 48 combinations / 270,725 = 0.000177 =
0.0177%

Example 4:

How many double-suited hands are there?

48 combinations for each 4 ranks × 13 × 12 × 11 ×
10 ÷ 24 = 34,320 combinations

34,320 ÷ 270,725 = 12.67%

Example 5:

What are the chances of being dealt a rainbow hand (four cards with four different suits)?

13 × 13 × 13 × 13 = 28,561 combinations

28,561 ÷ 270,725 = 10.54%

Example 6:

How many hands are exactly single-suited?

270,725 total combinations

− 28,561 rainbow combinations

− 34,320 double−suited combinations

= 207,844

207,844 ÷ 270,725 = 76.77%

PRE-FLOP HAND RANKINGS

——THE EXCELLENT——

Here is a list of the top 30 starting hands in Omaha:

1. A-A-K-K	11. K-Q-J-T	21. Q-Q-A-K
2. A-A-J-T	12. K-K-T-T	22. Q-Q-A-J
3. A-A-Q-Q	13. K-K-A-Q	23. Q-Q-A-T
4. A-A-J-J	14. K-K-A-J	24. Q-Q-K-J
5. A-A-T-T	15. K-K-A-T	25. Q-Q-K-T
6. A-A-9-9	16. K-K-Q-J	26. Q-Q-J-T
7. A-A-x-x	17. K-K-Q-T	27. Q-Q-J-9
8. J-T-9-8	18. K-K-J-T	28. Q-Q-9-9
9. K-K-Q-Q	19. Q-Q-J-J	29. J-J-T-T
10. K-K-J-J	20. Q-Q-T-T	30. J-J-T-9

For all hands, being double-suited (ds) is best, single-suited (ss) is next (and, when applicable, a strong preference for being suited with the Ace), and no suits is a distant third. This list represents about 3.5% of the total number of possible 4-card starting hands in Omaha.

——THE GOOD——

Hands that are double-suited with some connectivity are good hands:

KT98ds
QT86ds

These hands are good, but are played mostly for straight potential, with the flush as emergency backup.

Double-paired hands are considered good hands (and even better if suited or double-suited) and are almost always playable:

JJ55, 8877

Ace-suited hands with a medium or high pair and some connectivity are good hands.

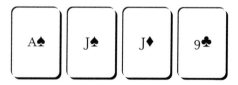

——THE MEDIOCRE——

Coordinated hands with a few gaps and a suit are mediocre.

    J986ds
    9754ds*
    J865ds

    Suited ace hands without much more going for them are considered mediocre, at best.

    A♠T♠7♣4♦

——THE UGLY——

Hands with only one low pair (2-7) are generally considered trash hands, unless there is another pair in the hand or the other cards have something seriously good going for them. A♣K♦2♣2♦ isn't a terrible hand, for instance, but J♣T♣5♦5♠ is considered ugly trash.

——THE WORST——

Any hand with trips (QQQX, TTTX, etc.) is trash and completely unplayable. Obviously, since trips are bad,

---

* Biggest downside with these hands is that they can easily flop a dominated wrap. For instance, 9754 on a flop of T82 could very well be up against QJ98.

quads are even worse. But don't worry, you'll only be dealt a hand this bad about 1% of the time.

PRE-FLOP PLAY

The starting hands in PLO are much closer in value than they are in Hold'em. Even the very best hands, like AAKK double-suited, are only marginal favorites over bad hands, like a J♣8♣6♦4♥ rainbow (which has approximately the same value as 85o in Hold'em), at 68% to 32%, or about 2-1. Many players presented with this information automatically assume that since the hand values are so much closer, almost every hand becomes playable. Those players quickly go broke. Hand selection, as in Hold'em, is still extremely important and sets you up for success later in the hand.

The "nuts," or the best hand possible, is very often the winning hand in PLO. Winning a pot with a hand other than the nuts is the exception, not the rule. With that being the case, it is crucial to play hands that will have many ways to make the nuts.

——PRE-FLOP FUNDAMENTALS——

In Hold'em, I advocate a "raise or fold" strategy. That is still the case in PLO: if I am the first player to voluntarily commit chips to the pot, I raise. I never limp in PLO (or any other poker game, for that matter).* My strategy is still "raise or fold."

I play hands that have a good chance of flopping the nuts or flopping a premium draw to the nuts—hands like JT98 have an excellent chance of pulling it off. Those hands are very playable, especially if they are suited or double-suited.

Hands with small cards (2, 3, 4, 5) are typically not playable. Many players overvalue hands with small pairs, like K855 and K744. The problem with hands like this is that unless you flop quads, it is nearly impossible to flop the nuts. Even if you flop a set, you have to play the rest of the hand defensively—players will almost always be drawing very live, and occasionally, they'll have you crushed with a higher set. My advice is to ignore 2, 3, 4, and 5 in your hand unless they are suited with an Ace.

I hate starting hand guides, but here is a good look at requirements for opening the pot in PLO. Notice that playing extremely tight from early position is correct, and that most decent hands become playable from late position.

---

* Late in PLO tournaments with an average stack of around 30 big blinds, limping *might* be acceptable if there are many short stacks at the table.

PLO Starting Hand Guide

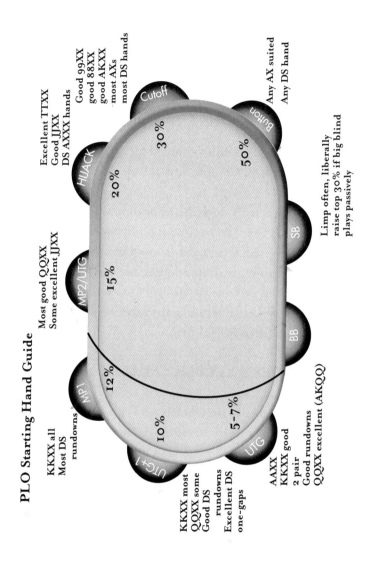

MP1
KKXX all
Most DS
rundowns

MP2/UTG
Most good QQXX
Some excellent JJXX

HIJACK
Excellent TTXX
Good JJXX
DS AXXX hands

Cutoff
Good 99XX
good 88XX
good AKXX
most AXs
most DS hands

Button
Any AX suited
Any DS hand

SB
Limp often, liberally
raise top 30% if big blind
plays passively

UTG+1
KKXX most
QQXX some
Good DS
  rundowns
Excellent DS
one-gaps

UTG
AAXX
KKXX good
2 pair
Good rundowns
QQXX excellent (AKQQ)

12% MP1
15% MP2/UTG
20% HIJACK
30% Cutoff
50% Button
10% UTG+1
5-7% UTG

——EQUITIES ARE VERY CLOSE——

Pre-flop equities are very, very close in PLO. Even hands that look dominant aren't extremely likely to win against even the trashiest looking hands at showdown:

AAXX* vs. JT98 double-suited 56% to 44%
AAKK vs. 4567 double-suited 60% to 40%

No hand is truly dominating against any other hand. In Hold'em, AA vs. 72o has about an 87% chance of winning. In PLO, AAXX vs. 7422 is only about 70% likely to win. Although the pre-flop equities are very close, post-flop playability is extremely vital. In PLO, multi-street betting and hands that go all the way to showdowns are much more common than in Hold'em.

——VERY LITTLE STEALING——

In PLO, there really isn't much of a chance to steal the blinds—it is a very rare occurrence. If I am the first player to raise the pot, I expect to get at least one caller, and I'm not at all surprised to face multi-way action. Even when I raise from the button, I expect to get called (or raised) from the small or big blind around 50% of the time.

At an average table against normal, tight, aggressive

---

* AAXX is used to represent AA with any other two random cards.

competition, when I open from middle position in a nine-handed game (under the gun in a six-handed game) here is what I expect:

Win the blinds (steal)	3%
Heads up, out of position, or three-bet	28%
Heads up, in position, or three-bet from the blinds	20%
Three-way action	35%
Four-way action	14%

Three-betting pre-flop in Hold'em will result in many folds and easy pre-flop wins. In PLO, three-betting does not win the pot very often at all. Most players will call a three-bet once they have opened the pot. In PLO, I never three-bet and expect to win the pot pre-flop. When I three-bet in position, I hope to isolate and play with a hand that has good equity and excellent playability. When I three-bet out of position (from the blinds), I'll always have a first-tier, premium hand.

——HEADS UP VS. MULTI-WAY HANDS——

Some hands in PLO play best when heads up. Hands like AAXX rainbow, KK97 rainbow, AK97 all play better if up against one player. These hands can (and will) win with one or two pair. In multi-way pots, it is rare to see a hand as weak as two pair take down the pot.

Other hands in PLO play best in multi-way pots. Most of these are the "rundown" hands—hands like JT98, T987, and 9876 that play well against many opponents. I either flop a huge draw, the nuts, trips, or I can easily get away from the hand without investing much money. With the lower rundowns (8765, 7654, etc.), the hands become weaker in multi-way action—weak flush draws, straights, and two pair are unlikely to be good if facing significant action.

With the hands that play better heads up, I am always trying to limit the field and play against as few opponents as possible. I will risk a three-bet in an effort to limit the competition. With hands that play better in multi-way pots, I will simply call a pre-flop raise and allow other players to enter the pot behind me more easily. Bottom line: In some hands, usually the high pairs, I want to push people out of the pot. With the straight and rundown hands, I don't mind pulling opponents into the pot.

	J♣ T♣ 9♠ 8♠		A♣ A♦ 9♠ 7♥	
Opps	My Win%	Opps Win%	My Win%	Opps Win%
1	44%	56%	63%	37%
2	31%	34%	43%	28%
3	24%	25%	30%	23%
4	19%	20%	22%	19%

As you can see from the chart, playing JT98 against two opponents only lowers the win rate by 13% (44% to 31%). Playing AA97 against two opponents lowers the win rate by 20% (63% to 43%).

——IMPORTANCE OF POSITION——

Position is even more important in PLO than it is in Hold'em. As there are so many multi-street, multi-way pots, being in position is a tremendous advantage. It is much easier to extract value from the "nuts" and save money with second-best hand when in position. It is also easier to bluff successfully.

I strive to play as many pots as possible in position in PLO. If there is a decent chance that I'll be out of position in a hand, there is a decent chance I'll just fold all but the best, most playable hands.

——THOUGHTS ON AAXX——

AAXX isn't as powerful as AA is in Hold'em. That should be fairly obvious—in Hold'em, AA is dealt only 1 out of 225 hands, while in PLO, a player is dealt AAXX about 1 out of 40 hands. Many players just lose their minds when they pick up Aces pre-flop in PLO. While AAXX should always open the pot for a raise, it isn't always worth three- or four-betting.

For three-betting purposes, AAXX hands should be subdivided into good, mediocre, and bad subcategories:

Good AAXX hands are double-suited or have another pair (AA55, AAJJ, etc.) A♣A♦K♦Q♠ is a great hand as well—it is suited with the Ace and has strong connectivity. Good AAXX hands can three-bet from any position and play well against any number of opponents.

Mediocre AAXX hands are usually single-suited with the Ace not having much connectivity: AA96, AAK9, AA52. Mediocre Aces should three-bet in hands where it is likely to be heads up, in position. I rarely three-bet these hands from the blinds—playing out of position is just too difficult.

Bad AAXX hands are usually rainbow hands without connectivity. These hands should rarely three-bet. I will three-bet AAXX from the button against a late position raiser—that is my best shot at getting this hand heads up. These hands are best played for set value.

Many players make the mistake of three-betting bad or mediocre Aces when out of position. The pre-flop raiser will almost never fold, and playing bad or mediocre AAXX out of position is very difficult. You don't have to play in many of these spots to realize that this is a recipe for disaster. A better play is just to flat-call these hands and then check-fold if the flop isn't good for your hand. Don't put another chip in the pot on boards like QJ8 and JT7. AAXX just plays like crap on so many different flops that it isn't worth a three-bet, despite the fact that you have the best hand at the moment. Remember, opponents aren't going to fold to a three-bet, and it will be extremely difficult to maintain the lead post-flop.

If you are new to Omaha, odds are you will be excited about seeing AAXX. That excitement will quickly fade after you misplay a few of these "monster" hands and get stacked a few times. Soon, you'll see bad Aces for what they are: a decent hand that has a hard time flopping the nuts and won't make much money in most cases when you do. New PLO players might be better off never three-betting mediocre or bad Aces and playing them solely for set-mining purposes.

When playing deep stacked, I am very cautious with this hand. If I open from middle position with mediocre or bad Aces and I get three-bet by a deep-stacked opponent who has position on me, I will not be four-betting very often at all. I'm just going to call the three-bet and check-fold if the flop is scary. When I four-bet pre-flop, my hand might as well be played faceup—a deep-stacked opponent will be able to put tons of pressure on most flops, pressure that a bare pair of Aces will have a hard time standing up against.

For example, playing with $2,500 on the table (250 big blinds deep) at a $5–$10 table, I raise from middle position with A♣A♦7♥2♠—bad Aces—and make it $35 to go. My opponent three-bets to $110 from the button. I four-bet the pot to $330. He calls. $675 in the pot. The flop is J♦6♠5♠. I bet $440, he moves all-in. I hate my hand. Even against my "best case" of A♠J♠T♣9♣, my hand is only 43%

195

to win. Against KQJJ or QJJT, I'm toast and only win 9% of the time.

If I face a three-bet after opening with mediocre or bad Aces and I can't get about a third of my stack in with a four-bet, I usually just call the three-bet and reevaluate after the flop. If I can get a third or more of my chips into the pot, I'll go ahead and four-bet and then get it all-in post-flop most of the time.

If I'm fortunate enough to pick up AA, but unfortunate enough to have AAAX or even AAAA, I realize that these hands still have some value. Of course, I'm not likely to flop anything substantial, but these hands have good bluffing potential on almost every "flush" board. Dumping these hands pre-flop isn't a mistake, but if I'm willing to get creative, I can pull off some spectacular bluffs.

——THOUGHTS ON KKXX——

Playing Aces in Omaha is very tough. Playing KK hands is just as difficult. KKXX is almost always a pre-flop opening raise if I'm the first to voluntarily enter the pot. There are some very, very bad Kings that might be a fold UTG in a full nine-handed ring game: Rainbow KK72, KK94 at very active tables probably deserve a tight, early position muck.

If a player opens in front of me, I am only three-betting very good Kings, and then only against a middle- or late-position opening raise. Ideally, I want to play KKXX hands heads up, in position. This is where Kings are the most effective. I am a little more willing to three-bet mediocre KK hands when I have an Ace in my hand—that Ace will decrease the chance that my opponent has AAXX by about 50%, based on straightforward card elimination.

If I open from early position with mediocre or bad KKXX and I get three-bet by a good player in position, I seriously consider dumping my hand. Playing a big pot out of position with a hand that isn't going to flop well most of the time isn't my idea of a good time.

For example, if I open K♣K♦9♠5♦ from early position and Phil Galfond three-bets me from the button, my most profitable play is folding (and quickly changing tables).

Bad KKXX hands can call an opening raise for set value if the pot looks like it will go multi-way.

——THOUGHTS ON QQXX, JJXX, TTXX, 99XX——

These hands come in a few versions, some with straight potential, others that are mainly played for set value:

Good: QQ JT double-suited, Q JJT, TT98, TT97, 9987, KsJsJT

Mediocre: QQ98 single suit, KJJsTs, JJ97 double-suited

Bad: QQ84 single suit, JJ83 double-suited, TT72 double-suited

These medium-strength paired hands, even double-suited and with straight potential, aren't as good as they appear to be. When I flop a flush draw, it won't be the nut-flush draw and I'll have to play conservatively. If I flop a set and get action, I can be sure that my opponents will be drawing very live. QQ84 can easily be a significant underdog on a QT7 two-tone board.

Most of the big pots with these medium-paired hands come in set-over-set situations. Realize that the lower your top set is, the more often you'll be facing a lower set that has good draws against your hand as well:

Example: Q♣J♠T♦T♥
Flop: T♣7♦5♦

If I open this hand for a raise and get a few callers from the blinds, I might be brilliantly ahead in a set-over-set situation. But, the hands with 77 and 55 that will call a pre-flop raise will also have some connectivity that will hit that flop hard for draws, with hands like 7789, 8776, 6554. Although ahead, Q JJT isn't much better than a 2-1 favorite against any of those hands.

These hands do not play well in multi-way pots. I really only want to play these hands in position against a single opponent—that means that they are really only playable from late position when I can open the pot for a raise. Calling a pre-flop raise, even with "good" versions of these hands, can lead to some serious problems post-flop.

Opening bad, uncoordinated queens from any position except the button is too loose. Calling a pre-flop raise with these hands out of position against an early or middle position raise is too loose. Playing these hands in multi-way pots is too loose. Get the idea?

——THOUGHTS ON RUNDOWNS——

Rundowns, hands like JT98, KQJT, AKQJ, 9876, are all very, very good hands, and in fact, they are my favorite type of hand to play. Not much can go wrong for these hands pre-flop. I will open them from every position and three-bet pretty much indiscriminately. These hands play well when heads up, and they play well in multi-way action too. When I pick up one of these hands, I consider it a green light to get active. Even against AAXX, rundowns hold up well: A rainbow JT98 is about 40% to beat AAXX at showdown.

One of the nice properties of rundowns is that they are relatively easy to play post-flop. If I flop two pair, I'll have at least a premium straight draw to go with it:

JT98 on a J84 or J93 board, 9876 on a 762 board

All of these flops allow extremely aggressive post-flop play with very little possibility that I'm drawing dead or slim. When I'm in late position and I'm facing an early or middle position raise, I'll most likely three-bet bad rundowns (T987 rainbow) and try to get heads up in position. With premium rundowns like JT98 double-suited, I'll most likely call the pre-flop raise and hope to draw some other players into the pot.

——THOUGHTS ON
MEDIOCRE, UNPAIRED HANDS——

Mediocre, unpaired hands can definitely be playable and profitable. Hands like "skip-straights" QT86, J986 certainly have potential, but they are markedly inferior to the "pure" rundown hands. Even hands with only one gap (JT87, 9865) look better than they really are. But if double-suited, these hands become very playable.

Unlike the pure rundowns, these hands play better against limited competition. If I'm in late position and facing an opening raise from middle position, I three-bet with these hands quite liberally and try to isolate in position to give myself the best chance to win the pot with two pair.

If I three-bet and face a four-bet with these hands, I'm definitely going to call if I'm in position. I'm most likely against AAXX-type hands. I can really have my opponent in bad shape on some flops, and my all-in equity against AAXX is 45%. Better yet, after 40% of the flops, I'll actually be in the lead (though I may not know it).

Omaha Hi Hand vs. Hand Equity Graph
10000 flops dealt
Minimum Equity for 9c 8c 6d 5d (vs.[AA**])

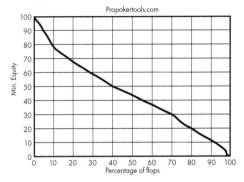

Bottom line: I play these hands in position and I try to isolate when possible. Post-flop, I get away cheaply when I don't flop at least top two or a premium draw. Flush draws are viewed as emergency backup, not a feature.

Other playable hands have a suited Ace and some connectivity between the other three cards: A♠9♠8♣7♦, A♣5♣6♦7♥. These hands are particularly playable if I'm the first to open the pot from late position. I never fold A♠9♠8♣7♦ to a single raise. I'll call a raise with A♣5♣6♦7♥ if I'm on the button, but not from the blinds. Any suited Ace is playable almost without regard to the other cards in a four-way pot on the button. A522 with a suited Ace is (marginally) playable from the blinds, A368 double-suited should probably fold to a pre-flop raise from the small blind, but may be playable three-way and definitely should be played in a four-way pot. Almost all of the playability of these hands comes from the flush draw and flopping trips—every other flop leaves these hands vulnerable and weak.

——THOUGHTS ON TRASH HANDS——

Hands like 5568 and 2235 are bad hands with huge reverse implied odds. I occasionally play some of these weaker holdings from the button when I can open the pot for a raise, but only if the blinds are weak: passive players and easy to read.

Playing these hands multi-way is a quick and effective way to go broke. You might as well just take out a lighter and set the money on fire. If I just have to play 5568 against a late position opening raise, I'm better off three-betting and then barreling off.

——THREE-BETTING——

Three-betting, a key strategy in most Hold'em games, is very important in PLO as well. Three-betting in Hold'em often results in winning the pot pre-flop. In PLO, that is not the case. It is extremely rare to see a player fold to a three-bet pre-flop in PLO—they are going to see the flop.

So, consider these two facts:

1) I will almost never get a pre-flop opener to fold pre-flop when I three-bet.
2) Position is more important in PLO than in Hold'em.

Considering those two facts, it is very clear that three-betting from the small or big blind is a very big no-no. Even with mediocre and bad AAXX, I am very reluctant to three-bet out of position.* Let's drill down here a bit using the Graph tool at ProPokerTools.

A♣A♥9♠7♦ vs. a cutoff position opening raise with a typical 35% opening range:

Pre-flop all-in equity: 63% for AAXX, 37% for cutoff.

Here is a graph of post-flop equities for the cutoff hand:

Omaha Hi Hand vs. Hand Equity Graph
10000 flops dealt
Minimum Equity for 35% (vs.[Ac Ah 9s 7d])

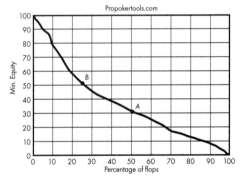

On 50% of the flops (Point A), my opponent will have at least 33% equity (probably some sort of flush draw

---

* Against the extremely wide opening range of 70%+ that I find in higher-stakes games, I three-bet much more liberally even out of position—very often my opponent will be opening a hand (and calling my three-bet) with hands that have very poor playability.

or straight draw), and there is no chance I'm going to get him to fold to a post-flop bet. Worse, on 25% of the flops (Point B), I'll actually be behind. So, I'm out of position in a three-bet pot, and I'm about to fire a bullet when it is unlikely that I'll get my opponent to fold, and there's a decent chance I'm actually behind. Worse yet, when I three-bet out of position, my opponent will be able to put me on a very, very tight range of hands and will be able to peg me with AAXX quite often and accurately.

As an aside, contrast that last graph to the equivalent Hold'em graph, a 35% opening raise and a three-bet with AA:

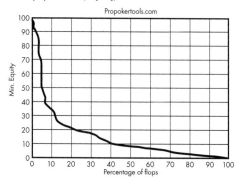

Hold'em Hand vs. Hand Equity Graph
10000 flops dealt
Minimum Equity for 35% (vs.[AA])

There are very few flops that significantly improve a 35% opening range against AA in Hold'em.

In PLO, the pre-flop three-bet serves just two purposes:

1. Trap the dead money and isolate the weak post-flop players when in position.
2. Build a pot with a big hand that has an excellent chance to flop the nuts or a big draw to the nuts.

If neither criteria is met, three-betting pre-flop isn't the best play.

——THREE-BET DEFENSE——

If I open the pot for a raise and get three-bet, most of the time my decision is easy: call and take a flop. Occasionally, I will four-bet. Very rarely, I'll choose to fold.

In Position

When I'm in position against a three-bettor, I almost never fold. I consider dumping only the very worst, paired hands. If I've opened hands like QQ96, JJ54, 9976, and TT85, I might fold to a three-bet. If my hand is unpaired, no matter how bad it is, I'm going to call the three-bet and take a flop in position.

At *deep* effective stacks of *at least 150 big blinds,* I four-bet liberally with my premium, rundown hands. I want the ape playing AAXX to go crazy out of position, 300 big blinds deep, when I can have him in such bad shape post-flop.

Out of Position

Getting three-bet and playing out of position can be very problematic. Because of my good hand selection skills, I won't be out of position often in PLO. Here are some general guidelines for this spot:

♦ Four-betting out of position is not normally a good idea unless I have AAXX and can get at least a third of my stack in pre-flop. The quality of my AAXX hands isn't as important as the effective stack sizes. If I can get a third of the money in with a four-bet, I do it and then fire a pot-size bet (the rest of my stack) on most flops.

♦ The worst of the paired hands can be folded without much regret. If I open a bad KK hand from early position in a nine-handed game (KK96) and get three-bet from the button, I can comfortably fold. Same with a QQT7-type hand from the cutoff. Paired hands have very little playability post-flop out of position.

♦ Unpaired hands that were good enough to open should be good enough to call all three-bets. That is actually a pretty good indicator when considering opening from early position—if I won't be happy to call a three-bet and play out of position, I should dump the hand and refuse to open the pot.

♦ Excellent AAXX hands, like AAJ9ds, can four-bet, even out of position.

—COLD CALLING A THREE-BET—

If I have a premium rundown and there is a bet and raise in front of me, I don't get scared off my hand—these are still excellent hands. Other hands that are playable in this spot are two pair hands like 9988, 8866. Hands like QQ JJ are worse than they look—your opponents will very often have "blockers" to hands like this (AKQ J, KQ JT, Q JT9). As a result, those hands are less likely to flop a set. Even if I do flop a set, my opponents will often have big straight draws and not be all that far behind.

—SQUEEZES—

When I'm in late position and there are several limpers, I will "squeeze" with a big pot-size bet on a wide range of hands. This is one spot where I expect my opponents to fold and I might be able to isolate some fishy money and play a pot in position. I'll almost never make this play from the blinds, however. I don't want to play a big multi-way pot out of position, even with AAXX. Out of position in what will be a 4- or 5-way pot, I'll just play my bad AA hands for set value. Players making the transition to PLO from Hold'em are really surprised that the pre-flop squeeze, one of the bread-and-butter plays in Hold'em, just doesn't work in PLO.

——REVERSE SQUEEZES——

While squeezes (especially out of position) aren't very effective, reverse squeezes can be an extremely good play. Again, a reverse squeeze operates when you flat-call an early position opening raise, get three-bet from behind, and then put in a big four-bet after "trapping" the pre-flop opener and three-bettor. Mostly, I'll make this play when I have bad AAXX-type hands that weren't good enough to three-bet pre-flop, but am more than happy to four-bet and get a significant amount of my stack in.

An early position player opens for a pot-size raise to $35 in a $5–$10 game. With 150 big blinds in my stack, I don't feel comfortable three-betting with A♣A♦9♠5♥. I call. The button, a frequent and aggressive three-bettor, raises the pot to $140. The opener calls. Now, I can four-bet to $575 with what is almost assuredly the best hand and get in a little more of a third of my stack pre-flop.

——TOURNAMENT PLAY PRE-FLOP——

In PLO, limping into the pot pre-flop might be a viable play. Early in the tournament, there are plenty of fish taking a shot at the game without much experience. Raising pre-flop chases away all the fishy money. I don't really want the Q♣7♦5♠4♣ to fold when I have A♣Q♦J♣8♥. I want that fish to get in the pot, flop a flush or flush draw and go broke. If I raise, the fish will almost certainly fold such a bad hand.

Late in most PLO tournaments, the stack sizes will degenerate to around 20–40 big blinds. Here, too, I might consider pre-flop limping from early and middle position. With short effective stacks, there simply isn't enough maneuverability when I raise pre-flop.

I play extremely, ultra-tight from the blinds in PLO tournaments. I simply don't want to play pots out of position when there is no possibility of a re-buy. If I'm short-stacked in a PLO tournament, I don't rush to three-bet or four-bet pre-flop out of position. As a short stack, I am never going to get my opponent to fold pre-flop. The "stop and go" from the blinds is a better short-stacked play: call the pre-flop raise, and then fire "pot" after the flop. That play is much more difficult to combat and gives me a chance to win the pot without going to showdown. With the stop and go, I also have the luxury of deciding to give up on the worst of flops and preserve the small amount of tournament equity I have left.

Example: I have JT98 and I have 11 big blinds left in the big blind. Middle-position player opens the pot, and I consider a three-bet all-in. But that play will never win the pot right away—my opponent will call my three-bet 100% of the time. A better play is to just call the raise and then fire at the pot.

FLOP PLAY

In PLO, almost every hand is contested and goes to the flop. Playing well post-flop is required to be a winning PLO player. A player with fire-hose-sized leaks in the pre-flop game can still win if he possesses great post-flop skill, but the opposite is certainly not true.

——VISUALIZE THE TURN——

The key to good post-flop play is to visualize the turn. To put in much action on the flop, I really want to either already have the nuts or have at least 8 cards that can come on the turn that will give me the nuts. When I don't have the nuts and there aren't many cards on the turn that can make me the nuts, I play cautiously (unless I'm bluffing).

It is important to also visualize the turn with respect to the opponent's range of hands. There are many instances where I can currently be in the lead with the best hand, but will likely be behind if the hand goes all the way to showdown.

——BEHIND WITH THE NUTS——

There are many times in PLO where you will flop the stone-cold nuts and actually not be a favorite to win the hand at showdown. These situations are much more frequent than you might expect, but taking a look at them will give you a good idea about the challenges and subtlety you will face in post-flop play.

Hand: Q♣J♦9♠8♠

A middle-position player opens for a post-size raise and I call from the button. The flop comes perfect for my hand and gives me the nuts:

Flop: A♠K♥T♥

The action on the flop is fast and furious—raise, re-raise, raise, re-raise, all-in. I couldn't be more thrilled, until my opponent turns over A♠A♥J♥7♠. They have top set, a gut-shot straight (to tie), a flush draw, and a back-door-flush draw. An equity analysis shows that the "nuts" just cost me a ton of equity:

Q♣J♦9♠8♠ = 31.71% equity
A♠A♥J♥7♠ = 68.29% equity

On the same flop with that action, it isn't inconceivable that my opponent is free-rolling against me with a hand like A♥K♦Q♥J♦. We both have a straight, but he has 9 outs to a flush.

Q♣J♦9♠8♠ = 22.99% equity
A♥K♦Q♥J♠ = 77.01% equity

——FOLDING THE NUTS——

In multi-way pots, it isn't unheard of to flop the nuts and be forced to fold before putting a single chip in the pot. For example:

A middle-position player opens the pot, cutoff calls, and I call from the big blind with a decent rundown hand 9♠8♠7♦5♥.

Flop: J♦T♦7♥

I check (intending to check-raise), opener bets the pot, cutoff raises the pot, and the action is on me.

Despite the fact that I currently have the nuts, this is a clear fold. If my opponents are rational, I'll be up against a minimum of a wrap (AKQX) and a flush draw, and it could be even worse:

Flop: J♦T♦7♥

A♣Q♠J♠J♣	38% equity
K♦Q♦J♥9♣	50% equity
9♠8♠7♦5♥	12% equity ← My hand is nearly dead

Take a long, careful look at this hand. After flopping the nuts, the hand has only 12% equity. There aren't many players who can flop the nuts and fold; luckily, it doesn't come up often.

Yes, this example is extreme and contrived, but it should scare the living hell out of you and wake you up to the possibilities of getting your money in very poorly post-flop. Many of these problems can be mitigated with a "backup" plan—a draw, even a gut-shot or backdoor flush draw, can significantly improve a hand's overall equity. For instance, here, I flop the nuts but my "backup plan" is a King to make a higher straight, and runner-runner to make the Ace-high flush.

Flop: J♦T♦7♥

A♣Q♠J♠J♣	37% equity
K♦Q♦J♥9♣	40% equity
9♠8♥A♥Q♣	23% equity

On coordinated boards, the current nuts won't be the nuts very often on the river, especially in multi-way pots. Don't get carried away and play too conservatively. With 9♠ 8♠ 7♦ 5♥ on a 6-4-3 two-tone flop, just get as much money in as you can—your opponents are very unlikely to have a set and a flush draw on a board like that.

——WRAPS AND STRAIGHT DRAWS——

As we've seen, it is quite common to be "behind" after the flop, but have more than 50% equity if the hand goes to showdown. Most commonly, these are hands with huge straight draws. These multi-card straight draws are called "wraps" and can be played extremely aggressively post-flop:

K♠Q♦9♥8♣
Flop: J♣T♦4♥

Here, any A, K, Q, 9, 8, or 7 will make a straight. Better yet, only the K and Q make a straight that isn't the nuts. There are 20 cards in the deck that will make a great hand, and 14 make the nuts. Clearly, this is a flop combination that can be played very aggressively. Even against a set, with a wrap, you're still in good shape:

Flop: J♣T♦4♥

K♠Q♦9♥8♣   51%
JJXX   49%

Beware of straight draws that look better than they are—you should significantly discount the value of straight draws that aren't the nuts. When you have a hand like this and your opponent has the full wrap, you may be in bad shape:

My hand: K♣Q♣T♣9♠   38%
Opponent: A♠K♠T♦9♦   72%

Flop: Q♠J♠4♦

Here, I flop top pair and a wrap. And yet, against a flush draw and wrap, I'm a big underdog. The lesson here is clear: *When the flop is two-toned, a wrap should be played much more cautiously.*

——CONTINUATION-BETS——

If I'm in the betting lead after the flop, the natural tendency is to make a continuation-bet (C-bet). In PLO, the correct use of the continuation-bet is much more difficult than it is in Hold'em. There isn't some master chart of all situations, obviously, so here is a partial list of some things I think about before firing that post-flop continuation-bet:

♦ If I don't think I have the best hand and I don't have quite a few outs to the nuts, I rarely C-bet. Draws to second nuts and top two pair (where the second pair won't make a straight) can warrant a continuation-bet as well.

♦ If the board is extremely dry (8-5-2 rainbow) and I whiffed (say with KQJT), I might make a C-bet as a bluff; my opponents are unlikely to have good hands.

♦ The best dry flops to C-bet are King-high flops—K-8-4 or K-7-2–type boards. I will get credit for a King (maybe even pocket Kings) and I normally won't face much resistance.

♦ If I have "blockers" to the nuts, I am more willing to fire a C-bet. For instance, if I have TTXX on a J-9-4 board,

I fire away—the chances that my opponent will have a huge wrap are pretty small, and there will be tons of turn cards that will give me an excellent, profitable bluffing opportunity. My opponent doesn't know that I'm betting with blockers—I could just as easily be betting with a huge wrap.

♦ On monotone boards, I almost always make a C-bet. If my opponent doesn't have a flush, they will have a hard time continuing on with the hand.

♦ If the board has two cards of the same suit (two-toned) and I have the "naked Ace" of that suit, I frequently C-bet. If the board flushes on the turn or river, I will be able to bluff effectively.

♦ If there are many bad turn cards for my hand, I don't feel like I have to C-bet to "protect" my hand. Flopping top two pair on a J-T-6 board is good, but as we've seen I am a significant underdog to wraps. I can just check (and call) and reevaluate after the turn. There is no really good reason to blow the pot up out of position when my hand is so vulnerable. I'm more concerned with protecting my stack than my hand.

♦ C-bets can help me realize my current equity with hands that can pick up monster draws on the turn, but don't really have the right odds to check and call a pot-size bet. Essentially, with these hands I C-bet as a semi-bluff—I might get my opponent to fold, and if not, I might pick up a good draw on the turn.

My Hand: A♣J♠T♦8♣
Flop: 9♣4♠2♦

Here, I have absolutely nothing, but if I'm out of position with the betting lead, I C-bet anyway. If I get raised, I can dump it without worry, and if my opponent calls, I can pick up a nut-flush draw or a wrap or even a wrap and a flush draw on the turn quite easily. This hand has substantial equity, but I can't just check and call out of position hoping to pick up a draw on the turn.

♦ I C-bet when the flop is very unlikely to have hit my opponent's range. Say a player opens from late position and I three-bet on the button and get called. The flop comes 5-6-7 rainbow. This is a great flop to C-bet. My opponent will have a really hard time calling with over-pairs and big rundown-type hands—exactly the hands that make up a substantial part of his range.

♦ I consider making smaller than normal C-bets in three-bet pots. Bets as small as a third of the pot can be very effective. I can get away with cheap bluffs, or I can induce some monkey-action from opponents when I have the goods. My small bet will charge them for some bad draws like gut-shots and weak flush draws. I want to bet most flops, but I want to be able to bluff as well. Most players aren't capable of raising a C-bet without the nuts because they'll be afraid of getting it in really bad.

♦ If I make a small C-bet and get called, my opponent will have a very wide range. Wide ranges don't play all that well on most turns and rivers. On the turn, I'll have a good shot at taking the pot away against a range not worthy of raising a flop C-bet.

♦ If my C-bet gets raised, I need a big hand to continue on, especially if I'm out of position. Even folding J♥T♥8♦6♠ on a J♣8♣5♥ board isn't completely ridiculous or too tight against a good, tight player.

——CHECKING BACK——

If I have the betting lead and position and my opponent checks to me, it seems nearly automatic to make a C-bet. In PLO, though, checking back and seeing the turn has much more going for it than many players realize.

♦ I check-back when my hand is weak, but there are lots of good turn cards that could give me a hand that can continue aggressively.

♦ I check-back with weak draws when I can't or don't want to call a check-raise. If I flop a Queen-high flush draw with a gut-shot, for instance, this is a good time to check-back. I wouldn't call a check-raise with that hand, but it has some equity that can be realized by checking and seeing the turn.

♦ I check-back with top and bottom pair hands that have good showdown value but can't stand a raise. I might get more value from these hands by inducing turn and river bluffs than I'll get by betting.

♦ In multi-way pots, I check-back even more often—I am much more likely to face a check-raise when there are multiple players in the pot.

——TRAPPING——

Trapping (or slow-playing) is not very common in PLO given all the draw possibilities. But, occasionally, I'll have a hand like QQ76 and flop Q-5-4 rainbow, and trapping seems to be the best course of action. But, even with that flop, I'm not thrilled to see an A, 2, 6, or 7 on the turn—those cards might well make my opponent a straight. And I almost never slow-play on two-tone boards.

After trapping on the flop, I just barrel off and bet the pot on all turn cards and hope that my opponent picked up enough of a draw or hand to make a bad bet or call. I could even get lucky and get my opponent to do some crazy stuff on the turn when I slow-play a hand like this—perhaps they pick up second set, or a big wrap. Either way, with only one card to come, they'll be drawing to only about a 30% chance to win.

For a trap or slow-play to be prudent, everything needs to be locked up and the flop texture has to miss the opponent's range. "Trapping" with the nuts on two-tone locked-down boards can also be effective. With 9875 on a J♣T♠7♠ board, I might just check the flop and hope for a "safe" turn card. The danger in betting this hand is getting check-raised by straight-flush-wrap draws—I may have the nuts now, but my hand often won't be very good after the turn and river.

——CHECK-RAISING——

Check-raising on the flop in PLO is a great play, and often is the most effective weapon:

♦ I consider check-raising for a bluff on locked-down boards, like 7-5-4 rainbow. Unless my opponent flopped the nuts, I will win the pot most of the time. If I get called after check-raising, I reevaluate after the turn—against novice opponents who always three-bet with the nuts, I can make a small turn bet (a third of the pot) and then barrel off the river if the board doesn't pair—opponents are almost always on a set in these spots.

♦ If I'm going to check-raise-bluff on locked-down boards, then I should also check-raise with the nuts for balance. My opponents will start making very tight check-backs in position because they are afraid of my check-raise.

♦ I check-raise and barrel off on monotone boards when I hit the naked Ace (see page 223). If I play this hand aggressively enough, it will be nearly impossible for my opponents to keep making crying calls as the pot gets bigger and bigger.

♦ I consider check-raising with blockers to the nuts. If I have JJ77 and the flop is 9-6-5 rainbow, this is a good time to go for a check-raise bluff. With two sevens in my hand, my opponents are unlikely to have a straight.

♦ I am unlikely to pull off a check-raise bluff when the board is two-toned. I won't get my opponent to fold the nut-flush draw.

When I'm considering a check-raise on the flop, I usually have either the nuts or air. I'm also willing to check-raise with dominating draws when I have a pair with a good redraw.

——FLOATING——

Floating in PLO is just not very common. If my opponent bets the flop and I don't really have anything, it is usually not wise to continue. Very infrequently, I consider calling that flop bet and trying to hit a great turn card. For example, with KQ J9 double-suited on a T-6-4 board, I could consider calling a flop bet to try to pick up a wrap or a flush draw on the turn. Of course, I'll play AT98 exactly the same way on the flop, so I won't be giving much away. Now, if a Queen hits the turn, I'll be in excellent shape to call or raise a turn bet.

Essentially, I float the flop to pick up a draw to the nuts on the turn. Do not overuse this play—use it only for very specific, targeted situations.

——DONK BETTING——

Donk betting (betting into the pre-flop raiser before your opponents have been given a chance to act on their hand) is much more common in PLO than in Hold'em. With so many potential draws, donking with a strong but vulnerable hand has a lot going for it.

♦ Donk betting is fine if I think my opponent is likely to check-back with a hand that could pick up significant equity on the turn.

♦ I don't donk into locked-down boards—I go for the check-raise instead. This matters a great deal. Firing a pot-size bet on a 9-6-5 rainbow board isn't nearly as effective as check-raising. If I donk, my opponent will wonder why I didn't check-raise, and they are much more likely to play back.

♦ I donk with hands that aren't strong enough to call a post-flop pot-size bet and can't check-raise. Essentially, I'm trying to either take down the pot or give myself some equity when I get called.

♦ I donk bet in multi-way pots when it is very unlikely that I'll see multi-way action on the turn. For example, a player raises from middle position, the button calls, and I call from the big blind. The flop comes T-4-2 rain-bow. This is a good spot to donk with JJXX or KKXX. I don't expect to get two callers on a dry flop like that. Of course, I'll fold if I get raised, but I'll pick up the pot often enough to justify the investment. I will not be well balanced in this spot, but this play is difficult to exploit.

——THE POWER OF THE NAKED ACE——

The "naked Ace" is the Ace of the suit that has flush potential with the board. When I have that card in my hand, my opponent can never be drawing to the nut flush. I can play all of my draws more aggressively, and I can effectively barrel the turn and river if a flush card comes. It will be very difficult for my opponent to call a pot-size bet on the turn or river with the third or fourth nuts. I will get called, of course, but getting caught bluffing with the naked Ace will make the times that I'm barreling off with the made flush that much more profitable. And, because I practice good hand selection, I'll have a suited Ace many, many more times than I'll have the naked Ace—probably two to three times more often. Many players aren't willing to fire that third big bullet on the river—they'll bluff with the naked Ace on the flop, fire a second bullet on the turn, and then chicken out at the river. That river bet was the most important of the three, though—if you're not willing to fire three bullets speculatively, then don't fire the first two either. Note that stack sizes are very relevant here. If I'm not going to have a 3/4-size pot bet on the river, then this play will be much less effective.

——SMALL SETS——

I won't be flopping small sets very often—there aren't many hands with small pairs in my pre-flop raising or calling range. If I happen to have a small pair and flop a small set, they are extremely difficult to play. The biggest danger, of course, is running into set over set—when that happens, I'll be drawing to one out (quads) and be in some really big trouble. With small sets, the best course of action is usually to try to play small-ball on the flop and reevaluate on the turn. Set-over-set situations constitute almost the entire profit margin of many winning players. If for some reason I find myself playing 7789 against an early position raiser and the flop comes A-K-7, I realize that there are many more playable combinations of AAXX and KKXX than there are of AKXX for my opponent. If I face opposition on a flop like this, my opponent is very likely to have the nuts—this is a flop where I can definitely lay down the bottom set and feel pretty good about my decision.

I keep my options open for the turn and see how things develop. I'm not in a big rush to get my chips in the middle with small or second sets. There are many turn cards that can come that might give me a better chance to win the pot by turning my "made hand" into a bluff or semi-bluff. When I rush to get my money in on the flop, I can find myself in a set-over-set situation or up against a wrap—in either case, I don't like my hand very much.

——BIG STACKS——

Deep-stack PLO games are rare online, but it's easy to find live games where the average stack is 1,000 big blinds deep. With stacks this big, PLO becomes a very psychological game of cat and mouse and can be very profitable with some adjustments:

♦ All the real money is made on the turn and the river in deep-stack PLO games. You need to be willing to put in big bets when your opponent has a weak range and you're at the bottom of your range.

♦ Leverage position and be willing to three-bet on the button quite liberally. Hands that were easy folds to an opening raise when playing with 100 big blinds become near mandatory three-bets when players are 1,000 bigs deep.

♦ In a 6-max PLO deep-stack game, you can easily play a 50/40/15 pre-flop game without much difficulty if you're a good post-flop player. That means you're voluntarily putting chips into the pot pre-flop 50% of the hands, you're raising with 40% of your hands, and three-betting with 15% of your hands. Get in there and mix it up in position.

♦ Winning players are willing to risk bluffing on the river with a big pot-size bet. That takes balls. The difference between strong hands and weak is hugely magnified in deep-stack games.

——LOCKED-DOWN BOARDS——

Locked-down boards are hands where it is possible to flop the nuts and there are no flush draws present. Flops like 9-6-5, 6-7-8, 4-6-8 are all locked-down boards.* I am willing to make some fancy plays on boards like this—mostly check-raises, especially if I've called a pre-flop raise from the blinds. My opponents will have a very, very hard time continuing in the hand unless they flopped the nuts as well.

Another good, dry board to try this play on is an Ace-high board like A-7-4. Say I open from middle position and get three-bet from the button. I call. On a board like this, I can check-raise quite comfortably, even if I don't have much of a hand. My opponent will either have a rundown hand like JT98, KQJT, etc., or they'll have AAXX. In short, they'll either have the nuts or a hand that won't be able to stand a check-raise. Some combinatorics show that there are simply many more combinations of rundown hands than there are AAXX. A check-raise in this spot should show a nice profit. Again, it is important to note that I don't make this play against players who will only three-bet pre-flop with AAXX hands—that would be suicide. Even if they suspect that I'm making a play, not many players are willing to put me (and their stack) to the

---

* Q-T-8 rainbow isn't considered locked-down—there are too many possibilities of open-ended straight draws, sets, and top-pair-with-a-gut-shot combinations on a board like this.

test. (Note: Dry King-high flops are not at all good to get creative with—there are simply too many combinations that won't fold.)

If I get check-raised on a locked down board having flopped top set, my instinct is to get it all-in as soon as possible. However, this is usually a mistake unless I have an effective stack size of less than about 60 big blinds. Calling is a much better play. Most of the time, my opponent will be polarized with the nuts or air. If I shove against this polarized range, I automatically lose—they fold every hand I can beat and get it in with the nuts. I'm certainly not going to fold top set, so calling must be right if the stacks are deep. I'll give them an opportunity to barrel the turn with their bluffs, keep the pot small when they are probably drawing very slim, and keep my options open for the turn.

TURN PLAY

The turn is the most important street in Omaha—the bets are bigger and the consequences of being wrong are more severe. As the name suggests, the entire complexion of a hand can and often does change on the turn. With only one card to come, the turn is where I really put some pressure on opponents drawing to a flush or straight.

There are two key fundamentals to keep in mind with respect to turn play:

♦ If a player has 13 outs, the hands are in equilibrium.

♦ It is vital to keep your range uncapped.

Everything else in turn play revolves around those two principles. Let's see how it all works together.

—— 13 OUTS, TURN EQUILIBRIUM——

On draw-heavy boards, the player with the worst hand typically has 12 or 13 outs. For example, a flush draw with a gutshot straight draw versus the current nuts:

	Flop	Flop Equity	Turn	Turn Equity
Me: J♣ T♦ 9♣ 7♣	Q♠ T♠ 8♣	58%	2♦	70%
Opp: A♠ J♠ 5♥ 5♦		42%		30% (12 outs)

With 30% equity, it isn't a mistake for a player to call a pot-size bet getting 2 to 1 on his money:

There's $100 in the pot. I bet $100 on the turn. My opponent has to call $100 to win a pot of $300 ($100 ÷ 300 = 33%). Calling this bet is only slightly unprofitable, but the implied odds of hitting should be adequate compensation.

Note that even check-raising the pot doesn't gain all that much against a player with 13 outs:

There's $100 in the pot, I check, my opponent makes

a semi-bluff of $100, and I check-raise the pot to $400. They have to call $300 to win a pot of $600. Again, my opponent is getting the same 2 to 1 on their money and has an automatic call with 13 outs.

A check-raise did get them to put in $400 to win the initial $100 in the pot, so they did make a small equity error with that first $100 bet of about $44 or so.

Mashing "pot" bets against a guy with 13 outs doesn't really accomplish anything. In fact, it just balloons the pot and will make the river decisions much tougher. Betting does get some helpful information that will lead to some good lay-downs on the river, but the same information can often be gleaned with smaller bets.

——KEEP RANGE UNCAPPED——

Keeping my range uncapped on the turn is one of the most important betting strategies in PLO. If my actions and story cap my range, I become really easy to bluff. When I have the betting lead in the hand, the best way to accomplish this is by betting small (one third to one half of the pot) with my entire range on most boards. This small bet keeps my range uncapped—I could still have air, nuts, or anything in between.

Small bets have a lot going for them:

♦ When I have the nuts, I will get called by worse.
♦ When I have air, I occasionally elicit some folds.

♦ When I have a mediocre hand, I can get a little value when I'm good and save money when I'm behind.
♦ I get some valuable information at a cheap price, and can set up some good river bluffs and value bets.

I'm unlikely to induce an opponent with 13 or more outs to make a serious mistake. I give my opponents plenty of rope to hang themselves with when I make these small, balanced turn bets. This is a very difficult style to combat.

Here is an example of keeping range uncapped on the turn:

I raise the pot pre-flop from the cutoff with Q♠J♦9♦7♣ and the button calls. Flop comes T♠7♠5♦. I make a continuation-bet of 3/4 pot. My opponent calls. Turn: Q♣.

Here, I have top and middle pairs and a straight draw, but I'm worried about the flush. Many players check and fold or check and make a crying call. If I check-call, I cap my range and make myself really easy to bluff on the river. Instead, I lead a third of the pot, and here are all the good things that can happen:

♦ I might get a worse hand to call hoping to river a full house (Q965, 7654).
♦ I might get a better hand to fold (AKQT, no flush).
♦ I give myself a decent price to pick up a full house on the river if I'm up against a weak flush and my opponent doesn't raise.

♦ If my opponent calls, I can be pretty sure that he doesn't have the Ace-high flush. I can then make a pretty big bluff on the river and get him to fold the Q- and J-high flushes quite often—my opponent's call on the turn caps his range—exactly what I avoided doing when I made a small bet at the turn.

Maintaining balance in this spot is imperative. I bet small when I have it, and bet small when I don't. In the same spot, I'd make a one-third-pot bet with the nut flush as well.

This is a very difficult style to combat. Opponents might just put in a big raise with a non-nut flush, thinking that I have a set—when I have the nut flush in that spot, cha-ching!

——NUTS, STILL BEHIND——

It is important to understand that even on the turn you can have the nuts, and still be "behind" in expectation. These situations are rare, but when they come up, they can be punishing.

	Flop	Flop Equity	Turn	Turn Equity
Me: Q♥ Q♣ 4♥ 4♣	Q♠ T♠ 7♦	39%	5♦	35%
Opp: K♠ J♠ 9♦ 8♦		61%		65% (26 outs)

Many players would be more than happy to get in 500 big blinds in this spot—when you do, you can be absolutely certain that you're up against exactly this type of hand and you'll have to get very lucky to fade the river.

——ACE-HIGH BOARDS——

Ace-high boards are good to double-barrel on. On a flop like a rainbow A-J-7, opponents call a continuation-bet with lots of drawing hands (KQT9, QT98, JT98, AT97) and weak two-pair hands (JT97, J987, KJ97). A pot-size bet can set up the turn for another big bet that will really put the pressure on.

From my opponent's perspective, a hand like AT97 on a board of AJ73 could be drawing to as few as four outs, and probably doesn't have more than six. If my opponent calls my flop bet and the turn bricks off, firing another barrel can be extremely effective. This kind of play is so effective that I can do this without any equity in the hand—it might not be entirely smart, but I can get away with it occasionally.

——BARRELING AWAY——

There are many profitable spots for bluffing on the turn:

♦ On paired boards with a flush draw (7-7c-5c, 9-9c-5c, Jc-6c-6, etc.), firing a second barrel on any card that doesn't complete the flush has a good chance of success.

Opponents will have a fairly wide range on this flop and will peel one off with flush draws. But, now that the pot is bigger, it will be more difficult for them to continue. An Ace on the turn is the best card to barrel on—an opponent might have called a flop bet with QXX on a Q77 board and will likely now fold to a turn bet.

♦ When I have a pair, a flush draw, and over-cards that won't make a straight for my opponent, this is a good spot for a second bullet. My hand is unlikely to be good at showdown and I don't expect to get bluff-raised very often. For example: A♣Q♣9♦7♦ on a flop: J♣7♣5♦ and a turn of 3♥.

♦ Check-raising the turn for a bluff can be profitable against Ace-high boards when an opponent will try to represent AAXX quite often. I love to make this check-raise if I flop or turn a wrap. I'm credibly trying to represent middle sets with this play. For example, if the flop is A-J-5 and the turn is a 9, I will try to check-raise with KQT8, KKQT-type hands as well as Q JJT and 7655-type hands at times.

♦ When I call a flop bet and the board pairs the turn, check-calling with a draw is a weak play. With premium wraps and flush draws, I mix in a few bluff-check-raises—this will balance the times I actually have the full house or set and help me realize value with my premium draws. If my opponent knows I'm capable of this play, they'll check the turn quite often with mediocre hands and hope to get to showdown cheaply.

♦ When the board is locked-down on the flop (8-5-4 rainbow, 5-6-7 rainbow) and I called a flop bet with a draw, check-raising if the board pairs can be a great play—I try to represent a turned full house. For instance, on a J-T-7 rainbow flop, I check-called a flop bet with AKQT. The turn is 7♦. I check-raise representing JJXX, TTXX, J7XX, T7XX. My opponent will be hard-pressed to continue unless I'm representing a hand he actually holds (oops!).

RIVER PLAY

With all cards dealt and no more drawing, the die has been cast—you either have the best hand or you don't. The goal of river play is to respond as flawlessly as possible. Realize this: an omniscient opponent never calls a bet on the river—best hands raise and worse hands fold (or bluff). Obviously, there are times when you just have to call. I call with a hand that might be good if a raise will only get called by a better hand. Don't be too showdown-oriented in PLO. Go with your reads. Bluff when it is right, and make some hero folds.

——CHECK-RAISE MORE——

Before check-calling a bet on the river, I consider the possibility of check-raising. There are many hands in PLO that will fire a thin river value bet and call a check-raise.

Board: T♠8♠6♦2♣A♥
My hand: 9♣7♣6♦5♥

My opponent raised pre-flop from the Hi-Jack, I called from the big blind. We are playing very deep, 300 big blinds each. I check-call a pot-size bet on the flop because I don't want to get tons of money in the pot without a backup to the higher nuts or a flush draw. On the turn, I fire a pot-size bet and get called. I felt sure he was on the Ace-high flush draw or a set. On the river Ace, it seems right to go for a check-raise. I think he'll make a thin value bet with a hand like A♠ T♥ 5♠ 6♦. He'll certainly bet AAXX and all sets, and he'll pay off my check-raise with those hands as well.

On the same board with a river 5♣ (instead of the A♥), not much has changed in the hand—my opponent's range wasn't improved with that river card. Now, instead of going for a river check-raise, it is probably right to just fire at the pot again and hope to get paid off.

When I check-raise the river, I don't check-raise the "pot"—that is too big a bet. I check-raise the river to about 2 to 2.5 times my opponent's river bet. I need to be able to make this play with air as well as the nuts, and I don't want my check-raises to be too expensive when I'm bluffing and I get called. Even a small check-raise can be hard for a player to call with a non-nut hand.

The advantage of check-raising on the river quite frequently is that it makes thin value bets and bluffs much less profitable for my opponents. I force them into "showdown mode" after pulling off a few of these. They become predictable and easy to play against.

If you're playing against a "maniac" who check-raises the river quite frequently, you'd likely go into showdown mode with every hand, except the nuts and pure bluffs. You'd almost never bet two pair on the river because you wouldn't want to face what could be a very difficult decision.

There are plenty of hands where I've check-raised the turn and the correct play is to go for a check-raise on the river for value. These are usually hands where I've "backdoored" the disguised nuts on a river card that probably helped my opponent's range. For example:

A♣9♥8♣7♥
Flop: J♥T♥5♠

I raise from the cutoff, and get called from the button. I bet flop and get a call.

Turn: 2♣

I check-raise on the turn hoping to represent a set. My opponent calls.

River: 8♥

This is a great time to go for another check-raise. That card brought in almost all the draws, and my nut hand (straight flush!) is concealed. If I bet, I'll only get a call from non-nut flushes and straights. By checking, I also give my opponent a chance to bluff with the naked Ace of Hearts.

——INDUCE BLUFFS——

There are plenty of hands where I know that my opponent was on a busted draw. This is incredibly common in PLO. In spots like this, my opponent will never be in a position to call a river bet. The only way to make money is to give them a chance to bluff. If they don't bet the river, they weren't going to call a river bet anyway, so I don't lose value by checking in these spots.

——POLARIZED RANGES——

It is rare for players to make thin value bets on the river in PLO. Usually, the ranges are extremely polarized—they'll either turn up with close to the nuts or they'll have air.

Most of the time, two pair, small sets, and other weak hands are happy to just turn the cards up at showdown. Players who aren't willing to bet on the river for thin value are just too easy to play against.

——SMALL BETS——

Getting value on the river with made hands can be surprisingly difficult. Opponents are unwilling to call even 1/2-pot-size bets with mediocre hands. By betting small on the river with all made hands and bluffs, I give them a chance to pay me off when I'm good and a chance to fold when I'm bluffing. Best of all, I'm bluffing at a price that is quite favorable to my overall expectation. After all, a 1/2-pot bluff on the river only has to be successful 1 out of 3 times to break even.

——HERO FOLDS——

There are times when my opponent simply can't be bluffing often enough to make a call profitable. I might have second or third nuts, but my hand can't win. Folding full houses on the river isn't much fun, but there really isn't much option if I'm beat.

A♠ J♣ 9♠8♣
Flop: A♦A♥9♣   Turn: 6♣   River: T♦

I call a middle position opener from the big blind. I check raise after the flop and get snap called. I bet 2/3-pot on the turn and get called. I value bet 1/2-pot on the river and get raised—then puke.

There is almost no chance my hand is good even though I have the second nuts. Hero-folding is the winning option.

BANKROLL REQUIREMENTS

In PLO I'd suggest that you maintain a bankroll of 50 buy-ins or more. Higher variance demands a higher bankroll. It is also vital that you practice sound game selection, especially as the relative skill equals out at the higher levels and aggression increases. If you're new to PLO, I recommend that you buy in short, maybe 40 big blinds or so. With this stack size, you'll get to see lots of flops but you won't be making that big a mistake after the flop with any of your drawing hands. In fact, if you're the only player short-stacked in a game where most players are 100+ big blinds deep, you can have a significant advantage in the game. Practice some good hand selection, look for opportunities to put your stack to use post-flop, and see what happens. Have fun!

META-GAME
CONSIDERATIONS

The "meta-game" is the game-within-the-game. Hands are never played in isolation—there is often a great deal of history between players. That history can weigh heavily in the decision-making process. What I know or think about an opponent affects my decision making, and what they think of my game and mental state does as well. The meta-game is one of the aspects of the game that I find the most interesting and rewarding—the battlefield and its warriors are constantly evolving.

POLARIZED GAME TYPES

Almost every great player online will examine your stats with their HUD and come up with a game plan to exploit your weaknesses. Say you're a TAG (22/18/5)—you're playing 22% of your hands pre-flop, raising with 18%, and three-betting with 5%. Knowledgeable opponents have dealt with this type of opponent thousands of times before and already have a well-thought-out strategy.

Now consider what would happen to their strategy if you were to randomly decide to play half of your hands as a LAG (28/24/8) and half of your hands as a super-nit (16/12/2). After a few thousand hands, your stats would converge on 22/18/5—a TAG. Half the time, you would be playing a very aggressive LAG-style game, and the other half of the time you would be playing like a complete and utter nit.

When a player sees your HUD stats, they're going to be playing sub-optimally against your specific strategy just about every time: A typical 28/24/5 counterstrategy will be playing way too loose against the super-nit and way too tight against the LAG.

I use a similar strategy in live cash games, called "advertising." After splashing around for a few orbits, I just hunker down and wait for the nuts. Inevitably, by "changing gears," I get paid off with my big hands because of the monkey moves I made on those first few hands. If you're going to try to mix your strategies, understand that it is important to do it randomly, and not by position. The advanced HUD users will be able to pick up a positional polarization without much effort.

You can effectively mix more than just two strategies:

25% playing 32/28/9
25% playing 30/26/7
25% playing 26/22/3
25% playing 24/20/1
    = 28/24/5 profile

Remember that your opponent will be treating you as the average of those profiles, and they have no idea that you are switching your style of play from hand to hand. If you're in agro-mode at 32/28/9 and get three-bet, remember they aren't three-betting a 32/28/9, they are three-betting a 28/24/5.

Randomly polarizing your play on a hand-by-hand basis is the goal—a necessary technique to counter the geniuses who can look at your HUD and execute a near-perfect, exploitative strategy without breaking a sweat.

LEVELING

There are still plenty of players in the game who strictly play at what I call Level 0: They only give consideration to their hand. They never consider the hand or hand-range of their opponents. If they have AK on an A-J-9-8-4 board, they never fold, no matter what hand you're trying to represent. Remember, they aren't trying to figure out your hand, they are only paying attention to their own hand. Do not try to bluff these fish—they are simply unbluffable.

With a little more experience, players can move up to Level 1: They know what hand they currently hold, and they think a little about what hands or hand-range their opponent can hold. Against these players, you might be able to pull off some bluffs. They will try to narrow down your starting hands based on the action in the hand and figure out what you have.

More advanced players are at Level 2: They know what they have, they think about what you have, and they try to figure out what you think they have. These players are capable of some very advanced reasoning, and they are tough to beat.

The most skillful players can operate at Level 3: They know what they have, they think about what their opponents have, they figure out what their opponents think about their hand, and then, in a twist of mind-numbing proportion, they think about what you think about what they think about your range.

One big mistake that some players make (myself included) is thinking on too deep a level for the competition. As quickly as possible, I assign levels to each opponent at the table mentally. When I'm in a hand, I remind myself of the level I associate with that player and make my decisions based on that level. In general, I focus my thoughts and decision making one level higher than my opponent.

Say you raise from the button six times in a row and get a fold from a very nitty big blind each time. On the seventh time, you raise with AJo. The big blind three-bets. You start thinking, *Well, I've raised him seven times in a row, so he's going to start playing back with a really wide range. The AJo is actually near the top of my range, so I can four-bet here.* You four-bet, he shoves and shows you KK. Duh. You leveled yourself into making a bad play. The reason you were raising so liberally on the button is that your opponent plays too tight. When he finally decided to play back and three-bet, he had a hand. He wasn't thinking at all about the fact that you had raised his blind mercilessly, he was only thinking about the fact that he had KK. End of story, end of stack.

GAME SELECTION

The secret to being a winning player isn't being a math genius, having a million hands of experience, or playing a perfect TAG (24/20/5) style pre-flop. Those attributes help, of course, but there is one criteria that will be the biggest determining factor in your win-rate, and it has very little to do with the actual strategies you employ. The biggest, most important factor in your win rate is the game you choose. A great player who only gets involved in fishless, tough games with regulars will have a really hard time winning more than a mediocre, less talented player who always plays in fishy games.

If you don't know who the fish is at the table, you're probably it. This poker axiom is as valid as ever. Even a mediocre or bad player can beat the daylights out of a spewtard playing a 60/5/20 profile. And believe me, even with all the information available, all the training sites, all the poker on television, these whales still exist and still dump millions of dollars a year.

If you're lucky enough to find a whale and the game is particularly juicy, this is one spot where it might (with all due respect to Chris "Jesus" Ferguson) be okay to buy in at a stake a little higher than standard bankroll management rules would suggest. If the fish goes broke, what might have been a gold mine could turn into a land mine if you don't quickly exit the game and search for a freshly stocked pond. I see so many people get the fishy money only to turn around and donate it all back to the rest of the sharks once the fish leaves. My friend Erik Seidel said it best: "We're all just holding Phil Ivey's money. The goal as a poker player is to hang on to Phil's money as long as possible."

When you identify a fish or whale online, use the site's note-taking facility and color-code them. I mark fish as green, good TAGs as red, and whales as blue so I can quickly scan the lobby and immediately get in the right game.

Another way to find a fish is to look in the lobby and find the games with the long wait lists—you can be absolutely sure that there is a fish at the table. Add yourself to the list and hope that the fish gets lucky and busts a few of the regulars.

BIG POT VS. SMALL POT POKER

When there is a serious skill differential between you and the rest of the players at the table, there are some adjustments you can make to a standard strategy that will give you a better win rate and lower variance.

——BIG POT POKER——

There will be plenty of times when you will find yourself seriously outclassed at the table. Perhaps you entered a heads-up tournament and got unlucky enough to draw the toughest opponent in the field. Perhaps you're in a tournament playing shorthanded with more skilled players. Or, perhaps your game selection is sub-par and you're playing in a cash game with guys who are going to eat you alive.

Playing "Big Pot Poker" is one way to drastically reduce the edge that a better player has on you. Essentially, you create conditions at the table where your more skillful opponent won't have all his weapons available, and he is reduced to gambling a bit more or playing a much more straightforward style against you.

If you have effective stack sizes greater than about 30 big blinds, one key adjustment that you can make in this situation is to increase the size of your pre-flop raises from the standard 3 times the big blind to around one eighth of the effective stack sizes. For instance, if you both have 40 big blinds, you would raise one eighth of 40, or 5 times the big blind. When you do this, you effectively eliminate your opponent's ability to three-bet without moving all-in—any three-bet they make will get them completely pot-committed.

For example, if the effective stack sizes are 40 big blinds, I make it 5, my opponent makes it 14.

I move all-in for 40.

They have to call 26 blinds to win a pot of 80, so their break-even percentage is 26/80, or 32.5%—they are getting a little less than two to one on their money, and they are virtually forced to get it in.

Effective Stack Size	Pre-Flop Raise Amount
30	3.75
40	5
50	6.25
60	7.5

Since they can't fold to a four-bet, they are forced to either call your pre-flop raise or just move all-in. Either way, you've increased the variance (which is something you definitely want to do against a better player) and eliminated one of their most effective weapons. If you have a stack size of less than 30 big blinds, you could simply play a pre-flop shove-or-fold strategy. That is, you are either folding, or you're going all-in. Playing this method will give you something around a 35–40% chance to win against a single opponent.

—— SMALL POT POKER——

If you're one of the better players in the game, try to play smaller pots in marginal situations. Flipping QQ versus AK for your buy-in against weak opponents isn't really necessary. You'll be able to find much better spots to get the money in than a coin flip. As the best player at the table, you want to play small ball—just grind them down, wait for the inevitable big mistake, and don't give them an opportunity to collect easy chips.

TAKING A SHOT AT HIGHER STAKES

If you check your bankroll, you'll know when it is time to move up to higher-stakes games. At the higher stakes you can expect tougher competition, more aggression, and higher variance. Your first session at the higher stake is the most important. Do your best to employ superlative game selection in this first session.

After you identify a juicy table, don't just jump right in and post a blind. Lock up your seat, but sit out a few orbits and observe. Make some notes on some of the guys in the game. Form a game plan: Where are the weak players? Where are the players opening too many hands? Which of the players is three-betting the most? Who can you trap? Who bluffs?

Don't get out of line in the first few orbits. You aren't going to be comfortable, and you are likely to make some less than stellar plays because you're not used to seeing that much money in the pot. Just play a solid, TAG game. Build a tight image. Get a feel for the game flow. Going off on a weird triple-barrel bluff line to start your session will probably end very poorly.

If things do not go well at the start of the session, consider leaving the game and taking a short break or finding a different table. Many of the regulars in the games will know that you are "taking a shot"—if they don't recognize your screen name, they'll peg you for an easy mark. If you show weakness early, you can expect the pressure and tough decisions to multiply in future hands. You're much better off just saving it for another session.

ZERO TO HERO—BUILDING A BANKROLL ONLINE*

Success at poker comes from three things: skill, luck, and bankroll management. You can't control luck, so we can take that off the table. As for skill, hopefully this book has been helping you in that arena so far. Now let's talk about the third factor—bankroll management. Do this well and it's possible to grow a bankroll from nothing to $100,000.

---

* Please note that gambling is illegal in many jurisdictions, and on a U.S. federal level, the Unlawful Internet Gambling Enforcement Act of 2006 (UIGEA) prohibits businesses (e.g., financial institutions, credit card companies) from knowingly accepting payment relating to bets or wagers on the Internet. As a consequence, many online poker sites do not permit "real money" play—or in some instances, any play at all—by U.S. residents.

Do this wrong and you're on a guaranteed path to bankruptcy.

Bankroll management is how you budget your poker funds among your opportunities to play. It is choosing to play the right games at the right level so that when you lose, you'll always have another opportunity to play. It is an essential skill whether you play at $0.05/$0.10 or $5,000/$10,000. Believe it or not, successful bankroll management still evades many of the top players in the poker world today.

One of the foremost experts on bankroll management is a good friend of mine, Chris Ferguson. The 2000 WSOP Main Event champion has accumulated over $8 million in live lifetime earnings, including 64 WSOP cashes (which puts him third all-time) and five WSOP bracelets. He is one of the most legendary players in the game, not to mention one of the icons on the virtual felt after he recently turned a bankroll of $0 into six figures.

Playing on IRC (Inter Relay Chat) back in 1989, Ferguson was often faced with decisions in huge pots that could eventually move him up on the leader board. IRC wasn't real-money gaming; the leader board was purely points based, which suited Chris well as poker has never been about money for him. Chris thrives on the challenge of becoming the game's best player.

Many believe that at its highest levels, poker is meant to be played for large sums of cash. "I love that people play poker for money, but even if they didn't, I'd still be out there studying hard and trying to improve, much like a chess player," said Ferguson. "Playing for money has never been my thing. I wanted a challenge; something I could concentrate on that would motivate me to play my best."

So, if the money is insignificant, how do you keep things interesting? Simple: Bring on the "Zero to Hero Challenge" and try to build a bankroll online from $0 to $10,000.

Ferguson's "lightbulb moment" regarding bankroll management came during a televised panel discussion with many of the game's best players. The other players advocated taking bankroll risks as an inherent part of the game. They believed that every once in a while you should play in that big game and try for a big score—even though it is above your head and your bankroll. After all, they claimed, the only way you could get better was by playing against better players.

Ferguson could not be more astonished by their conclusions. "They said that it'll get your adrenaline going and keep things really exciting. I was floored that the pros said that. It was the worst advice I'd ever heard. What's even worse is that I know that all these pros believed what they were saying to be true."

If poker is indeed a game where the higher you play the more successful a player you are considered, Chris felt that a player should have to earn their way into those higher games, not just grab a spot and hope that luck was on his side that day. He believes that limiting your risk increases your overall enjoyment of the game. Ferguson's advice for players aspiring to higher stakes games: "Don't just buy your way in and overextend your bankroll. Earn your way in and prove you can handle it."

The consummate poker academic, Ferguson set out to prove how critical understanding and implementing bankroll management was to poker success. "I wanted to give people a set of rules to follow that guaranteed you wouldn't lose money. And the only way to guarantee that you won't lose money is to start with nothing. That way, you've got nothing to lose. I wanted to build from nothing to $10,000 very methodically to show that you could repeat this again and again. Above all, I wanted to show that it was skill, not luck, that got me there."

To prove his point, Ferguson implemented and followed four basic rules:

1) Never buy in for more than 5% of your bankroll in cash games or sit-and-gos.
2) If you have 10% of your bankroll at risk on any one table you must quit that table.
3) In a multi-table tournament, you can never buy in for more than 2% of your bankroll.
4) You can only enter a re-buy tournament if the buy-in is less than two-thirds of a percent of your bankroll.

There was one very small exception he allowed to these rules and that was his approach when he was just getting started. There were no games smaller than $0.05/$0.10, so once he had built up a bankroll, Ferguson would buy into those games for $2.50. Also, at any time during the challenge, if he could afford it, he could also buy into a $1 multi-table tournament and a $2.50 sit-and-go.

"Part of this experiment involved playing against a huge variety of players on the site. And that resonated with me because poker, at its purest, isn't just about the big games and the high-limit players. Poker is for everyone. So even when I had no money in my bankroll and no free-rolls were available, I spent my time honing my skills and chatting with the players in the play money games. It was a great opportunity to get to know players of all levels, all of whom shared a common love of poker."

Ferguson started out playing free-rolls on Full Tilt. Given the maximum capacity of these events (when he first started this challenge in April 2006), he had to set his alarm to be ready to register the second registration opened up. Now, think about that. You have a multi-millionaire setting his alarm to play in a free-roll where the most he could win was $5. Chris meant business.

Every time Chris made the money in these events (only the top 18 out of a field of 900 got paid), he felt relief and excitement. At the start of his challenge, he cashed in nine of them for a total payday of $22. At every money bubble, the poker legend recalled sweating out the possibility of bringing home a $2 win.

Those first $2 wins kept him up staring at the online lobby for hours. "I was always looking for the right spots to put my money into play," said Ferguson. "I didn't just want to play because I had $2 in my account. I always wanted enough money to rebuy once so I wouldn't have to miss any hands once I'd started."

"The first time I cashed in a free-roll, I thought for two days about what game I should play. For two days, I wondered what I should do with that $2. I finally decided to buy into a $.05/$.10 no-limit hold'em cash game. I posted the big blind and three or four hands later I was dealt A-Q and lost to T-T. Back to the drawing board I went."

Accumulating a couple of dollars proved difficult, but once he developed a small bankroll, Ferguson often looked to the $1 buy-in tournament, which is today aptly named "The Ferguson." With only a $1 buy-in it was one of his favorite tournaments to play throughout his challenge. Month after month his bankroll grew, and after nine months he had completed Stage I—turning $0 into $100. The $100 was a significant milestone—at that number Chris felt his bankroll rules could finally be applied and tested in a meaningful way.

With a $100 bankroll, he was on his way, but his biggest challenges were yet to come. Not only would Ferguson be faced with bad beats and tough situations, but how would the millionaire maintain the mental focus necessary to succeed day after day when playing at such insignificant stakes?

"I was always playing at the top of my game," Ferguson said recalling his play at each level. "I knew my bankroll rules were very powerful. At the time, I just didn't realize quite how powerful. My bankroll management rules kept me motivated 100% of the time. What I see players do all the time is win, move up in limits, and then go on a losing streak. On the way up they use the right bankroll management techniques, but once they're on a losing streak, they lose focus and discipline."

Chris recognized that it was hard for players used to playing at higher levels to play "down" a level (or more). "They think they are better than the game and their over-confidence leads them to play too many hands and play them poorly. If you see people playing below their bankroll, those are usually the guys you want to play against. They may be great players, but when they move down they don't play as well because they've lost motivation."

Ferguson knew he had to train himself to avoid that type of pitfall, but found it challenging nonetheless. "I found that in my own play, I went through that exact situation," he said. "I went on a terrible losing streak, and I went down to $.05/$.10 from $.25/$.50. It was hard for me too. That feeling that you want to play higher, that you should play higher. I could see how hard it would be to play well in those lower stake games without a set of rules you were 100% committed to.

"Losing streaks are going to happen to you. It's part of the game. Staying committed to your bankroll rules is the real challenge. I'm not saying my rules are easy, they're very hard. But they're essential if you want to be a successful poker player. With bankroll management, there is always a new goal you're striving toward. You can't jump into a bigger game without the necessary bankroll and you have to play well to be able to stay in the bigger games over a long period of time."

It was that motivation that kept him going throughout his quest from rags to riches. He kept his rules simple and reminded himself that there were *no* exceptions allowed. The challenge boiled down to adhering to his basic guidelines *no matter what* and having to earn entry into the bigger games that he desperately wanted to play.

Over the next nine months Ferguson built that $100 into more than $10,000. Having achieved his first goal, he then decided to see just how big he could grow his bankroll. Over the next four years, he built it up even further to $126,000. He is now working toward his next goal—$1 million.

Remember: Chris started with nothing—Zero to Hero. Not a bad ROI, if you ask me. If you really want to succeed as a poker player, you need to adhere to your own set of bankroll management rules.

THE WHIZ KIDS

I've always been confident in my abilities as a poker player. Since going pro in 2001, I've never had a losing year. But, in the last few years, as my edge has evaporated, I've felt my enthusiasm for the game waning. I had little or no desire to compete online or even live against the new class of super-stars and Internet geniuses, except for perhaps at the World Series of Poker. The rest of my life—kids, wife, business, philanthropy—became much more important and I focused almost all of my energy on those core areas of my life.

Still, I knew that poker was a passion, deeply engrained into my psyche. I've loved the game since I was seven years old, playing for pennies with my Great Aunt Lib.

When I decided to "get good again," I devoted myself fully to the cause and sought the best teachers I could find. I looked for players of character, strong ethical standards, and results that speak for themselves.

For PLO, a game I've come to love, there was only one standout in the crowd for me: Phil Galfond. I've been a huge fan of his style for many years. He is the consummate professional. Better yet, he's a gifted communicator and teacher. I was thrilled when Phil signed on and agreed to help with the "Gordon Project."

For years, I've watched the NL Heads Up specialists battle for millions of dollars online. One kid, Daniel Cates, seemed to be getting the best of everyone, including the intimidating Tom Dwan. I found out through some friends that Cates was taking students, and, despite the sky-high hourly rate, I paid. It was worth every penny and more.

Finally, I knew that my friend Annette Obrestad would be a great choice for NLH Tournament coach. If she can win a 180-player sit-and-go without looking at her cards,* she can teach me a thing or two about winning tournaments. Fortunately, she was already a dear friend and it wasn't tough to get on her calendar.

So, with my mentors set, I started off on a journey of rediscovery. Presented here, you have partial transcripts

---

* You can easily track down a video replay of this feat by searching "Annette Obrestad 180 player blind sit and go"—it is tremendously entertaining to see her fold KK under the gun and three-bet 8-4 offsuit. It is also very instructive.

and some of the hands that my teachers used throughout this long process. There were thousands of hands and many, many hours and days of training. I wanted to give you a feel for their teaching styles, the questions I was asking, and the lessons learned.

Not everything they taught ended up in this small sampling. But, much of the material covered earlier in this book is based on my experience with these players, as well as my online coach Anders Taylor.

I really can't thank my mentors enough—they have reinvigorated my passion for poker and they've given me the updated tools I needed to take on the game. I am working hard on my game all the time now. Thanks to Phil, Daniel, and Annette, I'm enjoying the game more than ever, and so is my bankroll.

PHIL "OMGCLAYAIKEN" GALFOND

——POT LIMIT OMAHA CASH GAMES——

Chris Moneymaker vs. Sam Farha. It was a story and tournament that gripped America: the amateur with the perfect name taking down the seasoned pro with the perfect cigar and sports jacket. One of the greatest, well-respected Whiz Kids, Phil "omgclayaiken" remembers being mesmerized by the game: "I loved watching Moneymaker win the title and all that money. The broadcast made the game look like so much fun. I could, and did, visualize myself there at the table pulling off that big bluff."

Moneymaker's victory was the spark. Galfond first played poker for "real money" at age twelve. Later, while a freshman at the University of Wisconsin, he made his first $50 deposit at an online site and played his first hands of Internet poker, a $5 nine-handed sit-and-go. That first deposit quickly evaporated. "I played every A-X hand like it was the nuts! An Ace would flop, and I'd just get it all-in. Of course, they called and had me dominated quite often. I'd say to myself 'how sick is it that they have an Ace with a better kicker! I'm so unlucky!' and then I'd hop right back into the next sit-and-go."

After the first $50 was gone, he decided he needed to be more rigorous with his approach to the game: "I found out about Sklansky's book *Hold'em for Advanced Players* and I also found the 2+2 forums." Those resources changed his approach to the game and gave him a small edge in the low-buy-in sit-and-gos he was obsessed with. "Believe it or not, Phil, I also learned quite a bit watching the celebs play on your show, *Celebrity Poker Showdown.* You did a great job highlighting and explaining the mistakes that they were making."

I know, it is hard to imagine the guy who is currently crushing the $500–$1,000 NL cash games and the $1,000–$2,000 PLO games for millions of dollars a year sitting in front of the television watching Ben Affleck, Nicole Sullivan, Don Cheadle, and Shannon Elizabeth play poker—and actually learning something from it. What's even more amazing is that he's willing to admit it!

After thoroughly digesting Sklansky and scouring 2+2, it was time for a second deposit of $50. That was the last deposit he'd ever need. Fast-forward to March 2011 and my lessons with Galfond: that $50 is now more than $10 million and there are few, if any, players who will voluntarily sit in a PLO or Hold'em game with him. When Tom Dwan issued the "durrrr Challenge" in 2009,* the only person who was excluded from participating was Galfond.

"The games were much softer back then. With just a few tips and some basic math, the $20 SNGs were profitable. With the edge I had, I thought I could ignore some of the more traditional bankroll requirements for these games. Fortunately, I never went on a really bad run early. If I had, who knows—I might have given up the game." His $50 quickly turned into $300, then $500. As his bankroll soared and he gained experience, his confidence soared.

By 2004, he finally felt like he could beat the games. He turned down a job offer to concentrate on playing online. "Why deliver pizza?" he said. "I still had no dreams

---

* Tom challenged anyone in the world to play 50,000 hands of either PLO or No Limit Hold'em at the $100–$200 level. If at the end of 50,000 hands his opponent was up, Tom agreed to pay an additional $1.5 million. If Tom was ahead at the end, the challenger would owe an additional $500,000.

of going pro, but I knew that I was a winning player, and I really enjoyed the game. Back then, it was all about grinding out small wins for beer money."

Everything changed shortly thereafter. A high school friend cashed in for $30,000 in an MTT. "I got serious after that. I started juggling my classes and playing twenty, thirty hours a week. I was obsessed with everything poker, and I was determined to get better."

By the time he turned twenty-one, he'd run the $50 up to $100,000 and was beating the $200 and $500 sit-and-gos. Now "legal," he decided to take a shot at the World Poker Tour and World Series of Poker Circuit events, both $10,000 buy-ins, in Tunica, Mississippi. He laughs. "Yeah, not the smartest bankroll management decision, for sure, but I wasn't worried about my ability to replenish my bankroll if things didn't go well. It seemed like a cool thing to do for my twenty-first birthday."

The $10,000 World Poker Tour event didn't go so well and he busted Day 1. Fortunately, the WSOP Circuit Event went much, much better. "There I was, Day 1, playing against some of my idols from the World Poker Tour. Daniel Negreanu was at my table a few seats away. I couldn't believe I was sitting there at the table with these guys, talking to them, competing, and getting the best of it on a lot of hands. I remember very clearly seeing one of my heroes at that tournament—he was completely bored and miserable, and I couldn't believe it! This guy was living the dream and couldn't have been more unhappy."

A few days later, Galfond busted out in eighteenth place and earned his first live tournament score, $23,000—a $3,000 profit for the two tournaments (not including travel expenses). It was a huge ego boost and whet his appetite for the tournament circuit and competing against the elite in the game.

After returning to Wisconsin, he "accidentally" decided to take a semester off to play poker. "I never intended to drop out, but because I made it so deep in Tunica, I missed the registration deadlines for classes. So, I was forced, essentially, into taking the semester off."

With time on his hands, a healthy bankroll, and the confidence that came from his score in Tunica, he redoubled his efforts and started grinding. He was playing 60–70 hours a week, multi-tabling, and getting deeply involved in the forums. "I was completely focused, and all I really wanted to think about was getting better. I knew that I was good, but I wanted to be the best, and I could definitely tell that the games were getting tougher. I knew that I'd need to improve if I was going to maintain my edge. As the sit-and-go tournaments got tougher and tougher, I knew that I had to find another outlet, and cash games seemed like the place to turn."

Although he dominated the cash games, Galfond took time out to play some tournaments. In 2008, he entered the $5,000 PLO (with rebuys) at the World Series of Poker. After two days of grueling play, he secured a spot at a star-studded final table that included David Benyamine, Johnny

Chan, Kiril Gerasimov, John Juanda, Daniel Negreanu, Phil Hellmuth, and Brian Rast. At age twenty-four, Galfond won the bracelet and the $817,781 first-place prize.

——LEARNING PLO FROM
PHIL GALFOND——

In March 2011, I had the honor of getting some private coaching from Phil Galfond. Before our lessons, I was at best a break-even $5–$10 PLO player, though I have played much higher both online and live. I asked Galfond to approach our lessons with a "Tabula Rasa" or blank-slate mentality and teach me the game from the ground up. Fortunately, he agreed, and very quickly he was able to plug some serious leaks in my game and overall approach. You'll recognize many of the fundamentals in the PLO section of this book.

GALFOND: If I could summarize good PLO strategy in one sentence, it would be this: always draw to the nuts. I'm one of the tightest players in the game pre-flop. I might even be playing too tight, but I avoid a bunch of tricky situations with very marginal positive expected value by doing so. My tight image also helps me immensely in spots where I need to bluff. I think my opponents have a hard time understanding that "pre-flop tightness" doesn't necessarily mean that I'm a tight player post-flop. As a result, I get a lot more credit than other players post-flop.

I found a $5–$10 six-max PLO table and bought in for $1,000. I was ready to impress and show this champion I knew what I was doing. Unfortunately, I made a classic pre-flop mistake on one of my very first hands.

5-10 PLO/6-handed table

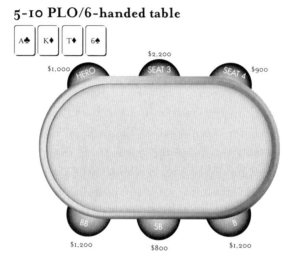

That looked like a pretty reasonable hand to me. I raised to $30. The pot went four-way, I missed the flop completely and had to give up.

GALFOND: Too loose, Phil, too loose. Look, it's close, but that's the way PLO is. There are very close equities in this game. But you're under the gun, you don't have a suited Ace, and if you get three-bet here from late position, you're going to be in a world of hurt. There are very few ways for you to flop the nuts as well. I would have folded this hand without even thinking about it.

Lesson learned. This hand would be marginally playable with A♦K♣T♦6♠ but is unplayable with the suited King from early position. Such subtlety and nuance I found very interesting. We explored it further while I folded a few hands.

GALFOND: Huge pots happen when there is flush over flush, especially second-nut-flush to nut flush. These are hands where you can get stacked or, better yet, stack someone. Why do you want to put yourself in a position to get stacked off or have to make a tough guess if your opponent is pushing hard with the naked Ace? I go out of my way to have suited Aces with these hands, and I fold a ton of hands that don't have more connectivity or something else going for them if I don't have the suited Ace.

This pre-flop theme would pop up over and over during our sessions. There were quite a few hands that I opened for a raise that Galfond would have routinely folded. Here are some examples, all from six-max $5–$10 PLO ring game:

UTG: J♣T♣T♠7♦
Hi-Jack: 9♣8♣5♦4♠
Cutoff: T♠9♠8♣4♦
Button: 4♣4♦A♥Q♠

GALFOND: Again, you're not necessarily making that big a pre-flop mistake by playing some of those hands, but you are setting yourself up for some very, very difficult and marginal situations post-flop. Even in PLO, tight is right pre-flop. Most of these hands have very good pre-flop equity, but play very poorly post-flop. You simply need to give more consideration to post-flop playability. This is a big mistake that Hold'em players make when making the transition to PLO. The equities are closer pre-flop in Omaha, which most players take as a license to play too many hands.

A few hands later, I was dealt a "monster" and made a monster mistake:

5-10 PLO/6-handed table

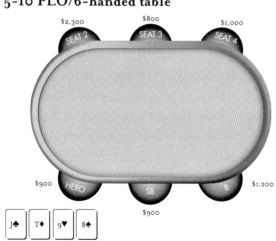

A good "rundown" hand in the big blind. UTG+1 raises to 30, everyone else folds to me. I re-raise pot to 100. My opponent called. Flop was 4♥5♥6♥. I check-folded.

I could sense some disappointment.

GALFOND: I don't think I would have three-bet out of position with that hand, even as pretty as it is. If you were double-suited, three-betting is fine, but without a suit, it just isn't that valuable—especially out of position. You're going to find yourself in some very tough spots when you three-bet this hand out of position against a good player. With this type of hand, it is very easy to get yourself stuck where you kind of have to get the money in, and then when you do you're going to be a huge underdog. Like on a J♠T♠6♣–type flop. You flop top two and a gut-shot, but any opponent that puts the money in post-flop will have either a set or a straight flush wrap.

Take a flop like A♠J♦7♠—here you have a pair, nine outs to a straight, but some of those outs might make your opponent a flush. Additionally, if you hit a Ten to make a straight (JT987) your opponent could easily have KQ for the higher straight. Even a great flop, J-T-4 rainbow, might not be so good. Run some equity simulations against AKQJ, AKQT, KKQT, AKJJ and you'll see what I'm talking about.

I stopped playing briefly, fired up a simulator, and put some hands in:

Flop: J♦T♣7♥

J♣T♦9♥8♠: 50%	AKQJ: 50%
J♣T♦9♥8♠: 46%	KKQT: 54%
J♣T♦9♥8♠: 13%	AKJJ: 87%

GALFOND: Position is so much more important in PLO than it is in Hold'em because draws are such an integral part of the game. When you're out of position, just keep the pots small unless you have a really, really great hand that is very playable. Hands like really good Kings (KKQJ, KKTT double-suited). Hands like really good Aces (AAK5 suited with the Ace). Hands like JT98, 9876 double-suited. Those are hands worth a three-bet out of position. Even bad Aces are best played conservatively out of position most of the time (AA94 rainbow). Of course, a lot of this has to do with the quality of your opponent and stack sizes, but even bad opponents aren't going to play too poorly against you if you are three-betting JT98 rainbow out of position. Hands that I like to three-bet out of position are hands that I'm more than happy to call a full four-bet with. If it is "close" and I'm going to be unhappy calling that four-bet, then I don't three-bet. Pretty simple.

GORDON: I watch the online high-stakes games all the time. Ivey, Dwan, Blom . . . they are all three-betting very aggressively from the blinds. I've seen them do it with hands much, much worse than the JT98 rainbow.

GALFOND: I know. That's great for me!

He was smiling from ear to ear. I knew that smile meant one thing: that was a weakness in their game that he was exploiting.

I played a few more orbits without much happening. But Galfond was intensely engaged. I was so impressed with his focus, his willingness to get inside my head and try to see my motivations for some of my bad plays without being condescending or having a big ego. I was having an unbelievable amount of fun, and I felt tremendously privileged to be able to pick his brain.

5-10 PLO/6-handed table

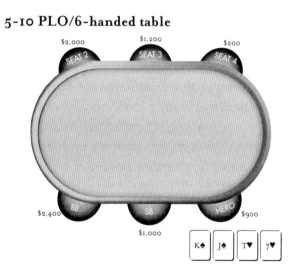

Cutoff opened for $30. I happily called with my gapped double-suiter. Big blind called as well and bet pot on a 9-9-6 board and there was nothing I could do but lay it down. After the hand was over, Phil actually made me sit out so we could talk. Evidently, this was going to be painful and important.

GALFOND: Look, calling with that kind of hand isn't necessarily a mistake, but it is not the best line to take. Think about this hand for a minute. When you call, you are setting up the blinds to get awesome pot-odds to call. Most likely, you're not going to be playing this hand heads-up in position, you're going to be playing this hand in a three-way or even a four-way pot. Hands like this play so much better heads up that it is worth the risk of getting four-bet to limit the field. The double-suited, gapper hands should three-bet from position for this very reason. Try to price out the suited-Ace–type hands that could have you in rough shape.

That made sense to me, and it immediately put me in a different mind-set about the game:

♦ Work to get heads up in position.
♦ Rarely play out of position without a premium hand, and when you do, keep the pot small pre-flop.

This is the same mind-set I have when playing Hold'em, but for some reason I didn't really carry this philosophy over to my PLO game. All the possible hand combinations led me to play a more passive, looser style pre-flop. Clearly, this was a big leak, and one that I am working hard to plug.

A few hands later, everyone folded to my button:

5-10 PLO/6-handed table

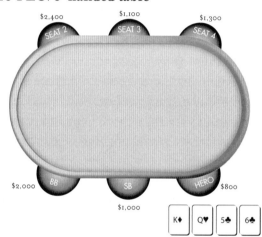

I raised to $30, knowing that I was playing a little loose. I preempted the impending criticism: Phil: This is probably a little loose, but at least I'll be in position.

GALFOND: It's not terrible, I'd probably play that hand, too.

Small blind folded, big blind called. Flop is J♣9♣6♠. Big blind checked.

Okay, gut-shot straight draw to the nuts, bad flush draw, small pair. I have to have enough equity to C-bet. I bet $50 into the $65 pot.

My opponent check-raised the full pot, and I had to fold.

GALFOND: That's exactly what you deserved when you bet that flop. Look, Phil, checking back in position is a very important concept to get right in PLO. Your hand has very little equity post-flop against the range of hands your opponent will play from the big blind. There is almost no chance that you were ahead post-flop, and there was a significant chance that you were going to get check-raised by wraps, higher flush draws with a pair, sets, and other hands. You were going to have a really hard time folding-out the hands that were ahead of you. There were tons of cards that could come on the turn that would have helped you proceed confidently: Tens give you the nut straight, a six gives you trips, and a club gives you a fighting chance of having the best hand with that anemic flush draw you had. You simply couldn't afford to get check-raised and be forced to give up the chance at that equity. Once you check this flop, a competent opponent will take the lead and bet into you on most turn cards. If you make the nuts, you can raise. If you make a flush or trips, you can call down, and if a blank like the 2♥ hits the turn, you can call and hope to hit your hand on the river while getting pretty good odds. The only line that you can take with this type of weak hand post-flop that eliminates all of that equity is betting and then folding to a check-raise.

I felt dumb, but also much smarter at the same time. Smart to have selected a coach like Phil. When he laid out the argument like that, it seemed to make so much sense, and I could definitely tell where I was spewing significant amounts of equity for no reason.

A few hands later, I found myself potentially playing a $2,000 pot:

5-10 PLO/6 max

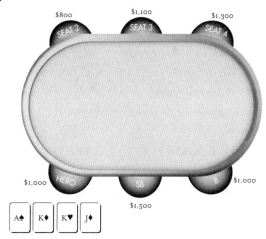

Cutoff player made it $30, Button folded, and I three-bet to $115, feeling very confident about my hand. Original raiser now four-bet to $350. Shit. I didn't feel like getting it in against what was probably AAXX, and I didn't have a ton of money in the pot already, so I reluctantly laid it down.

GALFOND: That was as tough a spot as there is in PLO. This situation was completely read-based, and you don't really have any reads. If you get it in against AAXX, you're going to be like 28% to win. If you get it in against a rundown hand like JT98 or T987 double-suited, at best you'll be about 56% to win. With only $115 in the pot, you're going to have to be right a significant portion of the time in order to justify going with that there. Against aggressive four-bettors, sometimes you simply have to get it in, but there are other players who simply never four-bet without AAXX. I think you did the right thing.

My first lesson came to a close. I was about $200 ahead in the game but millions up mentally.

——GET MORE PHIL GALFOND——

Phil Galfond is one of the most approachable, best-regarded teachers in the game. He offers private lessons (granted, they are extremely expensive) and also offers video coaching at BlueFirePoker.com. Search for some of

his posts on the poker forums—they are very well-written
and tremendously insightful.

ANNETTE "ANNETTE15"
OBRESTAD

Nine-Handed Tournament Play

If you're looking for a multi-table tournament genius to
teach you how to crush online, you might want to head to
Norway. Annette Obrestad has been crushing the online
tournament scene since age fifteen (hence, the screen name
"annette15"). She grew up in a small town and played poker
for fun after school. Her game of choice was seven stud
hi-low, and she killed the play money tables. Eventually,
she entered a free-roll and won a few bucks. She's never
looked back and never made a deposit. Soon, she was winning everything, built a nice bankroll, and decided to take
a chance at the WSOP Europe Main Event in London—a
$10,000 buy-in. At the ripe old age of eighteen, she won
her first WSOP Bracelet, overcoming 361 players to take
down the title and a measly $2,013,734.

Everyone was talking about this tiny, fierce, incredibly
talented girl from Norway. I met her shortly thereafter and
we hit it off almost immediately. I loved her enthusiasm for
the game. I loved her attitude. And I loved how she could

take over the table, dominate, and leave everyone else in the dust.

A few years passed, and Annette eventually signed as a red pro with Full Tilt. I was thrilled to have her as a teammate. When I started this project, there was only one person I knew who could teach this old dog some new tricks: Annette. I called her and she agreed to take me on as a student without hesitation. "I wondered how long it would take for you to reach out for some help, Phil. This will be fun! Let's play some FTOPS* events—you can sweat me and I'll show you exactly what I'm doing."

——PLAYING LESSONS WITH ANNETTE——

I arrived at her condo just before the MiniFTOPS Main Event was starting. The field had ballooned to more than 45,000 players. This $70 buy-in tournament had a prize pool of $3,000,000 and first place paid $450,000.

"Hope you have all night—this is going to take a while," she said. I liked the way that sounded. She bought in four times (FTP allows multiple entries to the same tournament in some instances). Soon, four tournament windows appeared on her monitor and we were off to the races.

---

* Full Tilt Online Poker Series, FTOPS, is the biggest tournament series on the site. Prize purses regularly reach more than $1,000,000 for the biggest events.

We started with 5,000 in chips with blinds at a very reasonable 15–30.

It didn't take long for her to find a hand to start the lesson:

NL 15-30

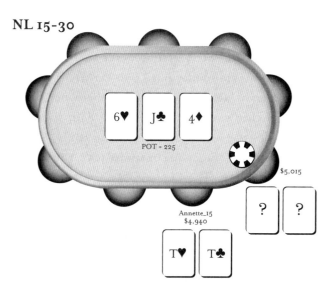

Everyone folded to the button, who raised to 75. Annette had TT in the small blind. This looked like an automatic three-bet to me. Instead, she called.

Big blind called the raise as well. Flop was J-5-3 rainbow. She check-called the flop. Turn came 8. She checked, button checked. River was an 8. She almost certainly had the best hand. She made a small bet, 120 into the 400-chip pot. Her opponent folded.

PHIL: Um, that looked like a pre-flop three-bet to me.

ANNETTE: I would never three-bet, I just wouldn't. Early in tournaments, I don't put too many chips into the pot unless I know I have the best hand. It seems really unnecessary. You don't need to double up because the structures are so good. I just think it is so dumb when people get it all-in with QQ or AK early in a tournament. Why do they do that? Honestly, Phil, I wouldn't even three-bet Aces in this spot. I just want to play small pots early.

PHIL: Come on, really? You wouldn't three-bet Aces?

ANNETTE: Say you're in the WSOP Main Event. The blinds are 50–100 with 30,000 starting chips. You have AA in the big blind. Someone opens to 300. You three-bet to 1,000. They call. The flop is Q75. You bet 1,500 and they raise to 4,000. What do you do? You are screwed and you have to throw it away. You'll either win a small pot or lose a big pot. And yes, I know this isn't how you played in the old days.

PHIL: You're right about that!

ANNETTE: Early in tournaments, I usually play a loose-passive style. I'm going to be opening a ton of hands, but I'm just not going to put many chips into the pot post-flop unless I flop something really, really good. I'm never three-betting. I just want to keep the pot small and hope to hit some good hands and give myself a chance to hit a flop really hard. If I ever run into any real resistance early, I'm just going to dump the hand.

I like to raise three times the blind early. Obviously, if I'm playing a hand and I'm first in, I'll always raise. But since I like to play so many hands pre-flop, I have to keep my raises small so I keep the pot small. Even if I open with AA and get raised, I'm not going to four-bet in the early levels unless I'm just going to move it all-in.

Now, this might not apply in like a $1,000 event at the WSOP where there are just so many bad players—there, you might just overbet AA and get a guy to get all the chips in with JJ or QQ. But in all the big $10,000 events where most of the players are pretty good and the stacks are deep, I don't see a reason to three-bet during the first few levels. By the way, this assumes that you are competent post-flop. So, if you're not confident in your post-flop abilities, you should definitely be three-betting and trying to get in as many chips as possible pre-flop. If you're going to lose your whole stack with KK post-flop on a Q-J-4 board, you might as well try to get as much of it in pre-flop as possible. But, I'm very confident that I can make good folds post-flop, even with over-pairs.

PHIL: How about pre-flop hand selection. What are you thinking?

ANNETTE: With deep stacks, say 150 big blinds or more, I'll play any pocket pair from any position. Under the gun, I'm pretty tight with unpaired hands. I'll open AT suited, but I'm folding AJo and maybe even AQ offsuit depending on the rest of the players at the table. But, again, any pair is good enough to open, even 22 under the gun,* I'm not all that worried about getting three-bet—that will be an easy call to try to hit a good flop [a set]. I do not have an open-limp range. I'm strictly raise or fold.

NL 15-30

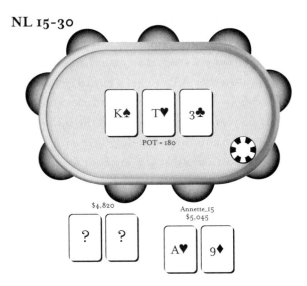

Everyone folded to Annette, who had A-9 in the small blind.

ANNETTE: Here you can do whatever you want. You can limp, raise, whatever. I see some players raise 4x,† but that is just so unnecessary. I just feel like players are calling with

---

* A range of 22+, ATs+, AQ+ is 8.9% of hands.

† Four times the big blind.

the same hands no matter how much you make it. If they have a hand they want to play, they aren't folding.

Flop came K–T–3 rainbow. She bet 120 into a pot of 180 and took it down.

ANNETTE: Standard C-bet.

PHIL: How aggressive are you playing from late position?

ANNETTE: Early in the tournament, I'm going to play a lot of hands from the button and cutoff if I'm first in. Certainly every suited hand, every pair, every Ace, King, any connected unsuited cards like Q9, 87, 64. It doesn't take much to get me in there. You'll see me tighten up considerably after the blinds go up, which is kind of the opposite of what people normally do. But that is because of my image—they just don't give me any credit for a hand.

When I'm deep in a tournament, I'm such a nit. People think I'm three-betting and playing trashy hands. They see me playing crazy hands early, and they assume that carries over when the blinds get higher.

PHIL: You definitely have the reputation as a player who gets in there and mixes it up!

ANNETTE: In live tournaments, I get that all the time. Early, I raise every button and the big blind just looks at me and is like, "You're raising again? What, you always get hands?"

Annette was registered for a higher buy-in event ($1,000) and a few tables popped up. She color-coded those tables by changing the background color to red. The Mini-FTOPS tables were blue.

ANNETTE: I'm color-coding these tables. In the higher buy-in events, I will assume that the players know what they're doing. In the smaller buy-in events, there are many more bad players. I adjust according to the field composition.

PHIL: What adjustments do you make against the lower-quality competition?

ANNETTE: Don't bluff them. And don't do anything stupid. They will bust themselves. My motto in most tournaments is: "Don't do anything that someone smart wouldn't do."

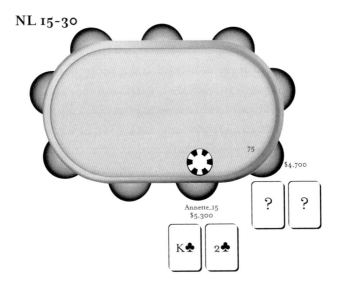

NL 15-30

75

$4,700

Annette_15
$5,300

K♣ 2♣

? ?

ANNETTE: Here is where I'm a fish. Now there is a raise and I'm not just folding my button. I'd call 6–7 off here. I'm certainly not folding K2 suited. I love my button and I'm not giving it away even though it seems like I'm a fish for calling. I'm not just going to fold if I miss either—I'll do some things post-flop.

Unfortunately for Annette, the pot was three-bet from the big blind and she was forced to fold.

ANNETTE: Obviously, I'm not going to call the three-bet. I'm not that fishy. If I had a pair, I'd call though. Speaking of small pairs, to call an open raise, I think you need about 20 to 1 implied odds. If I open a small pair and get three-bet, I need about 10 to 1 implied odds to call—but if they are a loose three-bettor, I probably need, like, 15 or 20 to 1. I see so many people call a pre-flop raise with deuces with like 30 big blinds. You're just never going to win the pot—it is hard to flop sets!

We were only about 30 minutes into our lesson, and already my head was spinning. The never-three-betting mentality had me a little confused.

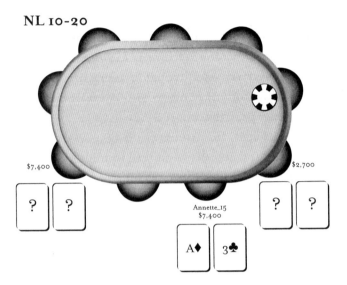

NL 10-20

$7,400

$2,700

Annette_15
$7,400

A♦ 3♣

UTG+1 limped, button called, small blind called, and she checked the A3 offsuit. 80 in the pot. Flop was 3♠3♦5♦. Small blind bet 55.

ANNETTE: I'm definitely going to raise. People think I'm full of shit.

She made it 200 to go.

ANNETTE: If the early position limper has anything good like 99 or TT, he's going to call. People that limp pre-flop are bad players who just don't fold over-pairs to the board in spots like this.

Sure enough, the limper called the 200 and the small blind folded. She was heads up with 535 in the pot. The A♥ hit the turn.

ANNETTE: That is a terrible card for me. Looks like a good card, but it is bad—it might scare him off the 99 or TT. If I bet now and get raised, I'm going to be very scared.

She bet 360. Scary Penguin quickly min-raised to 720. I guess she just has to call and then call the river. If he has AK, she'll lose some value, but she can't really beat anything else. She called. The river was the 8♥. She checked, he bet 180 into 1,975.

ANNETTE: Haha. Screw you with that small bet.

She raised to 2,000 and he snap-called with 55. Hard to believe he didn't just ship it instead of calling. Did he really think she had 33 or AA?

ANNETTE: Well, that wasn't much fun. But at least I didn't go broke. I was right—when he raised the turn, I knew I was screwed. If he had bet anything more than about one-third of the pot on the river, I was just calling. Guess he sort of suckered me with the 180, but then he didn't move it in after I raised . . . so weird. What a cooler!

A cooler, for sure, and yet, somehow, she had about 4,500 more chips at the end of that hand than I probably would have had. It is still the first level in the tournament. She has seven tables open and still has time to teach.

PHIL: You seem to play a bunch of very trashy hands from late position.

ANNETTE: Yeah, against early position raises, they usually have a very strong range. If you flop something good with one of the trashy hands, you can win a big pot. So many people play such a weak-tight post-flop game as well, I can just take the pots they are willing to concede and stay more or less even and wait until I hit something really good.

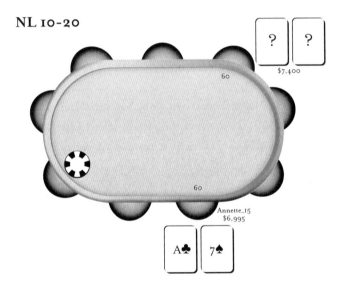

NL 10-20

60

? ?

$7,400

60

Annette_15
$6,995

A♣ 7♠

ANNETTE: Like here, I'm certainly behind his opening range, but I'm going to call anyway. I expect the pot to go multi-way and this hand has good multi-way implied odds.

Unfortunately, the player with the button spoiled the plan and three-bet to 270. She folded. With seven tables in play, there was almost always something interesting going on.

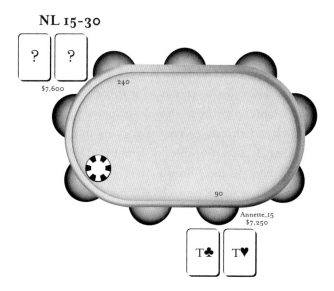

NL 15-30

Annette raised to 90 with TT from the Hi-Jack and the big blind three-bet to 240.

ANNETTE: I'm just going to call here, mostly to set-mine. I'm not going to be happy if the flop is all low cards.

Flop: J♦J♠6♥. Opponent led for 250 into the 495 pot.

ANNETTE: Or, something like that. I'll just call now and then give up on the turn if he barrels. People don't normally bluff the turn when you call the flop on a board like this.

Sure enough, she called, the turn was the 9♥, he bet half the pot again and she folded.

ANNETTE: I play lots of flops and then give up a bunch on the turn. They just usually have it if they keep betting, and I don't want to get into showdown mode in a big pot without the best hand. Are they really going to bluff me on the turn when I call a flop bet? I doubt it. Do they really think they can make me fold a pair of sixes or something on the turn? They just have to have a hand better than my pocket Tens.

PHIL: Man, it is really hard to get chips from you on the turn and river.

ANNETTE: Of course! People just don't bluff enough, so when they bet the turn and the river, I can just get away.

The blinds are up to 50–100, average stack is around 9,000. She's been playing now about ninety minutes.

ANNETTE: I'm going to start making it two and a half times the blind now. I don't really have a good explanation for why I do that, but it works for me. Raising 3x is fine too, it's just a personal preference. From the small blind, though, I still make it 3x—I'm out of position and I kind of want them to fold. I'll also start three-betting some hands now. It is time to start opening up a little. When I three-bet, I always know what I will do to a four-bet—I know I'm either going to call, ship it, or fold. If I don't know what to do against a four-bet, I won't three-bet.

This is going to make me sound like Phil Hellmuth, but I try not to go all-in unless I really feel it is necessary. I'm just trying to survive and weave my way through the pack. Sometimes you just have to, but I'm not ever really happy about it.

The blinds are now 300–600 with a 75 ante and we're approaching the money bubble. She's been playing for four hours and still has two entries remaining. Average stack was around 35,000.

ANNETTE: Now with an average stack of only about 60 big blinds, I only open for min-raises. There are way too many short stacks scattered around the table to open for three times the blind. I want to commit as few chips to the pot as possible in case I get shoved on by one of the short stacks when I'm going for a steal.

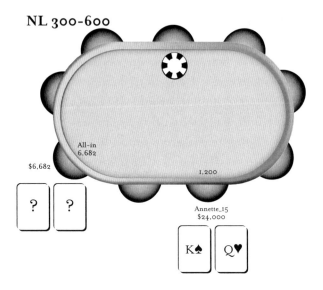

All-in
6,682

$6,682

1,200

Annette_15
$24,000

K♠ Q♥

Annette opened KQ from early middle position for a min-raise. A very short stack shoved for $6,600.

ANNETTE: Well, this really sucks. I guess I just have to call. KQ doesn't play that terribly against his range—he'll have lots of small pairs in his shoving range. People are shoving more hands than you think they are.

She called and the shorty had K♦Q♦. Fortunately, nothing terrible happened and she split the pot.

A few hands later, everyone folded to Annette in the

small blind. She raised to 1,800 with A♣6♠. Big blind
called.

NL 400-800

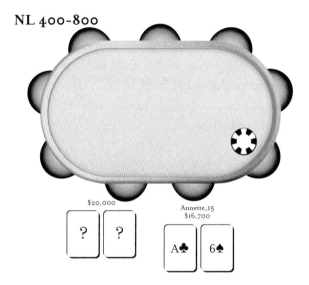

The flop was A♠K♣9♣. She fired a small bet: 2,050.

ANNETTE: I want him to continue with KQ, KJ type
hands and I'm trying to set up the stack sizes for a river bet.
Say I bet 2,000, and he calls. Now there is 8,000 in the
pot. On the turn, I bet 4,000 and he calls. Then on the
river, there will be 18,000 in the pot and I'll have 12,000
left. That's a good river shove.

He thwarted her well-thought-out plans, though, and raised to 5,400.

ANNETTE: So, you're saying that you have specifically A-9 or K-9, huh? Those are the only hands you can really represent with that raise. I don't believe you, and there really isn't much I can do. If you have it, at least I have runner-runner club outs!

She moved all-in.

ANNETTE: He could easily fold a better hand here. I wouldn't be surprised to get a fold from A8 or AT in this spot. And, if he has a hand like A5 or A4, it will probably end up as a chop anyway so moving in could earn me his half of the pot. He eventually tanked and called with A3— the pot was chopped.

Twenty minutes later, she was very short stacked with only 15 blinds:

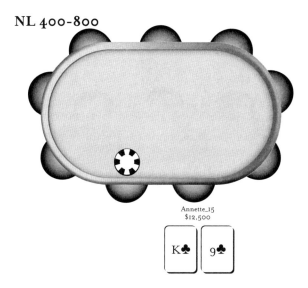

Annette_15
$12,500

K♣ 9♣

K-9 suited in the cutoff. She moved all-in.

ANNETTE: Short stacked, I really don't know all the math, but I think I have a pretty decent idea of what is right and what is wrong. This is a marginal all-in, but whatever. I want to play the hand and I really don't want to open-raise and then fold to a three-bet. I get very aggressive when I'm short stacked and there are antes in play. I'm either going to double up or get out, but I don't wait around and squeeze. I'm playing to win, not squeak into the money.

A few hands later, her short stacked 99 ran into AA. She was down to one entry.

NL 400-800

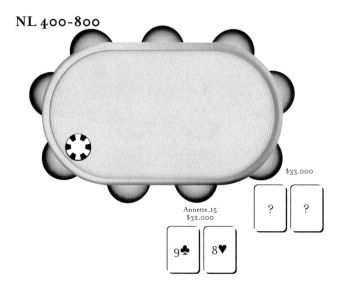

$33,000

Annette_15
$32,000

9♣ 8♥

ANNETTE: This guy has been opening too many pots. I'm going to try a little three-bet. I have to keep the bet size small, though, so I can follow through on the flop without getting too crazy. She made it 4,800. He called. Flop was J♦5♦5♥. He checked.

ANNETTE: I'm going to bet small now, 4,855. I want it to look like Queens or Kings. Even if I lose this pot, I'll still have plenty of room to maneuver with 30 big blinds. It is really vital when you're making plays with speculative hands that you don't give up flexibility if it doesn't work.

He folded and she added significantly to her stack, but not without substantial risk. A few hands later, a great opportunity for Annette:

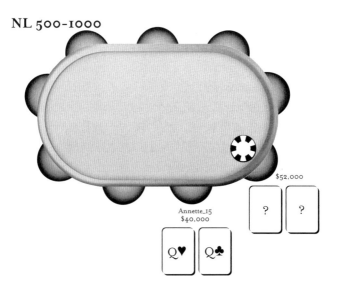

NL 500-1000

$52,000

Annette_15
$40,000

All folded to the button, who min-raised to 2,000.

ANNETTE: Come on, give me some action, please.

She clicked it back to 5,600.

ANNETTE: I make it 5,600 to give him what looks like good fold equity. I think he'll jam any pair or any Ace. If he calls that bet, he has to have King-high kind of hands, like KQ, KJ, KT.

He folded. Oh well. Our hero then went on a little bit of a heater. TT held over 99, then AK beat KT all-in pre-flop. She was well over average and had "in-the-money chips" with the blinds at 600 to 1,200 and a 150 ante.

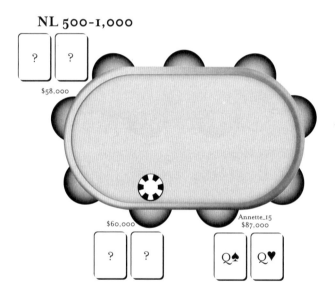

NL 500-1,000

$58,000

$60,000

Annette_15
$87,000

With the powerful 54 offsuit, she min-raised from the cutoff.

ANNETTE: These guys just aren't playing back too much, and I've shown AK and TT in the last few hands. I'll get respect.

The button called and the big blind hitched a ride to the flop: K♦9♦6♠.

ANNETTE: Crap, this is just a terrible board to C-bet. Whatever.

Action checked all around. Turn was 8♣. Blind checked.

ANNETTE: I really hate this, but I guess I have to make a play for the pot after they both were so weak. Maybe I can win by betting 6,245. I'm trying to get AJ, AT to lay down.

Button called. River was 6♥.

ANNETTE: I'm going to check-shove the river. My range is still uncapped—I could easily have been slow-playing a set or AK. There just aren't any hands in his range (except maybe 76 suited) that would check the flop, call the turn, and bet the river for values that are strong enough to call a check-raise on the river.

She checked, and he just went to showdown with 87 and took the pot with a pair of eights.

ANNETTE: Well, that sucked. But, I think my plan would have worked if he would have bet.

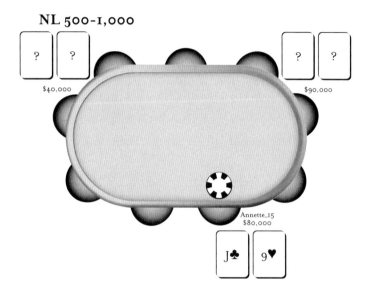

NL 500-1,000

$40,000

$90,000

Annette_15
$80,000

J♣ 9♥

UTG raised, middle position called.

ANNETTE: I'm going to be a huge fish and call here.

PHIL: What? Are you joking?

ANNETTE: Look, the under-the-gun raiser has a really strong range but is pretty short stacked. The caller is very deep. I have position, and if I flop something really good, I can win a really big pot. It looks crazy and I don't do this kind of thing regularly, but they will have to think I have a decent hand as well—there might be some spots where I can steal if the flop is favorable and neither has any kind of real hand. I'd probably be flatting Jacks and maybe even Queens in this spot, too.

Big blind called as well, so four-way action. I couldn't wait to see how this hand played out. Flop was T-T-7. Blind checked, Opener checked. First caller bet $6,200 into the $12,700 pot.

ANNETTE: I was going to check and take a free shot at the 8 if everyone checked. But this bet is bullshit. What, this guy has a Ten? Really? I have way more Tens in my range than he has in his range. In fact, he really shouldn't have any Tens in his range except maybe pocket Tens. Ace-Ten suited, Jack-Ten suited aren't going to be calling a pre-flop under-the-gun raise from middle position. After he calls, though, I can have tons of Tens in my range—ATs, KTs, QTs, JTs, T9s, T8s are all reasonable hands for me. He basically has small pairs and AQs as his range. This is too easy. I mean, if I raise, he has to fold, like, 88 now, doesn't he?

She made it 14,000, pretty much a min-raise, but setting up for a huge turn bet should that bet get called.

He folded. Of all the hands I'd seen her play, this was one of the most spectacular and interesting. Perceived range versus perceived range, deep and thorough analysis, and courage. With this one hand, Annette showed me how she has earned her reputation as one of the best in the business. It didn't take long for her to find another hand to show off.

NL 600-1,200

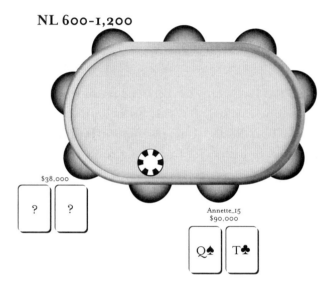

She min-raised from the cutoff and got called by the small blind. Flop was A♦K♥3♣. Small blind donked 4,500 into 9,800.

ANNETTE: What the hell, man? I'm going to float.

She called, he checked the turn (9♥) and she fired a small turn bet of 6,000.

ANNETTE: No idea why he was donking, but this just has to be a weak hand. When I bet 6,000 now, if he calls, the pot will have 30,000 in it and he will have 20,000 left. He should know that he will basically have to get it in if he's going to call the turn. I think I can get a fold from A-4, KQ, and other weak hands.

He folded, and Annette was up over 100,000 in chips. Brilliant.

Our hero went completely card-dead for the next 75 minutes. Eventually, the blinds were steep and she got it in with AK versus AQ. In typical donkament style, the AQ sucked out. She busted out just after the bubble burst, so at least she made a little money back.

ANNETTE: Oh, well, that's MTT life for you. Six hours of fun, one minute of misery, very little cash. Sorry I couldn't make a deeper run. Guess we'll have to save that lesson for another time. Hey, you know there is a $5,000 at the Wynn tomorrow, right?
PHIL: Sounds like fun. I can't wait to try out some of this stuff.

After Day 1 at the Wynn, I was tenth in chips with 100 players remaining. Her strategies worked beautifully. Annette was still in as well, but short stacked. At the end of Day 2, Phil Hellmuth put a sick beat* on me for about 200,000 in chips and I never recovered. Annette, meanwhile, rebounded nicely and cruised all the way to the final table. She ended up finishing in second place and winning yet another $200,000. It is clear I picked the right teacher.

DAN "JUNGLEMAN12" CATES

Heads Up No Limit Hold'em

It's hard for me to imagine what it must be like to be Daniel "jungleman12" Cates. He's a good-looking, slightly socially awkward phenom with a bankroll approaching eight digits. At twenty-two, he's a "regular" at the $500–$1,000 and higher games online. He's widely considered one of the best heads-up NLH specialists in the world. This kid is a winner, a big winner, in the mold of Tom Dwan and Phil Galfond. His star is on the rise, as is his bankroll.

---

* Okay, I hate bad beat stories, but I just can't resist: Hellmuth was on complete tilt and was splashing around (40/35/5) and had about 90,000 in chips. I was playing like a nit with 140,000. Average stack was around 70,000. Last hand before dinner break, blinds at 800/1,600. He raises UTG to 4,000. I three-bet on the button to 14,000 with A♠K♦. He called. Flop is K♣9♣4♦. He checks, I bet 20,000, he moved all-in, and I snap-called. He had A♣T♣. Turn was T♦, river T♠. Hellmuth then posted on his Twitter account how he was one of the chip leaders and was playing his "A" game. At least he bought me a latte during the break.

Fortunately, he's also available "for hire" for personal coaching, albeit at a rate that would make Warren Buffett think twice. But, hey, if I'm going to revamp my game, who better to learn from? In March 2011, I backed up the truck, took a mortgage out on my home, and bought a significant amount of time from the kid. I had one stipulation: as my Heads Up mentor, everything he taught me could go into this book.

Unfortunately, he wouldn't quite go for that last point. "Look, Phil, I'm willing to teach you, but there are some things I'm going to show you that I simply can't afford to have in print right now. If you really want this to happen, I'll need to edit the text before publication."

So, here you have it. Well, most of it. If you want the rest, find Daniel and pay. I can assure you it will pay for itself in a matter of weeks, if not days.

——MAKE MORE MONEY——

DANIEL: Before we start, Phil, I want to set a foundation for what we're trying to accomplish. What we're trying to do is simple: make money. Don't worry about balance or looking like an idiot. Don't worry about playing an elegant game. All we want to do is maximize our EV and make money.

There is always a best way to play a hand. For every spot, there is an ideal action. We're going to act based on what we know about our opponent, and we're going to play a maximally exploitative style, even if that makes us exploitable in a few spots ourselves. Every action has a justification, and every action adds to our overall expectation and long-term EV.

——HEADS UP——

DANIEL: First, assume that both players are 100 big blinds deep—that is somewhat normal for a Heads Up match. Now, let's start with play from the button.* Here is our general approach: at the beginning of a match we're going to play 100% of our hands on the button. We will raise three times the blind.

We will be making small adjustments to that strategy depending on how our opponent plays back and responds to our opening raises. Against the most aggressive players that will three-bet with a wide range and take more flops, it is acceptable to fold the very worst hands on the button, around the bottom 20% of hands. It is probably still more profitable to play 100% from the button, but it is difficult to deal with the human emotions of constantly having to fold to three-bets.

Now, change seats. We're in the big blind now. Against a 100% opening range, I defend somewhere around 42%

---

* In Heads Up play, the player with the button posts the small blind and acts first before the flop and then last on every subsequent round of betting.

306

of the time. As a default, I'm going to be three-betting with around 15% of my hands and calling with 25–27%. You must play-back [three-bet], and you're going to have to take some flops as well. If my opponent is folding to my three-bets too much, I'll open up my three-betting range and put on as much heat as I can get away with, but I don't ever get much higher than a combined 42% range from the big blind. It is very difficult to play more than a 50% range from the big blind—you'll find that you constantly just have nothing on the flop and have to play a really weak game post-flop, or you'll have to play "street poker" and start making all kinds of crazy-ass moves, like weird four-bet bluffs. If my opponent isn't folding to my three-bets and he is four-betting quite often or taking flops, I will slow down a bit and decrease my three-betting range so that I'll actually have a hand a little more often. I'll also start check-raising the flop more liberally.

All of this made total sense, and so far, I wasn't too far out of comfort zone. Thinking back to my limited Heads Up experience, I was pretty sure that I was playing a few too many hands and not three-betting enough, but not by a wide margin on either side.

DANIEL: I believe that three-betting a polarized range is one of the keys to Heads Up play. You want to three-bet with hands like 75 suited and hands like AK. You don't normally want to three-bet a hand like K9, QJ, or QT—when your three-bet gets called, most of the time your hand is dominated by their calling range. Against really aggressive players who call a ton of three-bets, you can start merging your three-betting range and including KTs, QJs type hands, but I wouldn't recommend playing against these types of players unless you play very, very well post-flop.

When you find yourself in a three-bet pot, out of position, with a dominated hand, you can be sure that you're in deep trouble. With a hand like 75 suited, I'm not going to be too concerned about being dominated if my three-bet gets called. On a J-7-2 board, there just aren't that many combinations that are going to be ahead of 75 that wouldn't have four-bet pre-flop. And, when I flop a flush or straight draw, I can really barrel off and put some big pressure on my opponent.

I stopped him a minute, took out a piece of paper, and drew a hand chart. "Okay, bud, let me try this on for size. We're playing 42%, which equates to around 550 combinations out of 1,326. I should be three-betting with about 200 of those, and calling with 350. My three-betting range should be polarized to include the best of the hands and the worst of the hands.

DANIEL: You got it.

Ten minutes later, I showed him this rough first effort:

	A	K	Q	J	T	9	8	7	6	5	4	3	2
A	3	3	3	3	3	C	C	C	C	C	C	C	C
K	3	3	3	3	C	C							
Q	3	3	3	3	C	C	C						
J	C	C	C	3	3	C	C	C					
T	C	C	C	C	3	3	3	3	C				
9	C	C	C	C	C	3	3	3	3	C			
8	C		C	C		C	3	3	3	3	C		
7	C						C	3	3	3			
6	C							C	3	3	3		
5	C								C	3	3		
4	C									C	3	3	
3	C										C	3	
2	C												C

Pre-flop big-blind strategy vs. a 100% opening range and raise. "3" represents hands that are three-bet, C represents hands that call pre-flop.

I had 376 combinations of pre-flop calls for 28% of my range and 190 combinations for three-bets for 14% of my range.

DANIEL: That's more or less it. You might be a little heavy with the 42, 43 suited hands, but this is a good start. As a default, you won't be doing too much wrong if you played this chart. At least you're thinking about the game the right way—knowing how to use combinatorics is vital.

When I was 10 I went to Vatican City and was personally blessed by the pope. Sign of the cross on my forehead, the whole deal. This felt better. And back then, I didn't know I was an atheist.

DANIEL: That takes care of a lot of pre-flop play. There are many adjustments based on game flow and your opponent's style, but we can get to that later. Let's talk post-flop. Here, you'll have to do some hand-reading and analytics to come up with the best line for every hand. And yes, there is a best line of play for each and every situation. There are standards that I have developed for every spot in No Limit, and I rarely deviate from those standards.

Now, here's the thing about post-flop play. I don't put much emphasis on the big pots. If both players flop a big hand, most, if not all of the money is going in. You can still misplay a big pot, for sure, but for the most part, there isn't much to be said about these hands. Making hero laydowns with big hands just isn't that big a part of Heads Up strategy. Those hands will even out over the long run. Post-flop, the game is much more about the small pots. Winning small pots is what drives up your EV, gives you momentum in a match, and makes your opponent overplay their marginal hands.

PHIL: What are some typical small-pot mistakes you see?

DANIEL: Giving up too easily and quickly. Not pressing implied odds. Being too showdown-oriented when betting is better. And, the big one, calling too light on the turn—

players love calling loose on the turn when they are beat and have a chance to suck-out. On the river, after they miss, they usually level themselves into making another bad, crying call on the river. That is how to turn what should have been a small pot into a big pot and a big mistake. Most of my focus and energy goes into these small pots—the big pots will take care of themselves.

Okay, back to post-flop play. After the flop, we're going to figure out how our opponent's range connects with the board and we're also going to think about how our perceived range connects with the board. We'll form a game plan and go from there. If we're on the button, there are only a few things that can happen: they can donk into us, or they can check to us. If they donk, we have only three responses: call, fold, or raise. If they check to us, we have only two options: check or bet. You can see where I'm going with this, I hope—the line we take depends on what we know about our opponent's range, what our opponent thinks of our range, what our opponent thinks we think of his range, the texture of the board, and our opponent's post-flop style.

DANIEL: Look, the best way to go from here is just to get you in a game and let me watch and comment after every hand. A lot of what I want to teach you can't be taught in the abstract—you just have to be in a hand. Are you ready to buy in?

Gulp.

PHIL: Sure. Let's try $5–$10.

DANIEL: Look for a table where a guy is sitting with less than a full buy-in. There is a better chance they are a weak player than if someone is sitting deep stacked.

I found a reasonable looking table at Full Tilt and bought in.

DANIEL: Oooh, I know this guy. He tried like hell to beat me a few years ago. Unfortunately for him, I played like God. I felt kinda bad about it. He's actually a very good player.

Translation: "Very Good Player" = "Not good game selection"—but what the hell.

——PLAYING LESSON——

Opponent	Me
1,000(B)	1,000
Raise 30	Qs 8s

My opponent raised on the button, I called. Flop was A♦K♦2♠. I check-folded.

DANIEL: I like to be aggressive and three-bet a lot more than 15% on the first hand of the match. It is really impor-

312

tant to figure out as quickly as possible how your opponent responds to three-bets.

Note: From here on out, I'll skip over hands that were just folded from the button or big blind and replay only the most interesting pots and lessons. I'm also skipping hands that Daniel asked me to edit out. For brevity, a few hands presented combine themes from multiple lessons and hands.

Opponent	Me
1,030	970(B)
	Ac 9d

I raise to 30. Opponent calls. Flop is J♥5♠T♠. Opponent checks, I bet $50 as a standard continuation-bet. Opponent folds.

DANIEL: Even though it worked, checking-back this flop is much better. I've run some simulations on this flop and they only fold to a C-bet about 30% of the time. Their pre-flop calling range hits this flop quite frequently. You're never getting a better hand to fold, and if you get check-raised, you'll lose the equity that you have in catching an Ace on the turn or catching a straight draw. Think more about your opponent's pre-flop calling range and how it intersects with the board—don't just mash the Bet button post-flop because you think you're supposed to make a continuation-bet. Figuring out how many hands call a pre-flop raise and then just check-fold on a J♥5♠T♠ board should be a key factor in determining whether or not to C-bet.

I play 15 more uninteresting hands or so, I've raised 100% on the button so far and my opponent just three-bet me twice in a row and I had to lay down bad hands.

Opponent	Me
1,200	800(B)
	Qc 4d

PHIL: I think I'll give him a different look. I don't want to three-bet again and have to fold again.

I fold.

DANIEL: Don't go on soft tilt, Phil. You haven't done anything wrong and nothing about this guy's play suggests that it's time to make an adjustment to a 100% pre-flop opening range. Not only that, but Q4 isn't in the bottom 20% of hands—it's more like a 65th percentile kind of hand. That was just weak.

A few hands later, I've made a little comeback.

Opponent	Me
1,140	960(B)
	Ac Jd

I raise, opponent three-bets, I call.

Flop: J♦4♣8♦. He bets 50. I call. Turn is Q♠. He bets 120. I call. River is 8♥. He checks. I check. I win. Opponent had AT♠.

DANIEL: I think you played that hand just fine. I probably would have value-bet the river, though. I don't think you're going to get called, but you really want to get paid off if your opponent has 99, TT, KJ, JTs. The only hands you should be concerned about are AQ and KQ, and you're probably not going to get check-raised by those hands anyway after the board pairs the river. Don't be too showdown-oriented.

Opponent	Me
920	1,080(B)
	8h 4d

I raise pre-flop to 30, opponent calls. Flop is Jc-9d-8d. He checks. I fire 50. He calls. Turn is Ts. He bets 50. I fold.

DANIEL: Your continuation-bet was okay, but I think you are probably one of those guys who C-bets too frequently. Victor* C-bets about 85% of the time. When you C-bet that much, you have to make some serious adjustments to the rest of your game. You have to barrel more often, you have to make some hero calls when you get check-raised, and you have to be very aggressive on the turn. I C-bet about 50% of the time, but against some tight post-flop players, it might be as high as 70%. Using a HUD to determine how often to C-bet is very useful. This is one of the biggest differences between live and online players.

He continued talking while I kept playing. I'd been at it for twenty minutes or so, sixty hands played, I was up four hundred. I could sense that my opponent was starting to get a little frisky—the bet sizes post-flop were getting a little bigger, and he seemed to be C-betting more often than he did when the match started.

PHIL: I think he might be a little tilted right now. He probably can't believe he's losing to me.

DANIEL: As the effective stack sizes get smaller, you can decrease the amount of your pre-flop raise. Make it two

---

*Victor Blom, another young whiz, otherwise known as IsildurI online. . . . Daniel and Victor have been battling it out at the nosebleeds for ultimate Internet heads-up superiority and unbelievable sums of money.

times the blind. You want to give yourself an effective four-bet pre-flop. Right now, if you make it 3, he'll make it 9. Now a four-bet is effectively an all-in. You can't really four-bet to 20 and then fold to a shove. If you double the blind and make it 2, his three-bet will be 5 or 6, and you can four-bet to 15 to 16 and still get away if you are making that move with a sub-optimal hand.

Opponent	Me
600	1,400 (B)
	9d 8d

I double the blind with a min-raise. My opponent three-bets to 60. I tank for a few seconds and four-bet ship it all-in. My opponent folds.

PHIL: I sensed he was getting antsy, and I don't want him three-betting me light. I was willing to double him up, but I still have pretty good equity against all but the best hands. I thought it was worth a shot—looks like I was right!

DANIEL: That was the best play you've made all match. You sensed weakness and pounded on him. One thing: I would have showed the 98s. You show him that hand and you own his soul. He won't mess around with you, and you should be able to grind him down. You'll definitely tighten up his three-betting, which is exactly what you want to do. If he knows you're willing to four-bet-ship a 98s, he'll really have to ratchet down the three-bets or be willing to call your four-bet very light.

We played a few more nothing hands and my opponent reloaded.

Opponent	Me
1,000(B)	1,260
	Q♣T♦

He raises, I call. Flop is K♣J♦7♣. I check with the intention of check-raising. He checks behind. Turn is a 7♣. I bet $50. He calls. River is 4♠. I bet $120. He calls and shows JT and wins the pot.

DANIEL: When I worked my way up to the $5–$10 and $10–$20 level, I started to realize that there are millions of spots where my action is going to be one thing, and one thing only. Say the flop is Q-T-4 and I check-raise with J9. The turn is a 7 and I pick up a backdoor flush draw. I fire at the pot and they call again. The river is a 4—this is a card where my opponent simply isn't going to fold very much. So I started thinking, "Shit, if I check on this river, I'm always check-folding. I'm exploitable!" So, I started check-calling and check-raising this spot more often. They always had a hand and I lost a ton of money making these

318

monkey plays. I realized then that although the situation was exploitable there was nothing that I could do about it. I just have to play my hand the best way I can play it. In situations like this, the best way to play the hand is to check and fold the river.

Opponent	Me
1,200	1,060 (B)
	J♣J♠

I raise to 30 with pocket Jacks, my opponent three-bets to 90, I four-bet to 220. He calls. This is getting serious. Flop is T-4-4 rainbow. I bet 350 in 440 and was prepared to call off the rest. My opponent folded.

DANIEL: In four-bet pots, the ranges are narrower, and you don't have to bet so much post-flop—it probably won't be much of a decision one way or the other, it will be either a clear call or a clear fold to a shove. You're normally not deep enough for it to matter. You want to bet small in these pots so that you can four-bet-bluff pre-flop and then follow it up with a cheap bluff continuation-bet. If you're just barreling and betting close to the size of the pot with all your four-bets, you'll be exploitable. I would have bet about half the pot on this flop.

Incidentally, you should be using a HUD. If I'm playing with a HUD and my opponent isn't, I just don't think it is possible for him to beat me in the long run. It is really hard to know frequencies without it—the human mind isn't really good at long-term trend extrapolation—we always rely on our most recent experiences more than the past. Perception can be way off, but a HUD doesn't lie. If you're going to take this game seriously, you simply have to play with a HUD.

PHIL: What keeps you motivated these days—besides the money, of course?

DANIEL: When you're used to winning so much, there is a weakness in that. You become complacent and don't work as hard. I've been lazy about my No Limit game lately. I'm really enjoying PLO and some of the mixed games. That is where I've been spending the majority of my time lately.

Opponent	Me
900(B)	1,400
	A♠8♠

Opponent raises to 30, I call. Flop is J♣-T♣-8♦. I check, he bets $50. I call. Turn is 7♠. I check, he bets $110. I call. River is 3♣. I check, he bets $300 into $380. Crap, I can't see him triple-barreling on this turn and river. I fold.

DANIEL: This is a classic mistake. Calling too light on the turn—that was a bad call. Your hand is just crushed by his range. You have to remember: he knows that a J–T–8 flop is likely to hit your pre-flop calling range, and yet he bet the flop and turn anyway. He almost certainly has to have a hand that can beat A8. You need to tighten up your turn-calling requirements substantially or you're just going to get murdered at the higher stakes. Yes, folding on the turn is weak. Yes, your opponent will be able to exploit you, but there just isn't much you can do about it—folding is still the best play.

A few hands later, I got another chance to screw up.

Opponent(B)	Me
1,200	1,100
	5♣4♣

Opponent raises to 30. I called. I meant to three-bet, but I just clicked the wrong button. Or maybe I just wimped out. Flop was Q♠2♣4♠. I checked, he bet 45, I raised to 145. He folded.

DANIEL: You played this hand like a live player.

I could guess that wasn't a particularly flattering remark.

DANIEL: Why did you raise?

PHIL: My hand is significantly ahead of his range, and almost every turn card in the deck will give me doubt. I thought I should just take the pot while I was pretty sure I had the best hand. If he plays back, I'll be able to get away as cheaply as possible.

DANIEL: Here is how I think about this spot. I have equity. A raise isn't a value bet and isn't a bluff. I can never get a better hand to fold. By calling, I mask my range. He won't know if I'm on a flush draw, a set, a Queen, 66, or the hand I actually have, 54. I have an uncapped range and have all plays available to me on the turn. I can check-call, check-raise, check-fold, or donk—all are viable options depending on the turn, and they will all make sense. I also have a pretty good idea of how my opponent will react to certain turn cards. For instance, I think this guy is very unlikely to barrel a 9 on the turn, but he'll bet every Ten or Jack. If the turn comes a 9, I will check and fold to a bet. If it comes a Ten or Jack, I will give him a little more rope and check-call again. You have to try to understand how your opponent thinks and how he will react to your action and the various turn cards.

When my session and first lesson ended, I was up $1,400 or so and was exhausted. The next day, I had a chance to try out my newfound skills in the NBC National Heads Up Championship. My first-round match, against Card Player of the Year Tom Marchese, was a seesaw battle. I eventually prevailed, much to the dismay of everyone on the 2+2 forums. Second round I had an early coin flip against Greg Raymer with AK versus QQ and won. I was in the money.

Third round, I ran up against Erik Seidel, the eventual winner of the tournament and one of the best in the game. There was no shame in losing to Erik. I had the chip lead briefly when the blinds were so high that we were forced to gamble a little, and things didn't work out.

You can get more information and contact information for Daniel at his website: Junglemandan.com.

HAND EXAMPLES

Here are some hands I've played that I believe are particularly instructive. I don't win every pot, I don't make the correct decision at every opportunity, but I did learn something in each hand. The hands that I misplay or miscalculate are the most instructive.

NO LIMIT HOLD'EM CASH GAMES

—REALIZING EQUITY—

2-4 NL

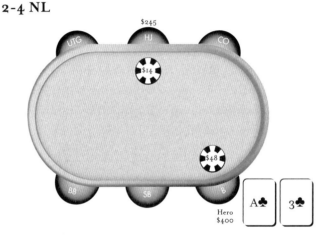

My opponent is playing 50/26/0 and opens to $14 from the Hi-Jack. I three-bet to $48, mostly to isolate the fish and play a pot in position. Of course, he calls. I'm fairly confident this player will just call my three-bet with many of his strong combinations, and also check-fold most flops that he misses.

Pot: $102   Flop: Q♠T♥5♣

Opponent checks. This is a very standard flop for a continuation-bet, so I fire $56—no reason to go crazy with a pot-size bet—against fit-or-fold types, a smaller continuation-bet in three-bet pots is correct.

He calls. After the call, I'm certain that he'll call a turn bet as well—no more bluffing for me.

Pot: $204   Turn: 2♦

I pick up a gut-shot straight draw and a little equity, but not enough to get me to try another bluff. He checks, and I check behind hoping to hit an Ace or a 4 on the river. I take my "free" card.

River: 4♥

Opponent shoves all-in for $191, and of course I snap-call. He had TT and flopped middle set.

By betting flop and checking the turn, I gave myself a chance to realize the inherent equity of my hand. And yes, I got lucky too.

1-2 NL

My opponent is playing 28/18/7 and opens from the button for $7. I three-bet to $23 for value with the K♥Q♥ and he calls. I think my opponent will have a wide range—he's the type that loves to play a pot in position (who doesn't?) and isn't afraid to mix it up a bit. He has a lot of small pocket pairs and Broadway (AJ, AQ, KQ, KJ) combinations in his range.

Pot: $48   Flop: T♥5♥3♣

I flop a very good hand: a flush draw and two over cards. This flop also misses my opponent's Broadway combinations. A continuation-bet is mandatory: $20 seems about right—I will make the same size continuation-bet with air as well on a flop like this. My opponent calls, and I suspect that there are quite a few "floats" in his range now, and very few strong combinations—I wouldn't expect him to slow-play a set in this spot. I plan on barreling most turn cards.

Pot: $84   Turn: A♠

The Ace looks scary, but it is actually one of the best cards in the deck if my range analysis is correct. My opponent has a few Aces in his range that floated the flop, but they are not as common as the times that he called with either air or a medium pair. I expect that my opponent will give up all the medium pair hands if I double-barrel. And, even if I get called, I've set up stacks nicely for a shove on the river if I hit my straight or flush.

Since there really aren't any extremely strong combinations in my opponent's range, I think a half-pot turn bet is all I need. I fire $42. My opponent sighs, shows 88, and mucks.

Use range analysis on the turn to figure out if betting will show a profit.

5-10 NL

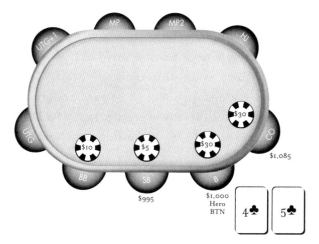

An unknown opponent raises to $30 from the cutoff. I call with 4♣5♣ on the button and the small blind comes along as well.

Pot: $100   Flop: T♣7♠4♦

The cutoff makes a continuation-bet of $80 and I decide to float. With bottom pair and a backdoor-flush draw, my hand is very well disguised and when I improve I expect to get paid when my opponent actually has something. When I don't hit, there will be a lot of good opportunities to bluff on the turn and make my flop call profitable. The small blind folds.

Pot: $260   Turn: 4♠

I improve to trips on the turn and my opponent continuation-bets again—this time for $140. This is a terrible card for my opponent to be continuing with as a bluff, but he's probably not a great player. His bet sizing is small relative to his bet on the flop, so I think he has either a weak made hand or a bluff most of the time. I elect to call because I get more value from this range by letting him value-bet thinly on the river and continue with his bluffs.

Pot: $540   River: 3♣

My opponent bets $290, I shove and my opponent folds. My read was right and I got more value by waiting for the river to raise.

1-2 NL

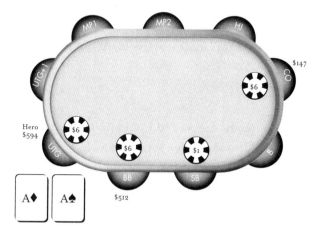

I raise under the gun to $6 with A♦A♠ and get called by the cutoff and the big blind. My opponent in the big blind is a solid regular in the $1/2 games on Full Tilt and the cutoff is an unknown.

Pot: $19   Flop: A♥3♦4♦

The big blind bets $10 and with stacks this deep, I would never be raising when he donks. I call and the cutoff calls. Slow play.

Pot: $49   Turn: K♠

331

The big blind bets $34 on the turn and after both the cutoff and I called, he continues betting with what looks like it could be a flush draw. I have blockers to him having an Ace, so he's pretty likely to have a set. I overbet the pot, making it $166 so that I can bet slightly less than the pot on the river. The cutoff folds and the big blind calls.

River: 8♣

My opponent checks and I put him in for his remaining $332 and he calls with a set, 3♥3♠. There wasn't much he could do and I don't think he could really get away from his hand, but the bet sizing and line of play made getting all the money in a certainty.

2-4 NL

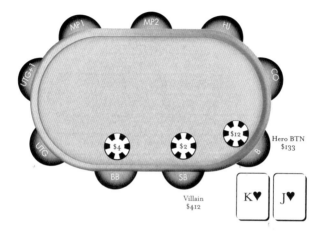

I raise K♥J♥ to $12 from the button and an opponent makes it $40 from the SB—I have a substantial number of hands with this player and my HUD tells me he three-bets 12% from the small blind. My opponent is re-raising with a wide range and I have position post-flop. KJ suited plays well enough to justify calling, so I do.

Pot: $84   Flop: K♣5♦2♠

My opponent continuation-bets $48. I think he'll make a continuation-bet on this board with his entire range. The flop hits his range harder than it hits my perceived range, but I have a blocker to him having a King. My opponent is very aggressive and I expect he thinks I will just call with my middle pocket pairs and top-pair–type hands to allow him to continue barreling.

This time, I get a little tricky and throw in a min-raise. I have every intention of calling a shove. Against a loose-aggressive opponent, this can be just the type of bet to help them spew. He knows that I would almost always four-bet AK pre-flop. My pre-flop calling range is fairly wide. He perceives my min-raise as a very narrow range of hands that include many bluffs.

He shoves, I call instantly, and he meekishly shows 6♣4♣ (gut-shot, backdoor flush draw.) I win the pot when the board bricks off and slow down his three-betting in the process.

——GETTING VALUE AGAINST A
TIGHT-PASSIVE PLAYER——

2-4 NL

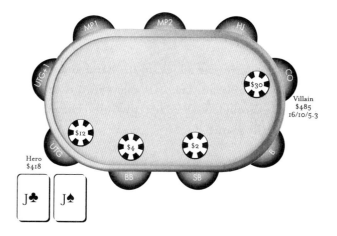

I raise to $12 with JJ under the gun, the cutoff re-raises to $30 and action folds around to me. Over a small sample of 49 hands, my opponent has played 16/10/5.3 pre-flop and has a low aggression factor of 1.0, so I expect him to be fairly straightforward post-flop. I call.

Pot: $63   Flop: J♣8♥7♦

I decide to donk bet $42. I need to start building a pot because my opponent is not very aggressive post-flop. The low aggression factor leads me to believe that he'll rarely bet this flop with air. If I'm going to get maximum value, I can't rely on him to bet for me. I'm hoping to bet two-thirds of the pot on the turn and three-fourths the pot on the river.

Pot: $147   Turn: 8♥

The turn gives me a lock on the hand and my bet sizing is the only relevant factor. I planned this on the flop and follow through with a bet of $98. Thankfully, my opponent calls again.

Pot: $343   River: 2♥

I shove for $260 and my opponent folds. I'm pretty sure my opponent folded an over-pair on the river, so I take a note: "Three-bet, called two donk bets, and folded to a third barrel on J8782 rainbow board." I'll be able to use this note to exploit his tendency to make nitty folds in three-bet pots by triple-barreling air on dry flops in the future.

2-4 NL

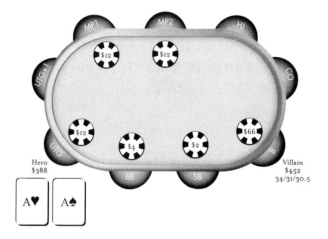

I raise to $12 with A♥A♠ UTG, two players call behind me, and an opponent playing 34/31/30.5 over 59 hands three-bets to $66 from the button. Even though my sample is small, I can be very confident that my opponent is trying to take advantage of being "anonymous." Unfortunately for him, I have a HUD and pocket Aces.

His range is very weak. I don't want to give him a reason to stop bluffing, so I call and the other two players fold. I'm hoping he'll put me on 99-JJ, AK, AQs+.

Pot: $162   Flop: T♣9♦5♥

I check and my opponent bets $160. If I shove, my opponent will be getting 3.7 to 1 pot odds and I don't expect him to fold if he has any piece of the flop or an over-pair. I move all-in for $334 and my opponent flashes AK and folds.

——BARRELING WITH IMPROVED EQUITY——

3-6 NL

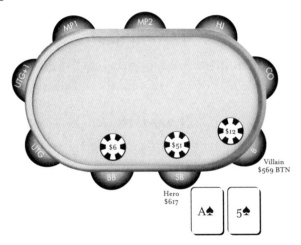

I'm in the small blind with A♠5♠ and my opponent, a smart LAG, opens to $12 on the button. I've played thousands of hands with this opponent and know that he opens

67% of hands on the button and four-bets 15% when he gets three-bet. He is a big winning player and I know that he knows that I three-bet from the small blind 10% of the time. I elect to re-raise to $51, and with the A♠5♠, I plan on bluff-shoving if he four-bets me small. This time, he just calls.

Pot: $106   Flop: T♣2♠8♦

I flop a backdoor-flush draw and the board is T high. There will be a lot of good cards I can barrel on if I continuation-bet—any spade, J, Q, K, or A. Since it's a three-bet pot, I don't need to bet much more than half the pot to threaten stacks. I bet $63 and my opponent calls. He will float often after he adds up the evidence: dry flop, wide three-bet range, dry flop, automatic continuation-bet.

Pot: $232   Turn: 8♠

I pick up a flush draw as the board pairs on the turn. My opponent knows that I know that this is a bad card for me to barrel as a bluff. He will not expect me to be bluffing very often when I bet. Since I actually improved, I barrel, making it $153 to go. My opponent calls and given how I've set up stack sizes, I can be pretty sure that he has a made hand that is not going to fold on the river.

Pot: $538   River: J♠

I river the flush and shove for $401. My opponent calls and mucks his KK when I show him the bad news.

Notice that he did not four-bet my raise out of the small-blind! That's wonderful news for my ability to five-bet-jam A5s profitably against this opponent in the future. He is capable of just calling the top of his range when facing a three-bet, and since he is four-betting so frequently, there are going to be many combinations of hands that will be four-betting and folding pre-flop to a five-bet shove.

——GIVING A LAGTARD PERCEIVED FOLD EQUITY——

3-6 /1 Ante NL

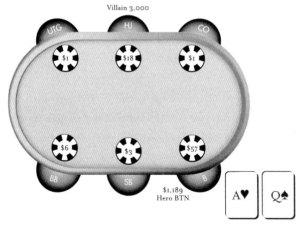

A LAGtard who opens a wide range of hands, calls three-bets too frequently, and plays too aggressively post-flop opens to $18. I pick up A♥Q♠ on the button and three-bet to $57. He calls.

Pot: $129   Flop: Q♦2♦2♥

I flop the world. After my opponent checks, my only consideration is how to get as much value as possible. I have almost 10x pot left behind, and I would often make a very large continuation-bet to leverage the power of my entire stack. But, after checking my HUD, I see that over my 300-hand sample, my opponent has check-raised 20% of his hands post-flop. I may not have enough data points, but I decide to bait him with a small bet of $75. He immediately comes over the top making it $244. Cha-ching. I want to keep the fish on the line, so I call.

Pot: $617   Turn: 8♥

My opponent checks a brick turn and I bet $285—a bit less than half the pot sets me up to make a similar size bet on the river. My opponent min-raises to $570 and I shove for a total of $947. With the flush draws on the board, I can never fold a hand as strong as AQ against this opponent. He calls with A♥T♥.

Of course, the river brings a heart and my opponent makes a flush. Sad. I won the battle but lost the war. Remember to give those LAGtards enough room to bluff—bet small and let them think they have fold equity.

3-6 NL

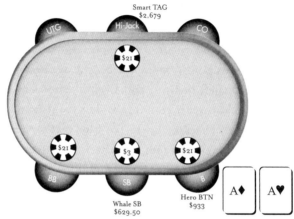

A smart tight-aggressive player opens to $21 from the Hi-Jack at a six-handed table. I would normally re-raise with A♦A♥ on the button, but an epic whale is in the small blind, so I invite him to enter the pot by calling. The whale obliges and comes along.

Pot: $69   Flop: K♣8♦2♣

The whale donks and bets. The smart tight-aggressive player re-raises to $144. KQ, KJ, Ace-high flush draws, and sets are all in the TAG's range. I just call to keep the

342

whale in the pot. He calls. I'm hoping to trap the TAG in the pot if the whale donks the turn.

Pot: $501   Turn: 3♦

With $466 left behind, the whale shoves and the smart TAG calls. Normally, with this action I would say that my TAG opponent's range is KK, 88, 22, AA, AK. Even though I am behind this range—there are six combinations of AK that I beat and nine combinations of KK, 88, 22 that beat me—the whale rarely has me beat and I can never fold getting 2.2 to 1 on my remaining stack.* I shove for $789. The smart TAG calls and shows A♠K♦. The river bricks with a 7♦ and the whale mucks 9♠4♥!

When you have a monstrous whale at the table, remember to play your hands in a way that gives him as many chances as possible to screw up.

——DEFENDING AGAINST A SMART LAG——

A smart loose-aggressive opponent with whom I have a lot of history raises to $25 on the button. I'm in the big blind with 7♠8♠. My opponent's aggression makes playing a hand

---

* $\dfrac{final\ pot}{stack} = \dfrac{1,756}{789} \approx 2.2$

like this difficult out of position when he has the lead, but he folds a little too frequently to my three-bets, so I re-raise to $90 and he calls.

5-10 NL

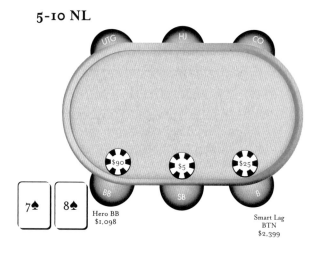

Pot: $185   Flop: Q♥5♦2♠

I make a small continuation-bet of $100 and my opponent calls. Since my opponent is a strong player, I probably should have given up on the flop. My HUD tells me that my opponent does not fold to continuation-bets in three-bet pots very often (50%) and this is a perfect flop for him to float because he knows that the flop improves his calling range more than my three-betting range.

Pot: $385   Turn: 6♠

The turn improves my equity dramatically, giving me a monster straight and flush draw. Time to barrel. By betting, I get to set my own price for my straight draw. He is unlikely to raise with any of his value hands because he has position and needs to balance the times that he is calling with a weak QX or 77-JJ. I also expect to fold out many of his hands that have me beat—mainly, his floats and his medium pairs. I bet $220, setting stacks up for a slightly less than pot-size river shove. My opponent calls.

Pot: $825   River: A♠

The river gives me the flush and I shove for $778. My opponent calls with A♦J♦ and mucks.

My read was spot-on throughout, and again, I got a little lucky on the river. But I was able to extract maximum value with my hand because I set up the stack sizes properly with my flop and turn bets.

——THREE-BETTING THINLY
FOR VALUE——

5-10 NL

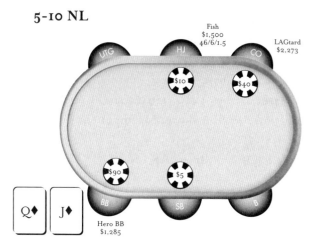

A loose-passive fish playing a 46/6/1.5 style limps the Hi-Jack, and a bad loose-aggressive player that has raised 40% of 86 times in the cutoff raises to $40.

I'm in the big blind with Q♦J♦ and I decide to three-bet for value and to isolate. The LAGtard in the cutoff only folds to three-bets 11% of the time and QJ suited plays very well against a 36% range—even out of position.

Another good reason to three-bet is that the LAGtard is playing deep and I can't buy-in for an amount that covers him. In these situations, I like to play a higher variance style to give myself more opportunities to increase my stack size and have the fish covered on future hands.

I make a tiny three-bet of $90. My goal is to keep the pot as small as possible while still getting the limper to fold. That way, I maximize my maneuverability and keep my option to triple-barrel open.

The limper folds and the LAGtard calls.

Pot: $195   Flop: 5♦4♥5♣

The flop is very dry and I expect this player will call a continuation-bet just about every time. A low paired board like this one will set up lots of profitable turn and river bluffing spots, so I make a continuation-bet of $150 and my opponent calls. I want to set up about a 3/4-pot bet on the turn and 3/4-pot shove on the river.

Pot: $495   Turn: K♥

The turn is a perfect card to barrel. I might get a light call on the turn if he is suspicious, but he'll fold by the river unless he has some stupid 5X or KX hand. I bet $350 and my opponent calls.

Pot: $1,095   River: 6♥

The river brings in a backdoor-flush draw, but it's not important. Neither of us has many flushes in our range. I gulp, reexamine the hand from all angles, and follow through with a triple-barrel shove for $700. My bluff only has to work 39% of the time to break even, and I expect my opponent to have enough weak hands in his range for my bet to be profitable. However, this time, he turned up with K-5 for a full house.

Even though I lost the hand, I believe my line is profitable over the long run against this player. I hope my wife wasn't watching.

——ADJUSTING RANGES AND EXPLOITING REGULARS——

3-6 NL

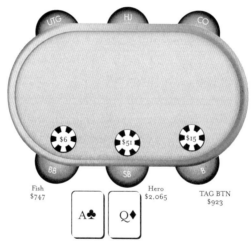

My opponent raises to $15 on the button. The only fish at the table is in the big blind, so even though my HUD tells me that my opponent raises 50% of the time on the button, I think his range is closer to 70% or 80% this time—he'll be picking on that fishy player in the big blind with just about every hand.

I wake up with A♣Q♦ and three-bet to $51. The fish folds and my opponent calls.

Pot: $108   Flop: J♦7♦7♠

The flop is dry and I make a continuation-bet of $70. I have been pretty quiet this session and I think this player is capable of folding a hand as strong as KJ to a triple barrel if he doesn't improve. I make a medium-size bet, which will allow me to set up stacks for a pot-size shove on the river. I estimate my opponent's calling range to consist of floats, flush draws, middle pairs, some suited connectors that hit trip sevens, and Jacks as weak as J9s.

Pot: $248   Turn: 2♣

The turn changes nothing and I continue with my plan. I make a bet of $190, which sets up a pot-size bet on the river when I'm called. My opponent calls.

Pot: $628   River: 3♣

I shove for $627 and my opponent folds and shows QJ.

It takes serious balls to triple-barrel into a guy when you feel strongly they have top pair. I only make this play against good players that are actually capable of laying down top-pair–type hands.

——TRIPLE-BARREL BLUFFING
A CALLING STATION——

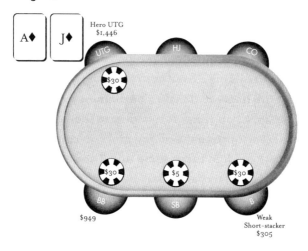

I raise to $30 under the gun with A♦J♦. I get called by a weak short-stacker on the button and a loose-passive player in the big blind.

Pot: $95   Flop: 2♥T♥5♦

Against two bad players and a short-stacker who has position on me, a continuation-bet is mandatory on this flop. Frequently, the button will fold and I'll gain position on the fish for the rest of the hand.

The big blind checks and I bet $70. The button folds and the big blind calls. I have a note on the big blind that says he plays very loose with draws and weak pairs. He raises his medium-strength made hands. After the call, I assume he is calling with all sorts of flush draws, gut-shot straight draws, weak pairs, and even over-card hands like QJ.

Pot: $235   Turn: 6♠

My opponent checks and I bet $220. I bet big to set up what I think will be a very profitable triple-barrel shove. I expect him to call with a wide range of weak made hands that will fold when I bet big on the river. I also expect him to raise now if he has a hand that will call a river shove.

He just calls, and I believe the stage is set. Cock the gun.

Pot: $635   River: 4♣

My opponent checks again and I follow through with my plan—I go all-in for $657 and my opponent quickly calls with Q♥3♥ and I lose to a rivered straight. Oops!

3-6 NL

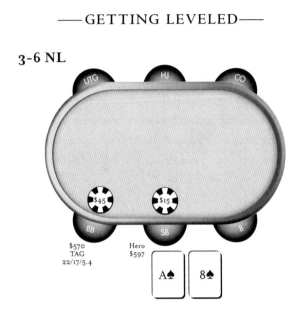

Action folds around to me and I raise to $15 from the small blind with A♠8♠. My opponent is playing a 22/17/5 style and aggressively defends his big blind versus late position raises. He three-bets to $45 and I make a loose call.

    Pot: $90   Flop: 9♦6♠5♣

I look at my HUD and see that my opponent makes a continuation-bet 70% of the time in three-bet pots. With a gut-shot, Ace high and a backdoor flush draw, I have good equity against my opponent's three-betting range so I'm not giving up easily.

I donk into my opponent with a bet of $72 hoping to either win the pot right away or get a read. Read this: my opponent raises to $153.

I should just fold, but I know that he knows that these small raises are very effective against an aggressive opponent and I think he is polarized between air and a very narrow range of sets and AA and KK. I make a pretty bad, spewy call.

Pot: $396   Turn: 4♦

The turn is a meaningless 4♦ and we both check. I'm very surprised that he checked behind. I believe he must be playing a hand like AK, AQ, or a very small pair (22–44).

Pot: $396   River: 6♣

This is a decent card to bluff. I do not want to check and then lose to AQ. I convince myself that my opponent will fold well over 50% of his range and I shove for $414. My opponent trapped me to perfection and shows 5♦5♥. Well played, sir. The check on the turn told a convincing story and really got me.

5-10/$1.50 Ante NL

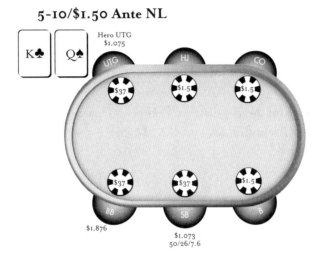

Hero UTG
$1,075

K♣ Q♠

$37 $1.5 $1.5

$37 $37 $1.5

$1,876
$1,073
50/26/7.6

I raise under the gun to $37 with K♣Q♠. The SB and BB come along. The SB is extremely loose and overly aggressive playing a 50/26/8 style.

Pot: $120   Flop: 5♥Q♦8♣

The small blind makes a small donk bet of $40 and the big blind folds. My opponent in the small blind has been very loose with his calls and very aggressive with a weak range of made hands. He is very unlikely to have a strong hand with this bet and the best play is to raise for value while setting up a pot-size river bet. I make it $120 and my opponent calls.

Pot: $360   Turn: 6♦

This 6♦ doesn't change much and my opponent donks again with a $120 bet. I think that his range is something like QJ, QT, 67, 78, 89, A8, 57, 54. I am very confident that I have the best hand.

I raise to $320, setting up a slightly less than pot-size shove on the river. Perfect. If he calls, I'm also getting value from his weak paired hands. He calls.

Pot: $1,080   River: J♣

The river definitely could have given my opponent the best hand, but he checks and shoving with thin value is the best play. Since the pot is so big and there is only $591.50 left in his stack, with any kind of very strong hand, I would expect him to shove either on the turn or the river. I'm hoping he has A8o or QT and digs deep to find a call. I shove and my opponent calls with A8 offsuit. Hee haw!

PLO HANDS

——ACES ON A DRY FLOP——

5-10 PLO

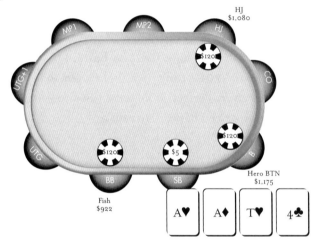

A strong aggressive player raises to $35 from the Hi-Jack and I re-raise to $120 with A♥A♦T♥4♣ on the button. A loose fish calls from the big blind and the Hi-Jack calls.

Pot: $365   Flop: K♣5♦2♥

BB checks, Hi-Jack donk bets $238. My opponent should know that this dry a board is perfect for me to continuation-bet. So, why did he donk? I expect that he'd check-raise KKXX every time. He has to have some sort of weird straight draw or KQT9 type hand. I should raise to protect my hand, but the donk bet confuses me. I decide to call and see the turn. Big blind folds.

Pot: $841   Turn: 2♠

HJ checks. The turn is a good card for my hand because it counterfeits all my opponent's two pair draws. If he has the KQT9 or similar, he's drawing to two outs. My only real concern is protecting against straight draws. But, sane opponents won't have that many straight draws. Maybe I'm leveling myself, but I check behind.

Pot: $841   River: J♣

HJ bets $562. This is a tricky river spot. My opponent is representing a full house. I'm really confused. I just can't see why he'd donk on the flop. Whatever, at the end of the day, if he checked the flop I'd probably go broke with this hand, so I might as well pay him off now. I call. And of course, he had K♦K♥9♠8♠.

I kept thinking about this hand for three days after, and I am still confused.

2-4 PLO

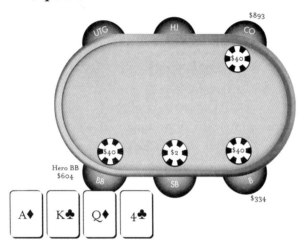

CO raises to $12. BTN calls. Hero raises to $40. CO calls. BTN calls.

A smart, aggressive player raises to $12 from the CO and an unknown player calls on the BTN. I three-bet to $40 from the big blind with A♦K♣Q♦4♣ (definitely a little loose, even double-suited) and both opponents call.

Pot: $122   Flop: 4♥4♦J♥

Nice flop—trips!

I make my standard small continuation-bet—$68. With trip 4's and only a flush draw to worry about, I bet small to induce a bluff from a naked flush draw. There are not many bad cards for me on the turn and I'm happy to let my opponents see the turn for a cheap price with a wide range. Both of my opponents call. I expect at least one (and probably both!) to have a flush draw.

Pot: $338   Turn: 6♥

The turn brings in the flush, and I know I'm beat. I check and hope that my opponents are too afraid of the paired board to bet their flushes so that I can get a free attempt at making my boat on the river. Unfortunately, after the cutoff checks, the button shoves for $266.

A quick pot-odds calculation ensues:

266 / (338+266+266) = 0.32 = 32% Break Even
    Point

With at best 10 outs, the rule of 2 says I'll make a full
    house 20% of the time:

10 outs × 2 = 20%

Since I will only win the pot 20% of the time and my break-even point is 32%, I must reluctantly surrender.

A short stack limps from middle position and the small blind completes. I check my option in the big blind with J♠T♠9♥3♣.

5-10 PLO

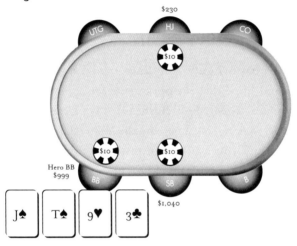

$230

$1,040

Hero BB
$999

Pot: $30   Flop: T♦9♠4♦

SB bets $25, Hero calls $25, MP raises to $50, SB raises to $205, Hero?

The small blind bets $25. On a board as draw-heavy as this one, I expect him to have a lot of draws and strong made hands. We could easily have the same hand, but if I raise, I don't expect to be getting in my 100 big blinds with the best hand. There are also *a lot* of bad turn and river cards that make my two pair worthless. So I just call.

The short stack min-raises and the small blind comes back with a raise to $205. With the action back on me, my choice is now clear: *fold.* At best, I expect to be flipping against one player, and against my opponent's combined ranges, I'm toast. After the showdown, I see that I made the correct fold. The small blind shows A♦K♦Q♣J♥ and the player in middle position had a set with 9♣9♥J♦7♣. I had less than a 15% chance to win.

——BLUFFING WITH BLOCKERS——

$2/4 PLO - 9 Handed

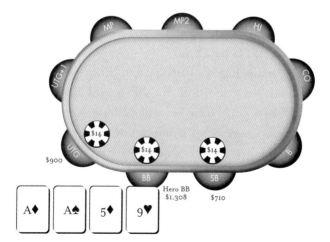

A player opens under the gun to $14 and the SB calls. With weak Aces (A♦A♣5♦9♥), I decide to just call and avoid playing a big pot out of position against a strong under-the-gun opener—he is capable of using his position to make good multi-street bluffs, and I avoid a lot of difficult decisions by just calling. I expect him to be playing many premium rundown hands.

Pot: $42   Flop: 4♣5♦9♠

SB checks, Hero checks, UTG bets $30, SB folds.

The flop is good for my hand, but the board will often develop poorly and make my hand difficult to showdown. I check, and my opponent makes a continuation-bet of $30. After the SB folds, I have an easy call.

Turn ($102): T♠

I check, UTG bets $78.

The turn brings a difficult card. Since my opponent opened from early position, he will usually have two pair with 9TXX or a wrap. If he has a flush draw to go with these hands, I expect him to bet almost all of the time. With AA, I may have the best hand against his wraps. With the naked Ace of Spades, I can also represent the nut flush if a spade hits the river.

River ($258): 7♠

With the nut blocker, I find myself in a great spot to bluff. My turn range analysis leads me to believe that my opponent has some combination of a flush draw with a wrap/pair/two-pair—type hand. Since my range consists mostly of wraps and two-pair hands on the flop and turn, my opponent will likely try to bluff if he can't beat the 8-high straight. He may also give up occasionally and let me win with AA.

I check and he bets $192. I'm a little surprised by his river-bet size. If my opponent had a flush, I would expect him to bet smaller since he can't have the nuts and my most likely hand is a non-nut, 8-high straight. I could also have a weak flush, but when he bets this big, he can't really be expecting me to bluff-catch very often.

My bet-sizing read combined with the nut blocker in my hand makes a river-bluff check-raise a must. I re-raise the pot to $834. After a mournful sigh, he folds.

——LOCKED-DOWN BOARD IN A MULTI-WAY POT——

An opponent raises under the gun to $7, UTG+1 calls, and I make a loose call in the small blind with J♦T♣8♦6♥. The big blind comes along and we have four-way action on the flop.

1-2 PLO

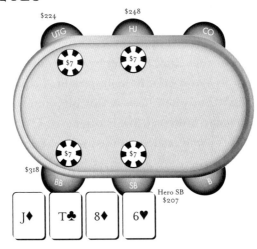

Pot: $28   Flop: 8♣7♣5♦

The flop is fairly locked-down, but it's not a good spot to check-raise. If the flop was lower and I was heads-up, I could make a move. But trying to make this move on this board in a four-way pot is crazy. In addition, my relative position is terrible because the SB is the most likely player to wake up with 96XX and the UTG and UTG+1 player are most likely to bet and call a check-raise with hands that have good equity against the current nuts.* I make a small bet of $12 with back-door diamonds, a gut-shot straight draw, top pair, and a blocker to the nuts. The big blind folds and both my other opponents call. I expect my opponents to have a range that consists of over-pairs with backdoor-flush draws, two-pair hands, and wraps.

Pot: $64   Turn: 3♦

I expect both of my opponents to have draws against the range I represent if I bet again—(96XX, 88XX, 77XX, 55XX)—and it's extremely rare for either of them to show up with 96XX or a set themselves. With this in mind, I don't expect my opponents to be betting or raising this turn card. I've improved my equity by picking up a backdoor-flush draw, so I bet $44 to set up stacks for a pot-size river shove. The player in the Hi-Jack calls.

River ($152): 6♦

I hit my flush, but there is not much value in betting. I decide to bluff-catch. I check, my opponent puts me all-in, and I call quickly for my remaining $151. He shows A♣9♣T♥J♦ and I win the pot with a flush.

_____

* Wrap hands like QJT9 that may have a flush draw as well.

5-10 PLO

The variance in PLO frequently leads to deep-stacked games. Live, this is even more common as the buy-ins are usually uncapped. This hand was played in a live PLO game at the Wynn.

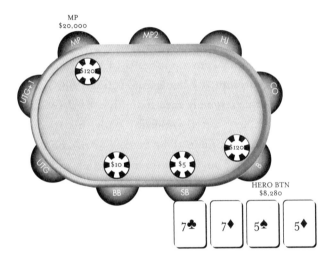

An opponent raises to $35 from middle position. He is a hyper-aggressive player who has been playing fearlessly and using his enormous stack to his advantage, winning lots of hands without showdown. I know that he either loves to run huge bluffs or he is getting really, really lucky by hitting the nuts way more often than expected.

I look down at 7♣7♦5♣5♦ and make a standard three-bet to $120 on the button. We are both very deep and I want to leverage my positional advantage with a hand that flops a set about 25% of the time. Even if I miss, I'll have a good shot to win the pot after three-betting. Everyone else folds and my mark calls.

Pot: $255   Flop: 5♥4♦J♣

I flop middle set and my opponent checks to me. I make a standard continuation-bet of $185 and get called. I think my opponent often has AAXX, KKXX, QQXX, or a J with backdoor flush and straight potential. A wrap is very unlikely because I have blockers with my sevens.

Pot: $625   Turn: J♥

My opponent checks. I'm not scared of quads or J4, so I value-bet. I'd also bet here with air for balance. I bet $225 and my opponent raises to $575.

The check-raise has me a little concerned, but I still expect to have the best hand much of the time. If I were playing 100bbs deep, this would be a simple "all-in" situation. However, since there is so much left behind and I'll never make the nuts, I need to be very careful not to put in too much money and value own myself.

I think my opponent's most likely holding AJ98 type hands. Less often, he will have a complete bluff or a better full house. I call. I have position and there is still over 4x the pot left in my stack after calling.

Pot: $1,775   River: 2♠

My opponent checks again and I think he's giving up. I think for a minute and decide to bet $725. I think I can get a call from a Jack or a rivered straight by betting small.

My opponent immediately pots, making it $3,950. Uh oh. Really? Pots like this make Omaha a sick game.

There is a ton of money on the line. He's representing J5XX or JJXX. Neither seem very likely. After I called the turn, there are many full houses in my range, including the hand I actually hold. Does he really think I'd make a thin value bet with AJXX? (I would.)

So I think his check-raise is a response to his perception that I'm value betting thinly with a hand like AJXX. Well, if he has AJXX as well, he might think he can blow me off my hand. I will not be at all surprised if he has some comical full house, but I just can't get myself to fold. I reluctantly call.

"Nice call, Phil. Chop it up." He flips over AJT9.

"No, thanks," I retort, "but I will buy you a drink . . . cocktails for the table, please!" The dealer pushes the mound of chips to me.

FINAL THOUGHTS

Overhauling my game has been a challenging journey. Writing the book was even more difficult. Add in the stress of "Black Friday" and, well, I'm completely spent. I have a few months before the World Series of Poker starts and I'll have an opportunity to put all that I've learned to work. Until then, it is family time.

One thing is certain: the game will continue to evolve. If you're reading this book in 2013 or beyond, it wouldn't surprise me in the least if the strategies I've espoused here have been completely discredited and won't beat a $2–$4 game.

An inquisitive attitude and a desire to improve will never let you down. As theories come and theories go, I'm just going to keep working on my game. I strive to learn from each session and each hand.

Of all the things I've accomplished in business and poker, I can tell you that nothing quite compares to having someone come up to me and tell me that they read my books and started winning. I love knowing that a few words can help a player get over the hump. That feels good and makes all the effort worthwhile.

I'd love to talk to you and learn from you as well. If you're interested in starting a dialogue, please feel free to reach out and let me know what you think I got right or wrong. Send me a hand history or two. Send me a picture of you with all the chips, the trophy, or the bracelet.

Feel free to email me directly. No PR filter, just me and you talking poker. Thank you for taking this journey with me—I sincerely hope you find gold at the end of the rainbow. If you feel like giving back, please consider donating 1% of your poker winnings to the Bad Beat on Cancer initiative. (See page 377.)

I hope to meet you at the final table soon. Until then, I'm all-in.

Phil Gordon
April 30, 2011

Email: gold@philnolimits.com
Web: www.philnolimits.com
Twitter: @philnolimits

Autographed copies of this and all of my books, as well as private lessons, are available through the Prevent Cancer Foundation's Bad Beat on Cancer website, www.badbeatoncancer.org.

ACKNOWLEDGMENTS

I'd like to thank the many people who made this book possible. As this was a collaborative effort, the list is not short.

A special thanks to my poker coach, Anders Taylor. Anders crushes the games online and worked long, tireless hours bringing my game up to speed. He gave up significant equity to do so. Without his incredible talent and efforts, this book wouldn't have happened. Other players who made major contributions to the book include "the kid" Austin Schaff and my cohort at ESPN.com, Andrew Feldman. Thanks, boys.

My mentors, Phil Galfond, Annette Obrestad, and Daniel Cates, were extremely generous with their incredible knowledge and time. As you've seen, they think about the game in deep and profound ways. Simply breathing the same air that they breathe made me a better player. Getting extensive coaching from each of them has made a permanent and lasting effect on me as a person and as a player.

My publishing team is the best in the business. Venture Literary—Greg Dinkin and Frank Scatoni—thanks for the nudge. To my editor, Tricia Boczkowski, and the guys at Simon & Schuster—you've been a dream to work with. I sincerely appreciate your herculean efforts to make my books look great.

I'm not a professional or even polished writer, that's for sure. As I've found out, writing a book that is clear, concise, and accurate is tough. Fortunately, I have an awesome team of friends who gave me extensive notes and provided feedback, criticism, and the occasional shoulder to cry on. Thanks to Dave Lambert, Rick Averitt, Kim Scheinberg, Bruce Hayek, Dave Tuckman, Andrew Jones, Shaun Wyman, Marissa Chien, Jay Greenspan, and Duke Dianni. Beer is on me, guys.

Finally, I'd like to thank my beautiful, intelligent, and very understanding wife for her love, support, and friendship. When I somehow convinced Barb to marry me and start a family, I sealed my status as the luckiest guy in the world.

PHIL'S OTHER WORKS

Poker: The Real Deal (a k a Phil Gordon's Little Black Book)
Gallery Books, September 2004
An introductory text to the world of poker

Phil Gordon's Little Green Book
Gallery Books, October 2005
A treatise on winning No Limit Texas Hold'em

Phil Gordon's Little Green Book (Audio)
Simon & Schuster, October 2005
Read by the Author

Phil Gordon's Little Blue Book
Gallery Books, October 2006
More than 100 instructive No Limit Hold'em hands
    examined

10% of Phil Gordon's share of this
book is donated to PreventCancer.org
and the Bad Beat on Cancer.